WRITER

Volume 3

WRITER

Volume 3

Richard A. Lupoff

Edited & Introduced by

Gavin L. O'Keefe

Surinam Turtle Press
RAMBLE HOUSE
2018

First trade paperback edition

Surinam Turtle Press
an imprint of
Ramble House
10329 Sheephead Drive
Vancleave MS 39565 USA

ISBN 13: 978-1-60543-878-8

Back cover photo credits
Clockwise from top left-hand corner:

Ethan Lupoff reading a copy of *Writer #1*; photo by Ken Lupoff
Dick & Pat Lupoff, Ann Bannon & Michael Kurland,
at the Vintage Paperback Show, L.A., 2015 (photo by Linda Robertson)
Don Thompson & Dick Lupoff
Dick Lupoff
Pat (foreground) & Dick (background) Lupoff, at NYCon 3.
© Photo by Andrew I. Porter
Fender Tucker & Dick Lupoff, Bouchercon 2010, San Francisco.
© Photo by G. L. O'Keefe

Interior picture credits

Page 14: *Two-Timers* cover art by Ditmar "Dick" Jenssen
Page 34: Photographs by Amelia Beamer, Locus Publications.
Pages 38 & 282: Photographs by Rachael Wenban
Page 43: Photograph by & copyright © Andrew I. Porter
Page 78: Photograph by Michael Zagaris
Pages 83 & 87: Photographs courtesy of
The Philadelphia Athletics Historical Society
Page 276: Photo by Ken Lupoff

Picture credits

Two-Timers cover art by Ditmar "Dick" Jenssen
Photographs in 'Frank M. Robinson' by Amelia Beamer, Locus Publications.
Photographs in 'We Didn't Know' & at end of book by Rachael Wenban
Group photograph in 'We Didn't Know' by & copyright © Andrew I. Porter
Photograph in 'In Another World' by Michael Zagaris
Photographs in 'The A's Bionic Pitcher' courtesy of
The Philadelphia Athletics Historical Society
Photograph in 'Learning to Read' by Ken Lupoff

Surinam Turtle Press #50c

TABLE OF CONTENTS

Time Kaleidoscope

WHAT IS TIME?

Is Time the number of passing of moments it takes to imagine a different reality?

Is Time the amount of breaths it takes to fashion words with a quill, or to type with fingers on a typewriter—and to then see a page filled with sentences previously unwritten?

Is Time the un-timeable space in which a writer meditates on past events and sees those things in a new light?

Is Time chronicled by the written word?

Is Time circular?

In his renowned story '12:01 PM' (first published in 1973, when I was eight-years-old), Richard A. Lupoff challenged the world with a concept of Time that was hard to shake: Time portrayed as the inescapable loop, where only thoughts and deeds could offer the individual some kind of ultimate redemption. Time, however, was delaying me in the meantime; I would not read '12:01 PM' until I met Dick Lupoff, became his friend and colleague, and was invited by him to illustrate *The Book of Time* (2011), a compilation of time-travel stories by H. G. Wells and Richard A. Lupoff, together with the latter's '12:01 PM' and that story's sequels '12:02 PM' and '12:03 PM'.

This was a cherished moment in my lifetime, and the continuum has extended—not simply through creative collaboration, but through the warmth of the friendship given to me by Dick and Pat Lupoff.

For a reader of science fiction and fantasy since my teens (living in an isolated country town in Australia in the 1970s)—and even then I was reading about Lupoff's writings in the field—finding myself with Dick Lupoff in Berkeley, CA in 2010, browsing in a science fiction specialty bookshop (no less), tossing around ideas for future projects, and then being invited to collaborate with this (to me) *famous* writer, seemed beyond even my wildest dreams.

Others more worthy ("more worthy," because they themselves are exemplary writers) have preceded me with their introductions to the writings of Richard A. Lupoff: Robert Silverberg (in *Before . . . 12:01 . . . and After*), Ed Gorman (in *Writer, Vol.1*),

Fender Tucker (in *The Book of Time*), Michael Kurland (in *Writer at Large*), John Pelan (in *Writer, Vol.2*) and Christopher Conlon (in *Dreamer's Dozen*), to name just a few. This introducer encourages the reader to seek out these prior introductions, because they admirably encapsulate Lupoff's writing achievements. If you don't already own these books—it may be that *Writer, Vol.3* is your introduction to Lupoff—they are recommended as fine collections of his fiction and essays.

As I enter my sixth decade, Dick Lupoff steps farther into his ninth—but there is no dulling in his enthusiasm for exploring those things which capture his imagination, and which he is moved to bring to life for us through his words. You will find in this third volume in the *Writer* series a wealth of writings gathered from throughout the author's career. There are the life-long passions (comics, Edgar Rice Burroughs, science fiction); but, in the end, the book reviews, the reminiscences of family and friends, the introductions to other writers' works, the sporting memories, and the rest, all exist because passion has sparked them. Even in the modest commission of a book review, Dick Lupoff spoils the reader with riches far beyond the traditional format.

It can be an invidious exercise highlighting certain works from a collection, but let me whet your appetite with a few examples of the treasures in this volume.

Take the piece 'The Key to Lafferty', a new introduction to a forthcoming volume in a series (published by Centipede Press) reprinting the short fiction of R. A. Lafferty. Where he doesn't have a lengthy experience of having known Lafferty in person, Dick Lupoff rewards the reader instead with a discursive exploration of his own early years of discovering science fiction through the numerous genre magazines (where he first encountered Lafferty's stories), Lafferty's religious perspective, the religion-themed works of other science fiction authors such as James Blish, Walter Miller and Jack Dann, the possible influence of George Orwell's *Nineteen Eight Four* on Lafferty—and more. By the end, one definitely feels introduced to R. A. Lafferty—and we are keen to read his stories.

Or, let's jump to the review section of this collection. In 'Two to Keep', Dick Lupoff reviews two books whose purviews overlap: *American Pulp: How Paperbacks Brought Modernism to Main Street* by Paula Rabinowitz (2015) and *When Books Went To War: The Stories that Helped us Win World War II* by Molly Guptill Manning (2014). Dick Lupoff doesn't jump cold into the lake here; an article by Louis Menand in *The New Yorker* had been prompted by Rabinowitz's book—and Dick's name and his own book *The Great American Paperback* had been referenced in both places. What follows is an objective review of *American Pulp*, informed by far more authority than we would usually expect. The second part of this article appraises the Manning book, whose subject matter overlaps with the content of the first book. By the end of 'Two to Keep' we feel as though we know how successful each book was in meeting its aims—but we've also been concisely, informatively, and generously briefed on the history of modern American paperback publishing, by a writer who knows the field.

And there are unexpected gems sprinkled throughout this already rich tapestry. For instance, during his tenure with the publishing house of Biblo & Tannen, Dick Lupoff met one of my favourite illustrators, the American artist Mahlon Blaine. Yet there is always more. Dick's personal reminiscences of Howard Browne, Frank M. Robinson, and E. E. 'Doc' Smith are golden . . . and I could keep on teasing you. I promise to bow out shortly and let Mr. Lupoff take the podium. You won't be disappointed, I assure you.

At the beginning of this introduction, I raised some questions about Time. I'm afraid I can't offer a convincing answer to the first of those questions—but the answer to most of the queries following it would be, I venture, a resounding "Yes." The last question ("Is Time circular?") must, I suppose, remain one of those vaguely-couched, possibly-unanswerable, questions. However, I distinctly feel the cyclic or connected nature of Time in my experience with Dick Lupoff, the writer and the man. I first read his words on the printed page; now I count him as a friend, and in this volume have the honour of compiling a selection of his writings. So . . . having entered that 'circle' many years ago, I haven't yet departed it (and, happily, can't imagine ever doing so). But what of Time, and its influence on the writing of Richard A. Lupoff? The following extract is from a letter sent to me by Dick as we were working on this volume:

Human memory is a fallible whatchamacallit. I know mine is, anyway. The events described in this compendium of memoirs, essays and reviews took place anywhere between a sunny day in December, 1939 and this morning, January 28, 2016. In a few weeks I'll be 81 years old, an age that I never expected to reach. Some of the stories I tell recur, and the versions are not always consistent. Did my mother give Jerry and me twenty cents or twenty-five cents on that morning in 1939? I don't know. Did Howard Browne really meet Edgar Rice Burroughs in a saloon in LA, or did Burroughs send Browne a letter, or both? I don't know.

I can only quote Walt Whitman: "Do I contradict myself? Very well, then I contradict myself. I am large, I contain multitudes."

It take all kinds of individuals to make a world, and, within that world, it takes all kinds of writers to make a literary kaleidoscope. But even within that kaleidoscope there exists another—that of the written *œuvre* of Richard A. Lupoff—and I am honoured to recommend herewith that you turn the page (even as you might turn the kaleidoscope or the hands of the clock) and be drawn into the past, the present, and the future.

Gavin L. O'Keefe
South Berwick, ME
January 2016

Science Fiction

Two-Timers

Ray Cummings

THE MAN WHO MASTERED TIME

Malcolm Jameson

TIME COLUMN & TAA THE TERRIBLE

Introduction by Richard A. Lupoff

THE TWO-TIMERS:

RAY CUMMINGS & MALCOLM JAMESON

Ray Cummings

"TIME," SAID GEORGE, "why I can give you a definition of time. It's what keeps everything from happening at once."

That's one of the most famous sentences in all of science fiction, and it has achieved considerable currency outside of the field. It's been attributed to many wits, but as far as I've been able to determine, it was first used by Raymond King Cummings (1887-1957) as the opening paragraph of *The Man Who Mastered Time,* one of the most famous works of this almost unbelievably prolific writer. And one who has been largely—and unjustly—forgotten by a generation who regrettably think that science fiction was invented by George Lucas or Gene Roddenberry or at the earliest by John W. Campbell.

Ray Cummings was writing science fiction before Campbell took the helm of *Astounding Stories* in 1938, before Hugo Gernsback inaugurated *Amazing Stories* in 1926, before *Weird Tales* made its debut in 1923. There's no definitive bibliography of Cummings' work, but he is known to have penned somewhere in the vicinity of 750 pieces of fiction, ranging from short stories to novels.

He wrote vast amounts of science fiction, as well as mystery stories, jungle tales, and an array of other works. He was immensely popular in his heyday, and if his stories tend to creak a little in this, the Twenty-first Century, we can still enjoy them as mind-stimulating and pulse-pounding adventure tales.

The Man who Mastered Time is one of his best. It was the second in a series of science fiction novels exploring, in Cummings' words, "time, space, and matter." The series was framed as a sequence of meetings by a Gentlemen's Scientific Association. While this concept may seem quaint today, an attempt was made to revive it as the Interplanetary Exploration Society in the late 1950s by the widely admired John W. Campbell. Further, even today there are organizations such as the Mars Society, the High Frontier, the Planetary Society and others dedicated to the promotion of scientific research.

The first in Cummings' series was *The Girl in the Golden At-om,* an early exploration of the notion that each atom is in effect a miniature solar system. Cumming was not the first writer to utilize this theme; that was almost certainly the Irish-American writer Fitz-James O'Brien, in a short story called "The Diamond Lens" (1858). Still, Cummings' use of the notion was far more extensive and influential than O'Brien's, and led to a great many pulp and comic book stories.

Cummings' debt to H. G. Wells was immense, and Cummings' use of Wells' works as a matrix for his own was overt. Wells' first use of the "club" format was in his own first novel, *The Time Machine* (1895). Wells' narrator, the Time Traveler, details his adventures in an extended monolog. The other members of the "club" are identified as the Medical Man, the Psychologist, the Mayor, the Very Young Man, and the Rector.

In tales the assembled group include the Chemist, the Doctor, the Very Young Man, the Banker, and the Big Business Man.

Like Wells' Time Traveler, Cummings' narrator first explains his theories of time and his attempts (in association with his father) to build a time machine. This machine, utilizing a "Proton Drive," looks like a cross between a World War One Fokker triplane and a Jules Verne dirigible. Cummings' narrator travels to a neo-primitive world tens of thousands of years in the future, sees a young woman held in bondage, returns to the present, and sets out on a second time-voyage to rescue her.

In Wells' novel the future humans have divided into the gentle, peaceful Eloi and the brutish, muscular Morlocks. In Cummings' novel, the future humans have divided into the gentle, peaceful Aran and the brutish, muscular Bas. There is even a significant character named Mogruud.

Cummings predicts particle-beam weapons, heat-seeking missiles, and aerial drones remotely piloted via TV viewers and radio devices.

Tempting though it might be, I will not divulge more. *The Man who Mastered Time* is a remarkable novel, an exercise in both prediction and speculation as well as a stirring adventure story. Early in his career and for several decades Ray Cummings was regarded as a pioneering creator of science fiction. As time passed, however, critics and fans alike came to regard him as stodgy and outmoded. In the years after his death, save for occasional revivals of interest, he seemed to become one of the many pulp writers destined to be forgotten by all save antiquarians, scholars, literary historians, and collectors.

There may well have been some validity to this critique, but if Ray Cummings was very much a man of his time, modern readers should be able to read his works with real enjoyment as well as sense of nostalgic innocence.

Malcolm Jameson

Planning to pursue a career as an officer in the United States Navy, Malcolm Jameson (1891-1945) found himself forced to take an early medical retirement. He turned to writing science fiction, both as a source of income and as an outlet for his immense creative talents.

His first short stories were published in 1938, when he was nearing fifty years of age. He produced short stories, novels, and essays at a prolific rate until his death in 1945. His novels included *The Giant Atom* (later retitled *Atomic Bomb)* and *Tarnished Utopia.* He is best remembered for his story cycle *Bullard of the Space Patrol.* All of these have been reissued by Surinam Turtle Press.

His short stories have been gathered by my friend and colleague John Pelan in two volumes issued by Dancing Tuatara Press, *Chariots of San Fernando and Other Stories,* and *Alien Envoy and Other Stories.* Further collections are promised.

The Jameson stories in the present volume, most notably his short novel *The Time Column,* are very much the product of their era. The Second World War was raging, the threat of Nazi domination not merely of Europe but of the world, was frighteningly real.

One can well imagine Malcolm Jameson, forced out of the United States Navy by a medical diagnosis, itching to get back into action and, as the phrase of the era had it, "to do his bit." If he couldn't don his officer's uniform and board a warship, he could at least promote the war effort by writing these stories about heroism and sacrifice.

He died on April 16, 1945, as the war was drawing to its close.

EDITING A TITAN

DOC SMITH'S ALLEGED unrealistic characters and wooden prose are often derided but I simply didn't notice them when I was a young science fiction fan. I was caught up in the astonishing ideas, the perilous adventures, the breathtaking action that filled his books.

I thoroughly enjoyed his Skylark novels and positively loved his Lensmen books. He was already a legend when I became part of the science fiction world in the 1950s, and the World Science Fiction Convention of 1963 was doubly thrilling for Pat and me. Our fanzine, *Xero,* had been nominated for a Hugo (and in fact, it won) and we got to have dinner with Doc Smith and his wife, Jeanie. I don't remember anything about the décor or the food but I remember Doc and Jeanie. Just imagine a rock music fan having dinner with his favorite musician, or a movie lover having dinner with her favorite star.

Doc was a pulp writer in his spare time. His "day job" as a nutritional chemist kept him and Jeanie traveling from city to city, consulting with food manufacturing companies, helping them to develop appealing, nutritious products. In fandom he was sometimes referred to as "donut maker to the stars."

By 1963 I had started working as an editor at Canaveral Press. Well, without bragging I suppose I should say, "*the* editor at Canaveral Press." We were a small company, and as far as editorial staff was concerned, I was it.

I was also on friendly terms with my opposite numbers at other publishing houses: Don Wollheim and Terry Carr at Ace Books, Larry Shaw at Lancer Books, Robert W. Lowndes at Avalon, Donald Bensen at Pyramid.

Doc Smith had published a short story called "Subspace Survivors," and over dinner he mentioned that he was planning to expand the story into a novel. He had a contract with Pyramid Books to publish it as a paperback original.

I jumped at what I considered an opportunity. At Canaveral Press our mainstay was Edgar Rice Burroughs. We'd reissued many of his older books and we were on our way to getting rights to his uncollected magazine stories and unpublished manuscripts. We were also working to broaden our line, and had projects under way with James Blish and Norman L. Knight, L. Sprague de Camp and Catherine Crook de Camp, and a promising younger writer named Ed Ludwig. Some of these would eventually see print; others fell by the wayside.

At that historic dinner party—it was in Washington, D.C.—I asked Doc Smith if he would like to see a hardbound edition of the expanded "Subspace Survivors" and he welcomed the idea. At my next chance to speak with Don Bensen I broached the idea of Pyramid's delaying their edition of the book and releasing rights to us at Canaveral for an edition to precede the Pyramid edition. This practice is known as "back-selling."

Doc had also spoken about his dicey relationship with John W. Campbell, Jr., the editor *Astounding Science Fiction*. Campbell was a strong-willed individual, and reportedly made attempts to dictate story content to his writers. I never had any dealing with him and cannot give direct testimony on the subject. However, at least one of Campbell's writers, Donald E. Westlake, did describe the situation in his classic essay, "Don't Call Me—I'll Call You."

Don agreed, contracts were signed, and—lo! and behold—here I was, a young rookie editor working with the legendary Edward Elmer Smith, Ph.D.

When Doc turned in his completed manuscript, I was thrilled beyond words. Once I started reading I realized that, although Doc was well into his seventies, he'd lost none of the energy that had propelled him through his earlier novels. I was reluctant to touch a word in the manuscript, but in fact there were two problems.

One was, for want of a better word, political. The book involves labor relations in the future. There are some pretty nasty, corrupt union bosses in the story, and Doc made a passing remark about all labor leaders being pretty venal.

The second problem arose from a quirk that I suppose many authors with long and productive careers face. Namely, Doc had plagiarized himself, repeating a major incident from one of his earlier novels. Fortunately I was enough of a fan of Doc's to recognize this as soon as I spotted it.

I certainly didn't want to dictate story content to Doc Smith— no way did I want to offend him, the way Campbell had done. But I felt that I had to bring these matters to Doc's attention.

I wrote to Doc, describing the two problem areas. Almost at once I received a letter from him. I wondered if he was going to breath fire and brimstone at me. I'd previously encountered at least one established author who practically exploded with rage when I pointed out a problem with his manuscript. In that case, fortunately, we hadn't yet issued a contract for the author's book—and we never did!

But Doc Smith's letter was brief, calm, and to the point. Don't worry, he told me. He would take care of everything. And he did. In short order I received a replacement page for the one slamming all labor leaders as greedy and corrupt. The new text merely pointed out that some labor leaders are greedy and corrupt.

Fair enough.

As for the self-plagiarized chapter, Doc provided a complete new chapter to replace the one that had caused our problems.

That's the kind of man he was, and the kind of writer. Here he was, one of the titans of modern science fiction, widely regarded as the father of space opera. And here I was, little more than a young fan, just cutting my teeth as a professional.

Doc Smith, as far as I am concerned, brought luster to the term, *professional.*

He was also an immensely practical man with skills developed in the hard years of the Depression. I remember his telling me how to save money on typewriter ribbons by unrolling a spent ribbon, re-inking it, and winding it back onto its spool. It was cheaper, Doc explained, to buy a bottle of ink than a new typewriter ribbon! I never tried that, myself, but Doc insisted that he had done it repeatedly.

We published his book in 1965. Its title was *Subspace Explorers.* The dust jacket was typographical but we did add one graphic to the book, a terrific frontispiece by Roy Krenkel. I was proud of that book, and prouder still to have been Doc Smith's editor.

I will confess that I haven't reread any of his books in many years. Frankly, I'm afraid to. Will the magic still be there, or were Doc's books only wonderful for me because I was young and innocent and read them with stars in my eyes?

Tell you what. I'm going to risk it. I'll wager that the magic is still there. I'm going to find out!

THE KEY TO LAFFERTY

IN 1949 MY parents scraped together the necessary dollars and treated me to a couple of months at summer camp. I spent my days swimming, sailing, playing baseball, and engaging in other healthful and wholesome activities. Nights were devoted to amateur theatricals, story-telling contests, and ping-pong tournaments. Off-hours were spent in our cabins either playing penny-ante poker or reading. Uncounted comic books and pulp magazines were passed around.

You are probably wondering by now what this has to do with Rafael Aloysius Lafferty. Well, it has a lot to do with him. It will just take me a little while to get to him. But trust me, please. Just trust me.

Several weeks into the season the parents of one of my cabin-mates sent him a box of books. Among them was the first American edition of George Orwell's important novel *Nineteen Eighty-Four.* I was already a nascent science fiction aficionado, and when I saw the title of that book I immediately entered my plea to borrow it, once my friend had finished reading it.

Although I read the book chiefly for its story content, its deeper meaning was not lost on me. I'd been old enough to be very much aware of the Second World War and the horrors of Nazism. After a brief period of euphoria, the Cold War had set in. I didn't know that Orwell had been a disillusioned Communist but I had an inkling of what totalitarianism and oppression were, and I like to think that I understood *Nineteen Eighty-Four* better than the average kid of my age.

Among the concepts to which this book introduced me was that of *doublethink.* Orwell defined this process twice, and if you will forgive my doing so, I will quote both definitions:

"To know and not to know, to be conscious of complete truthfulness while telling carefully constructed lies, to hold simultaneously two opinions which cancelled out, knowing them to be contradictory and believing in both of them, to use logic against logic, to repudiate morality while laying claims to it, to believe that democracy was impossible and that the Party was the guardian of democracy, to forget whatever it was necessary to forget, then to draw it back into memory again at the moment when it was needed, and then promptly to forget it again, and above all to apply the same process to the process itself—that was the ultimate subtlety, consciously to induce unconsciousness, to become unconscious of the act of hypnosis you had just performed. Even to understand the word 'doublethink' involved the use of doublethink."

That's pretty longwinded but it's damned powerful stuff. You can feel Orwell's passion as he pounds home the concept as if his words were a hammer and he strikes with it again and again and again. And then he defines doublethink still again, a little more succinctly and a little more directly this time:

"The power of holding two contradictory beliefs in one's mind simultaneously, and accepting them both . . . to tell deliberate lies while genuinely believing in them, to forget any fact that becomes inconvenient, and then, when it becomes necessary again, to draw it back from oblivion for just as long as it is needed, to deny the existence of objective reality and all the while to take account of the reality which one denies—all this is indispensably necessary to exercise doublethink. For by using the word one admits that one is tampering with reality; by a fresh act of doublethink one erases this knowledge; and so on indefinitely, with the lie always one leap ahead of the truth."

After all these years I remember an example that Orwell cited of this mental phenomenon. The stars, he said, were giant blobs of burning gas incalculable millions of miles from Earth; they were also tiny points of light placed in the sky by the Party as navigation aids for mariners. At least that's the way I remember it, and if I have it wrong I apologize,

Well so much for the summer of 1949.

The next ten years were a very busy decade for me. I suffered through an abominable high school career, partied through an enjoyable college life, spent a few years in uniform defending my nation from the clutching tentacles of the Red Octopus of Communism, married the loveliest and most wonderful woman in the world, and took a job in which I masqueraded as a junior executive in one of the pioneering corporations of the then-fledgling computer industry. (Anybody want to hire a gray-haired oldster who remembers how to program a Univac II?)

I had also become a confirmed science fiction fan. I'd read every word of every story ever published in *Galaxy Science Fiction* and *The Magazine of Fantasy and Science Fiction,* along with a smattering of *Astounding Science Fiction, Thrilling Wonder Stories, Amazing Stories, Fantastic Adventures, Planet Stories* and a couple of dozen other periodicals.

One of these others was a low-budget digest called *The Original Science Fiction Stories,* edited by a sweet-natured man named Robert W. Lowndes. The last issue of that magazine published in 1959, although it carried a cover date of January, 1960, contained a story called "Day of the Glacier," by one R. A. Lafferty.

Ah, you knew I was going to get around to Lafferty eventually. I thank you for hanging in there with me, even if you did skim a little bit.

While Lowndes gets credit for being the first editor to publish a Lafferty story in a science fiction magazine, other credits are not as clear-cut. Another early Lafferty story, and an important one, was "The Six Fingers of Time," that appeared in *IF: Worlds of Science Fiction* dated September, 1960.

IF had experienced a troubled history including a revolving door series of editors. Initially, publisher James Quinn hired Paul W. Fairman to run the magazine. When sales were unsatisfactory, Quinn dismissed Fairman and there began a series of brief editorships: Larry T. Shaw, Damon Knight, Quinn himself, and (after Quinn had sold the magazine) Horace Gold and Frederik Pohl. Whoever bought Lafferty's story is apparently lost to history.

"The Six Fingers of Time" is implicitly a deal-with-the-devil story. These things are generally regarded as fantasies, but Lafferty had sent it to *IF* anyway, and the editor *de jour*, whoever he was, bought it.

Near the end of "The Six Fingers of Time" Lafferty's protagonist, Charles Vincent, soliloquizes: "I understand that the life I have been living is in direct violation of all that we know of the laws of mass, momentum, and acceleration, as well as those of conservation of energy, the potential of the human person, the moral compensation, the golden mean, and the capacity of human organs. I know that I cannot multiply energy and experience sixty times without a compensating increase of food intakes, and yet I do it. I know that I cannot live on eight minutes sleep in twenty-four hours, but I do that also. I know that I cannot reasonably crowd four thousand years of experience into one lifetime, yet un-

reasonably I do not see what will prevent it. But you say I will destroy myself.

"I will have it both ways," he said. "I am already a contradiction and an impossibility."

I do not know whether Lafferty was consciously paraphrasing
Orwell, or even whether he had read *Nineteen Eighty-Four* before
writing "The Six Fingers of Time." But deliberately or not, he
managed to summarize Orwell's rather overheated explanation of
the concept in just over a dozen words. "I will have it both ways. I
am already a contradiction and an impossibility."

While my own career in science fiction overlapped somewhat
with Lafferty's—by the time I was a newly-fledged professional
fictioneer he was a popular if eccentric established writer—I
didn't really know him well. We met a couple of times at conventions or conferences, but our encounters were little more than
handshake-and-howdy-do moments. I remember him as a rough-
edged individual, more than twenty years older than I was. I was
rather in awe of him. Born in Iowa, he'd lived most of his life in
Oklahoma, making his home in Tulsa, a town that Jim Thompson
would have loved.

It was my notion at the time that fiction was primarily a medium of entertainment, a position which I maintain to this day, ideo-
logically driven works like *Nineteen Eighty-Four* notwithstanding.
Certainly I read Lafferty as a storyteller with a unique outlook on
the world and on his craft. I could imagine him as an oldster sitting
by the fireside in an Irish pub, a bottle of John Jameson at his elbow, spinning enchanted yarns of saints and leprechauns and
damning the English and the Protestants and charming everyone
within earshot, especially generously-endowed crimson-tressed
serving wenches wearing low-cut blouses.

My personal Ray Lafferty fantasy, okay. But as is often the
case with enchanted (and enchanting) yarn-spinners, there is a
deeper meaning to many of Lafferty's works. Take "Guesting
Time" (*IF*, May, 1965). It's a hard-to-categorize little story. Is it
science fiction? It's an alien invasion tale of sorts, but hardly scientific. Perfectly human aliens start turning up on Earth. Zillions
of them. No explanation of how they got here. Is it fantasy? Well,
it feels more like fantasy—maybe fable would be a better word—
than science fiction.

These aliens—Skandians, Lafferty calls them—are committed
to the joys of fertility. They just keep on piling up—literally—
until they have to stand or sit on one another. They're sweet-

natured and gentle but they are filling up the Earth, eating all the food, breathing all the air, and—obviously—bringing about universal disaster if they are not stopped and—preferably—removed.

As for that doublethink, now. The Church to which Lafferty gave his loyalty has always maintained that any form of artificial birth control was forbidden, a mortal sin. Nobody pays much attention to that doctrine any more; at least available statistics indicate as much. But Lafferty, remember, was about as devout as he could be. He reportedly attended Mass every morning and today lies in consecrated ground, per his own wishes. He was not a "cafeteria Catholic," accepting such Church doctrines as suited his personal lifestyle and ignoring those he found inconvenient.

No.

He bought the Faith; he bought the whole nine yards.

But he was an electrical engineer by profession, meaning that he had a good understanding of the physical principles by which the world functions. And as a science fiction writer he must surely have had at least a general understanding of the hugeness and ancientness of the cosmos. Since Lafferty's day we have learned that our universe is even more vast than previously believed, and may be only one of an infinite number of universes. And the whole notion of God's creating the world in six days and resting on the seventh has largely given way to the Big Bang theory and various complex notions of cosmic evolution, planetary formation, and the development of life.

How could a man of Lafferty's intelligence and education take the Bible and Church doctrines as literal truth? Was "Guesting Time" a sly dig at the Church and its teachings? It reads almost like an anti-Communist satire written in an Iron Curtain country and passed around in clandestine *samizdat* publications at the height of the Cold War.

Let's look at another Lafferty story. Consider, if you will, the following speech from "Animal Fair," published in *New Dimensions IV* (1974), edited by the estimable Robert Silverberg:

"There is a wide misconception as to what happened in the beginning and as to what unfolding or evolution means. There is nothing new under the sun, and the sun itself was never so new as some have said. Too many persons have looked at the world as if it were indeed the product of natural-selection evolution, as if it were the result of purposeless chaos rather than purposive order. Enough persons have seen it so as to make it to be so for all impractical purposes. But every thesis, if acted upon wisely enough, comes to its in-built conclusion. The only possible conclusion to the natural-selection thesis is total pollution unto suffocation and death: the effluvia of organized and widespread idiocy brings always this suffocation. And the last choking voice of the chaos-origin believers will croak, 'It is the fault of others, of those who said that it began in order; they caused the whole breakdown.' "

These are the words of one Drakos, a character in the story, not directly those of the author, and such is a common enough device (I've used it myself) to make an implicit point without quite putting one's own name on it. But here I think we can fairly attribute Drakos's argument to Lafferty, and the argument is identical to that used today by advocates of Intelligent Design, itself a transparent repackaging of Creationism, long the argument made by Lafferty's Church.

Please pardon me if I keep coming back to this, but I truly believe it's the key to understanding Lafferty. As a devout Catholic, he believed that the Jewish Communist revolutionary Joshua ben Joseph was both God and Man and the Son of God. That he could turn water into wine (okay, a parlor trick). He could raise the dead (Lazarus the zombie). Was killed and rose from the dead (Jesus the zombie). Then ascended to Heaven to be welcomed back by his Father (who, uh, was also himself).

I'm sorry if this offends any readers, but to me it all sounds like a somewhat incoherent fairy tale. I don't want to insult my Catholic friends. Hey, I can tell you that one of the best people it has ever been my privilege to know is Father John O'Leary, whose home parish straddles the border between the Irish Republic and Ulster. (Talk about doublethink, hey?) A dozen years ago he saw me through the worst medical and emotional crisis of my life, and I'm grateful that I was able, in return, to help him through a spiritual crisis of his own. I believe that we loved each other and helped each other as two decent men, both of us in severe pain.

Back to Ray Lafferty. And if you'll forgive another digression, I'll tell you that my dear, lost friend Joe Gores used to explain a crucial point in writing, thusly:

" 'The king died, and then the queen died.' That's a story.

" 'The king died, and then the queen died—of grief.' That's a plot."

In other words—forgive me if I'm gilding the lily now—a series of events make a story, but those events must be organized into a coherent whole through logic and emotion to give that story a plot.

Some of Lafferty's stories are *only* stories, unless I'm missing something in my reading of them. Which is by no means impossible. But some of them had real plots, and some of those plots are devilishly clever and satisfying. One of my favorites is "Heart Grow Fonder" (1975) first published in *Future Corruption*, edited by Roger Elwood. In this story one Simon Radert, until now happily married, begins to suffer the proverbial seven-year itch. He becomes involved in an unusual wife-swapping scheme based on personality-switching. Into this apparently simple and fairly safe arrangement, Lafferty mixes a tale of embezzlement; he complicates and re-complicates matters until a nightmare scenario emerges.

More than this I will not tell you. Sooner or later you must read this story for yourself. Although originally published in an anthology of science fiction stories, "Heart Grow Fonder" might as well have run in *Ellery Queen's Mystery Magazine*, had Lafferty (or his agent) seen fit to offer it to that prestigious market.

Yes.

Here's another guess on my part. You'll recall that in Orwell's definitions of doublethink he asserted that the final ingredient in this exercise in mental self-deception was that one would erase from his mind the very fact that he had committed doublethink. At times, Ray Lafferty seems to be quite aware that he is performing doublethink. At others—well, maybe not so much. I mention this relative nit in passing, and will leave it to you to examine Lafferty's works and decide for yourself.

Lafferty was undeniably one of the more distinctive and praiseworthy science fiction writers of his era. His short stories are intricate and deceptive. His novels are at least a little bit calmer, nor are all of them science fiction. *Okla Hannali,* for instance, is a glowing example of both regional and ethnic prose.

And speaking of prose, Lafferty had a poetic talent that came into public display on rare but notable occasions. Consider the following:

The Reefs of Earth

To Slay the Folks and Cleanse the Land
And Leave the World a Reeking Roastie
High Purpose of the Gallant Band
And Six Were Kids, and One a Ghostie

A Child's a Monster Still Uncurled
The World's a Trap, and None Can Quit It—
The "Strife Dulanty" With the World
Was Mostly That They Didn't Fit It.

No Setting For the Gallant Brood
In Sacred Groves of Yew or Linden
They Found a Hold More Near Their Blood
A Mountainful of Murdered Indians

In Brazen Clash of Helm and Greave
Fit Subject for Heroic Chantey
He Battle Joined That Could But Leave
Or Altered World or Dead Dulanty.

(1968)

Well, the title is a dead giveaway but whence came that poem? Answer: It's the table of contents of the book. Each line of the poem is the title of a chapter. Four quatrains, rhyme schemes nearly perfect ABAB, CDCD, EFEF, GHGH. Well, one might pick a nit over rhyming *Linden* with *Indians* but I've certainly read far worse and I imagine that you have, too.

Lafferty was part of a glorious tradition of blue-collar raconteurs who had the gift of gab and a style all their own. Jack Vance was one of them. A former merchant seaman and truck driver, Jack would happily play his banjo and sing old songs for anyone who would listen when he wasn't busy writing space operas in his wonderfully ornate and captivating style. Eric Hoffer was another, blinded in an accident in his youth, he regained his eyesight, worked for decades as a longshoreman, and went home at night to write a series of books that were astonishingly erudite and influential. The most successful of them, *The True Believer,* bears rereading to this day. And Ray Lafferty, yes, belongs in that distinguished company.

If Lafferty is being rediscovered today—and this series of Centipede collections will undoubtedly go a long way to accomplish that—Lafferty was not unappreciated during his career. He received repeated Hugo and Nebula nominations, and his short story "Eurema's Dam" received the Hugo Award in 1973. In 1990 he received the World Fantasy Lifetime Achievement Award. In 1995, the Oklahoma Department of Libraries Arrell Gibson Award, and in 2002, the year of his death, the Cordwainer Smith Rediscovery Award. In his book *Modern Fantasy: The Hundred Best Novels*, editor and critic David Pringle includes Lafferty's *Fourth Mansions*.

Nor was Lafferty's talent unappreciated by his contemporaries. Consider the following comments:

Poul Anderson: . . . wild, subtle, demonic, angelic, hilarious, tragic, poetic, a thundering melodrama and a quest into the depths of the human spirit.

Terry Carr: R. A. Lafferty is one of the most original writers in science fiction. He bends or breaks normal story restrictions apparently at will, pokes fun at serious matters and breaks into a kind of folk-lyricism over grotesqueries. All this, plus the most unfettered imagination we've enjoyed in years.

Samuel R. Delany: The Lafferty madness is peppered with nightmare: witches, lazarus-lions, hydras, porsche's-panthers, programmed killers that never fail, and a burlesqued black mass. One hears of black comedy? There are places in *Past Master* where humor goes positively ultraviolet.

Harlan Ellison: As with everything the man writes, the wind of imagination blows strongly, with the happy difference that in a novel he can reach full gale-force . . . This is a great galloping madman of a novel, drenched in sound and color.

Judith Merril: It is a minor miracle that a serious philosophical and speculative work should be written so colorfully and so lyrically. There is, happily, no way to categorize this book: it has elements of science fiction, of pure fantasy, of poetry, of historical fiction; it is sharply critical and marvelously gentle; very serious and irrepressibly funny; profoundly symbolic and gutsy-realistic by turns. A first rate speculative work."

Fred Saberhagen: Lafferty's stories, like Philip K. Dick's, are not susceptible to being confused with the work of any other writer.

Theodore Sturgeon: R. A. Lafferty is the result of the ecstatic union of a power shovel and a moonbeam. One of his eyes is a laser and the other an x-ray, and he has a little silver anvil on which, warmed by laughter, he shapes logic to his own ends. For breakfast he eats pomposity, for lunch he nibbles on the improbable, and he dines on fixed ideas (yours or mine) which he finds about him in great abundance . . . some day the taxonomists, those tireless obsessives who put labels on everything, will have to categorize literature as Westerns, fantasies, romances, lafferties, science fiction, mysteries . . . .

Gene Wolfe: Lafferty is the ambassador dispatched to the Late Twentieth Century by Dr. Johnson and Benjamin Franklin, Socrates and St. Paul.

Roger Zelazny: I read *Past Master* in one sitting. I couldn't put it down. Lafferty has the power which sets fires behind your eyeballs. There is warmth, illumination, and a certain joy attendant upon the experience."

And still we wonder at the paradox: How could Lafferty believe simultaneously that the Earth was flat and that the sun and stars revolved around it—as he would have believed, had he lived a few centuries earlier than he did—and that the Earth is round and revolves around the sun, and the stars are balls of burning gas untold millions of miles from the Earth? Lafferty would have been a good citizen of Orwell's *Nineteen Eighty-Four.*

Religiously-themed science fiction is not very common, but it is far from unknown. Perhaps the finest religious science fiction novel—at least in my opinion—is *A Case of Conscience* by James Blish. Jim told me that the manuscript was returned by one editor after another. They considered it too controversial. Finally Larry Shaw bought it for *IF: Worlds of Science Fiction.* Shaw didn't break it into chunks and sneak them into the back pages of the magazine, either. He honored *A Case of Conscience* with a striking cover, and it was an immediate success. Jim and Larry were both friends of mine, and Blish told me that he was personally a committed agnostic in his personal life, but when he set to work on *A*

Case of Conscience (or other religiously-themed fiction) he became a temporary Roman Catholic.

Walter Miller's *A Canticle for Leibowitz* also has a Catholic orientation. And for any reader interested in pursuing Jewish-themed science fiction stories I would recommend Jack Dann's two fine *Wandering Stars* anthologies. I particularly recommend the short stories of Bernard Malamud, Isaac Bashevis Singer, Carol Carr, and Grania Davis.

But I digress. I'll confess that, like Lewis Carroll's White Queen, when I'm in the mood I can believe six impossible things before breakfast. We all have our own little imaginary moments that we hope someday to experience. If they're real—or at least possible—the current term for them is a Bucket List. If they're impossible dreams, I suppose they're all the more precious to us.

Here's my personal fantasy: I'm in Ireland on a walking tour with my pal John O'Leary. After a long day trekking through the glorious green countryside John and I will wander into a picturesque village where in a friendly pub we will purchase a bottle of Jameson's from a generously endowed, crimson-tressed serving wench. We'll recognize a paunchy, balding fellow sitting beside the fire. He'll look up and recognize us.

"Father O'Leary," he'll exclaim. "And by the saints, do I actually recognize that Lupoff person!"

Father O'Leary will reply, "If it isn't Rafael Aloysius Lafferty! May we join you, sir? And would you honor us by sharing a friendly libation?"

Ray Lafferty will motion us to a couple of vacant chairs. Then, "If you gentlemen won't mind waiting for a few minutes . . ." He nods to a heavyset fellow sitting nearby, a banjo in his arms. " . . . we've been saving this one for the right moment." He counts out, " . . . six, seven, eight," and proceeds to deliver the lyrics to "At the Sign of the Bonny Blue Bell" in a remarkably pleasant tenor voice, skillfully accompanied by the banjo player who also provides a delightful harmony to the song. The two of them follow with "Molly Brannigan," then a rousing rendition of "Bold Fennian Men" that brings the pub to a round of cheers and applause.

Now Lafferty waves to O'Leary and Lupoff.

"I was just about to tell my friends here a little story that I've been thinking of writing down. And my pal here"—he'll gesture to the banjo player—"my very good pal Jack Vance has agreed to provide a little musical accompaniment."

Jack hits a couple of banjo chords.

Lafferty says, "I think I've even got my opening worked out. The story goes like this: 'There was once a very peculiar fellow named Monahan. You wouldn't know it just from looking at him, but he was the possessor of certain talents and certain objects that it would not be advisable to learn too much about . . . .' "

If there is a God after all—on this question, I'm with my old pal Jim Blish— She just might grant us forgiven sinners those wondrous moments that we dream of, after we leave this world. We love our wives and children but sometimes there are pleasures to be had that do not necessarily require family participation. I'm sure that my loved ones will forgive me my golden hour with my friends John O'Leary and Jack Vance and Rafael Aloysius Lafferty.

It isn't guaranteed.

But pending that, we can have the next best thing. We can read Ray Lafferty's enchanting stories. And that's a joy, because for all that Lafferty was appreciated during his lifetime—I've given you a few salient details about that—his works have almost all been out of print in recent years. Searching even for battered reading copies will turn up too few books, and too many of them at astonishing prices. Glory be to Centipede Press and its editor John Pelan and publisher Jerad Walters for bringing back what will eventually be the complete Lafferty short fiction in this series of beautifully crafted volumes.

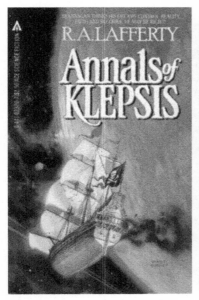

1983, cover art by Jim Gurney

1977, art by Ron Walotsky

1982, artist unknown

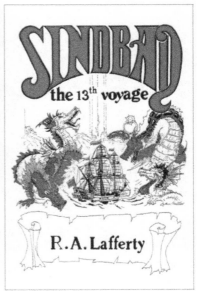

1989, art by Lissanne Lake

Robert Silverberg, Richard A. Lupoff & Frank M. Robinson

FRANK M. ROBINSON

1926-2014

ANYONE WHO VISITED Frank Robinson's San Francisco home and happened to peer into his office might have seen a framed copy of *Le Zombie*, a fanzine published by Wilson Tucker in 1942. Frank contributed the cover for that issue, and kept it on his wall to remind him of his roots.

He told me that he was raised in a home which his step-father, a voracious reader, kept well supplied with pulp magazines. His favorite was *Weird Tales*, and surely his early exposure to the fantastic stories in that magazine had a lifelong effect on Frank.

By the early 1940s Frank landed the dream job of any starry-eyed science fiction fan. He was hired as an office boy at Ziff-Davis Publications in Chicago. He worked for that company's fiction group that included such titles as *Mammoth Detective, Mammoth Mystery, Mammoth Adventure,* and—most relevantly—*Amazing Stories* and *Fantastic Adventures.* Half a century later Frank revealed that he had started what would become his world class pulp magazine collection by smuggling file copies of back issues out of the Ziff-Davis building, hidden under his coat.

The editors included Ray Palmer, Bill Hamling, and Howard Browne, all of them legends in the history of science fiction. In the spring of 1988 a luncheon was held in San Francisco in observance of Browne's eightieth birthday. As Browne, who was notoriously near-sighted, was escorted into the restaurant, he overheard Frank's famous and distinctive laughter. "That's Robinson the office boy," Browne shouted.

Frank was drafted into the United States Navy during World War Two. After the war he returned to civilian life only to be called back into the navy during the Korean War. Assigned to a ship in the Mediterranean—thousands of miles from the combat zone—he was placed in charge of the ship's library. One of his duties was to go ashore whenever the ship was in port, find an English-language bookstore, and buy paperbacks to replenish the ship's library. The two authors in greatest demand, he later said, were Mickey Spillane and Edgar Rice Burroughs.

Although he obtained a degree in engineering, he decided that his real talent was in writing, and over a span of sixty-four years, from 1950 to 2014, he produced some eleven novels, five of them in collaboration with Thomas M. Scortia.

Frank's first book, *The Power,* was published by the prestigious firm of Lippincott in 1956. It was also featured as a complete novel in *Bluebook* magazine, where a college kid named Richard Lupoff read it, and was scared out of his socks.

After *The Power* there was a long hiatus between novels, as Frank concentrated on editing for periodicals ranging from *Science Digest* to *Playboy,* where he wrote the Playboy Advisor column. His next novel, in collaboration with Tom Scortia, was *The Glass Inferno,* a major best-seller that became the basis for the film *The Towering Inferno.*

This and most of Frank's collaborative novels—with Scortia or John Levin—were borderline or hybrid books, combining elements of the mainstream thriller and science fiction. *The Prometheus Crisis,* for instance, warned of meltdown in a nuclear power station, years before Chernobyl, Three Mile Island, and Fukushima. *The Gold Crew,* filmed as *The Fifth Missile,* concerned a rogue, nuclear-armed submarine commander.

In 1991 Frank returned to mainline science fiction with *The Dark Beyond the Stars,* a Lambda Literary Award winner. Two more science fiction novels followed, *Waiting* (1999) and *The Donor* (2004).

Many of Frank's nearly fifty shorter works were collected in a massive volume, *A Life in the Day of . . . and Other Short Stories* (1981), and a smaller collection, *Through My Glasses Darkly* (2002), selected by Robin Wayne Bailey. Of Frank's many short stories, the two very best may be "East Wind, West Wind" and "The Hunting Season." The first of these is a powerful cautionary tale, years ahead of its time, concerning atmospheric pollution. The second is a tense chase story with a major time travel element.

And any coffee table would be enhanced by Frank's important contributions to cultural history, *Pulp Culture: The Art of Fiction Magazines, Science Fiction of the Twentieth Century: An Illustrated History,* and *The Incredible Pulps: A Gallery of Fiction Magazine Art.*

Possibly because he was sometimes seen as a mainstream best-seller writer, Frank may have been unrecognized as a major science fiction writer. This oversight was corrected just weeks before his death when he received an award in special recognition from the Science Fiction and Fantasy Writers of America. Even so, a few years earlier he had received the Emperor Norton Literary

Award in San Francisco. His acceptance speech was brief and as modest as Frank himself: "I thought you were gonna give this to somebody who deserves it."

At the same time, Frank had finally completed his autobiography. We may all look forward to reading this fine book.

Now I would like to add a personal note to the foregoing. Frank Robinson was my friend, and a friend to my wife, Pat, for more than forty years. We visited each other's homes many times. Often Frank would arrive at our house in Berkeley and chat briefly, then sprawl on our couch for an afternoon nap.

After this we would engage in shop talk. Often he would talk about current or planned projects. Frank would lay out possible plot developments, enumerate various options, bounce ideas off me. As a decidedly junior practitioner of the art of fiction, I would offer whatever notions and advice as I could. I would surely not claim to be a ghost collaborator or editor of any of Frank's memorable novels. I do like to think that I provided some modest assistance with them.

His plots were always constructed with the care and precision of his engineer's mind. They can stand as models of science fiction and of fiction in general. He was a fine craftsman as well as a fine human being and a fine, unforgettable friend.

And as a friend, Frank would sometimes come up with wonderful surprises. I guess I should have seen this one coming, as he was proud of the kitchen he had built in his home in San Francisco. Still, when he invited Pat and me to a dinner party at his house, we didn't know what to expect.

There were half a dozen guests present. Frank started us off with a crisp green salad. Then came the best fried chicken that I've eaten in my life. Amazing. With it, of course, mashed potatoes, gravy, green beans. And for dessert, a choice of chocolate cake or lemon cake, both baked by Frank himself. Absolutely gourmet quality!

He was a man of many talents, many virtues. He left behind many friends and many wonderful memories.

Dick & Pat Lupoff

WE DIDN'T KNOW

WHEN WE STARTED out we didn't know what we were doing. Well, we were newlyweds or nearly so and I suppose a lot of young couples don't know what they're doing. I was recently out of the army and Pat had even more recently completed her degree at Connecticut College. We were living in Hartsdale, New York, a suburb of White Plains, New York, itself a suburb of New York City. I was commuting to a day job in Manhattan and Pat was trying to settle into the life of a young suburban homemaker, and neither of us was very satisfied with that life.

So with the help of Pat's parents we found a great apartment in the city, packed up our meager belongings, and bid good-by to our life as would-be Ward and June Cleavers.

It didn't take us long to start interacting with a more interesting crowd of self-styled creative intellectuals, bohemians, ambitious literary wanna-be's, cartoonists, graphic designers, editors, musicians, and science fiction fans. Everything changed then and our apartment in the city soon became the nexus of a constantly swirling population of unconventional characters.

One thing that a lot of our contemporaries were engaged in was the publication of science fiction fanzines. I'd been involved with fandom since my high school days, so I was at home in this milieu. To Pat it was clearly new and wonderful, and she took to it like a rocket to outer space.

There was no such thing as comics fandom in those days. I'm talking about 1959. There had been articles about comics in science fiction fanzines from time to time, as fans wrote about Flash Gordon, Buck Rogers, or Brick Bradford. There was a flourishing Burroughs fan movement, which of course brought about discussions of John Carter of Mars, Carson of Venus, and David Innes in Pellucidar. And of course there was Superman—created by Jerry Siegel and Joe Shuster, a couple of science fiction fans themselves.

There was also EC fandom, a specialized, narrowly focused community devoted to the fine comics edited by Al Feldstein and illustrated by an amazing array of fine cartoonists: Bernie Krigstein, Wallace Wood, Frank Frazetta, Graham Ingels, Al Williamson, Roy Krenkel.

So science fiction fandom and comics were by no means strangers. But there were no fanzines devoted to the broader field of comics and cartooning, and there were certainly no comics-oriented conventions.

Pat and I wanted to get into the swim of our new cultural community, and it seemed that the way to do this was to publish a fanzine. We chose a suitably exotic name for it. We would call our magazine *Xanadu.* A young Indiana fan, Joe Sanders, sketched out an image of Kublai Khan's fabled pleasure dome for the cover of our first issue.

Even though we were now part of the fan community—or so we believed—we weren't very well connected with fan writers and illustrators, so we did what many youngsters in that position have done from time immemorial: we wrote and illustrated the first issue ourselves.

Pat wrote a review of *Brood of the Witch Queen,* a marvelously lurid novel by English thriller writer Sax Rohmer, the creator of the sinister Dr. Fu Manchu. She also wrote a longer and more serious essay about another English fantasist, Mervyn Peake. Our friend Joe Sanders had put her onto this writer's dense, eccentric works, and she had become a devotee of Gormenghast and its strange denizens.

We happened to cross paths with Harlan Ellison, and when he heard that we were planning a new fanzine he offered a contribution to the first issue: a review of the recently released film version of Robert Bloch's novel *Psycho.*

That left me, and when I started casting around for a topic to write about I thought of my childhood fascination with comic book superheroes. My favorite were the Marvel Family—Captain Marvel, Captain Marvel, Jr., Mary Marvel, and assorted ancillary Marvels.

Here was my chance to rhapsodize on a favorite topic, one that nobody else seemed to be interested in. Fawcett Publications had dropped its comic book line at that point, the Marvels were a rapidly fading memory in the rapidly evolving world of comics, and so I plunged into the depths of memory and wrote about my first encounter with Captain Marvel when my brother and I invested ten cents in the first issue of *Whiz Comics.* Ironically, it was marked Volume 1, Number 2, but that's a piece of publishing history trivia that's been recorded elsewhere.

I called the essay "The Big Red Cheese," and labeled it, with more hope than confidence, as the first in a series to be known a ". . . and All in Color for a Dime."

At the last minute we discovered that another fan had already laid claim to the title *Xanadu,* so we scanned the dictionary for another "X" title and settled upon *Xero.*

For the record, *Xero* didn't spring full-blown into existence. A few weeks earlier a group of fans had gathered in a city park for a picnic only to run into two gangs of self-styled toughs. They announced that they were planning a turf war that very afternoon, on the very picnic ground where we had planned to hold our festivities.

They warned us, very civilly, that it would be very dangerous for us to spread our blankets and baskets on the ground where they were planning to battle. At least one of us—yep, me, fresh out of the army and rarin' to do battle—wanted to defy the thugs and call their bluff. But cooler heads prevailed, and instead we retreated to a convenient apartment and held an indoor picnic.

Three of us—Pat and I and another local fan—wrote up a report on the event and published it as a slim one-shot called *The Rumble.* I've never seen a copy of this for sale, but I imagine that it would make quite a collector's item. In any case, we received a good many letters of comment on *The Rumble,* and these provided grist for a letter column in *Xero 1.*

We didn't have a duplicator so we paid another fan who was operating a small-scale mimeography business to run off a hundred copies for us. Allowing for spoilage, file copies, and the like, we actually distributed something like 90 copies of *Xero 1,* dated September, 1960, at the World Science Fiction Convention in Pittsburgh, Pennsylvania.

I remember running down the hotel hallway, literally chasing people, trying to get them to take copies of the fanzine. I think they go for several hundred dollars a copy now, and demand exceeds supply.

We encouraged readers to send letters of comment on that first issue—it ran something like 30 pages—and to our surprise, the LoCs came pouring in. People liked Pat's review of the Rohmer book and her essay on Mervyn Peake, and of course Harlan's review of *Psycho* evoked responses, but we were amazed at how many readers responded to "The Big Red Cheese." Apparently there was a deep reservoir of nostalgia and general fondness for the comics, and nobody had written about it in quite the way I did.

Once the floodgates were opened, people stood in line, eager to contribute essays to the series.

Xero was officially published on an irregular basis. I had a day job in the then infant computer industry. Pat was involved as a homemaker as well as tending to family obligations. But unofficially, we were turning out an issue every couple of months. The trouble was—if trouble is the right word—with each issue of *Xero* the magazine was growing in size and elaboration, and also in circulation. We declined to accept subscriptions at that point, or to sell copies. We would only give copies of *Xero* to contributors, to authors of letters-of-comment, or to other publishers who would trade their fanzines for ours.

Even so, circulation went from 100 to 120 to 150 to . . . we had no idea where we were headed!

For the second issue, my own crude design and illustrations were replaced by outside contributors. We had artwork by Dave English and Sylvia White, and articles by Ray Beam (yes, his actual name), Mike Deckinger, Les Sample, and Dick Schultz. Larry M. Harris (aka Larry Janifer) arrived as our regular book reviewer. And very much to the point, we had the second instalment of "All in Color for a Dime" (we'd dropped the ". . . and"), "The Spawn of M. C. Gaines," by Ted White. The issue ran to 50 pages.

Issue 3, dated January, 1961, also contained 50 pages. There was a variety of material in the issue, much of it attracted by a manifesto of sorts, in which we stated that we would welcome material for *Xero* on any subject, provided only that it be well written, and of interest to our readership. The fanzine world in that era had been swept by a movement called "fannishness," in which fan writers seemed obsessed by the idea of sheer cleverness to the exclusion of content. In *Xero* we insisted on content, and while a few fans seemed to be offended by our plonking serconnishness, many more responded favorably.

Science fiction writer James Blish contributed a fine essay under the pseudonym of Arthur Merlyn, giving the inside story of what it took to write for the Captain Video TV series. And "All in Color for a Dime" expanded to some twenty pages, with an essay by Jim Harmon on the Justice Society of America, "A Bunch of Swell Guys." In addition, I expanded on my "Big Red Cheese" essay, based on some actual research—I had written the original piece strictly from memory, and it was riddled with errors.

We had a wonderful essay by Otto Binder himself, the longtime chief writer of Marvel stories. I'd visited his office to drop off a copy of *Xero 1,* but run away, leaving the magazine at the receptionist's desk. I was too shy to actually meet the great man just then, although Pat and I would later become good friends with the Binders, visiting their home and entertaining them at ours.

And Ted White expanded on his tribute to M. C. Gaines. It made a sparkling section of the magazine. When I said that we hadn't known what we were doing when we started publishing *Xero,* I was slowly coming to an understanding. We'd thought that *Xero* was going to be a science fiction fanzine, but in fact it was actually—from the outset!—a wide-ranging journal of popular culture.

Xero 4 was dated April, 1961. The comics related material was spun off to create *Xero Comics,* published back-to-back, Ace Books fashion, with *Xero* itself. James Blish was back, writing under his own name now; we had commentary from leading fan Bill Donaho and from professional writers and editors F. M. Busby, Larry Shaw, Hal Lynch, and Larry M. Harris. Robert S. "Buck" Coulson joined our regular troupe with a fanzine review column.

Chris Steinbrunner, a film programmer for New York's Channel 9 and for a commercial airline, extended our reach into another medium with "Next Week: The Phantom Strikes Again," a marvelous survey of motion picture serials.

bhob Stewart, Chris Steinbrunner, Jack Gaughan, George Earley

Xero Comics was devoted to the ancestors of today's Marvel Comics empire, "O.K. Axis, Here we Come!" Don Thompson wrote this one, and I'm almost certain that it was the first serious treatment of Captain America, the Human Torch, the Sub-Mariner, and the lesser members of the Stan Lee universe.

Fifty-four pages for *Xero* plus eighteen for *Xero Comics*—a total of 72 pages. Oh, and did I mention, Pat was pregnant!

Xero 5 (July, 1961) shrank a little, to a mere 56 pages, but it featured our first offset-printed cover: a marvelous, evocative portrait of the original (1940s) character, the Atom. Artist was Larry Ivie, and the stark black-against-yellow design was a stunner. We'd also added an art editor (and chief designer), bhob Stewart.

An eager teenaged fan named Roger Ebert arrived as our resident poet, and we had contributions from James Blish, Ed Gorman, and Avram Davidson. We also had a growing crew of cartoonists including Jim Warren, publisher of *Famous Monsters, Creepy,* and *Eerie.* A very political fan named Art Castillo had sent us a series of postcards condemning us for wasting paper and ink and energy on such trivia as comic books and old movies when we should have devoted ourselves to deep analysis of the political issues of the world. He called our attitude "Relativistic Dadaism," a phrase so charming that we adopted it as our slogan.

You may have noticed that there was no instalment of "All in Color for a Dime" in *Xero 5* but we made up for that by featuring two instalments in *Xero 6,* September, 1961. This was the Willish, so named in honor Walter A. Willis, a popular Irish fan. We dedicated the issue to him, the front cover a portrait by bhob Stewart, and featuring a fine new logo that bhob also designed.

George Scithers, a career army officer and later editor of *Isaac Asimov's Science Fiction Magazine,* had lucked into a supply of brilliant, incandescent green paper, and donated it for use on the cover of *Xero 6.* We didn't have enough of this to use on all copies of the issue, so some of our subscribers (by now we'd given in and agreed to accept money) had to settle for covers printed on ordinary green paper.

Contributors included Willis himself and most of our regulars, plus Charles M. Collins, a bookstore manager who wrote knowledgably about book publishing and selling, Lin Carter who wrote about Jules Verne, and Wilson Tucker writing as "Hoy Ping Pong," with a devastating satire of Robert Bloch.

We sold the issue for an astronomical price of one dollar, evoking an angry letter of complaint from Marion Zimmer Bradley, and contributed proceeds to a fund designed to bring Walter Willis and his wife, Madeline, to the US for the Worldcon.

The two instalments of "All in Color for a Dime" were "The Several Soldiers of Victory" by myself, and "Me to Your Leader Take," a fine survey of *Planet Comics* by Dick Ellington.

Seventy-six pages. And Kenneth Bruce Lupoff was born on September 7, weighing in at seven pounds, two ounces.

Xero 7, November, 1961, filled a puny 54 pages. "All in Color for a Dime" was titled "The Wild Ones," and in it, Don Thompson lived up to that title. His subjects were Doctor Fate and the Spectre, surely two of the superest superheroes of all time.

Xero 8 had another incandescent cover (at least on the copies of the lucky subscribers), with an amazing op-art experiment by bhob Stewart. Believe it or not, the only date I can find on my file copy is the year—1962. Larry Harris had retired as our book reviewer, replaced by Lin Carter. In addition to his reviews, Lin initiated a series of essays called "Notes on Tolkien," which would eventually grow into a book.

An eccentric local fan, H. P. Norton, gave us an essay in tribute to Clark Ashton Smith. And sometime anthologist Henry Mazzeo recorded an odd encounter with our cocker spaniel, "The Shadow Meets Snoopy."

"All in Color for a Dime" was devoted to "The Education of Victor Fox," a remarkably well researched essay by Richard Kyle, about one of the more off-beat publishers of Golden Age Comics.

Seventy pages for *Xero* plus another 20 for *Xero Comics.*

By *Xero 9* we were starting to wind down. We felt that we'd pushed the fanzine about as far as we could. One hundred pages. I don't know our exact circulation, but it was somewhere around 300. Most of our regulars were back—Ebert, Carter, Tucker, Coulson. An array of artists including Englishman Arthur Thomson ("Atom"). Instead of carving ATom's work into the wax of mimeograph stencils, our friend Chris Steinbrunner got us access to a scanning electrostencil machine at Channel Nine.

A local fan named Norman Clarke did a superb essay called "The Greatest Shows Unearthly," about science fiction in turn-of-the-century theater. This, too, grew into a book.

"All in Color for a Dime"— A fine essay on the Fawcett comics line, backing up the Marvel Family. Author was a kid named Roy Thomas who wanted to get into the business himself. He was really talented. Wonder if he ever made good.

Another hundred-pager, with a raging back cover by Steve Stiles, done up in three different color versions. Nothing like making completest collectors and bibliographers tear their hair.

Xero 10 was the magazine's swan song. We had two covers, designated "Sword" and "Sorcery." Fine, collectable pen-work, one by Roy Krenkel and one by Eddie Jones. Rather than designate one as the front cover and the other as the back, we alternated them on copies of the issue. Issue dated May, 1963.

Lots of cartoons by Dan Adkins, "Bab," Cathy Bell, and the other *Xero* regulars. A long essay on Sax Rohmer by Bob Briney. This one grew into a book. For "All in Color for a Dime," Richard Kyle returned with "Sparky Watts and the Big Shots." And a brilliant cartoonist named Landon Chesney gave us an hilarious parody, "Two Flashes Meet the Purple Slagheap."

Again, 100 pages. But *Xero* would not go quiet into that good night. Local fan and burgeoning novelist Dave Van Arnam had promised an essay on Edgar Rice Burroughs for *Xero,* but the longer he worked on it, the longer the essay grew. Eventually it became so big, there was no way we could fit it into an issue of *Xero.*

So we obtained additional contributions by Donald A. Wollheim, Larry Ivie and myself, a superb gatefold map of Barsoom by Larry Ivie, and artwork by Roy Krenkel, bhob Stewart, and Al Williamson. We published it as a book, *The Reader's Guide to Barsoom and Amtor,* and it sold out before publication.

Dave Van Arnam was working on a revised and expanded edition at the time of his death.

And finally, there was the *Xero Index Edition,* comprising not just an index but also a final, final, final letter column.

Xero won the Hugo for best fanzine in 1963. Forty years later Tachyon Publications of San Francisco published *The Best of Xero* and that was a Hugo nominee.

Pat and I had been urged to turn *Xero* into a full-scale commercial publication, and it was indeed an intriguing idea. But she was raising three children as well as pursuing a career as a retail bookseller. And I was writing novels and short stories and editing novels and anthologies. Maybe if we'd had clones, that would have worked. But as things stood, we couldn't do it. We just couldn't do it.

So *Xero* stands. It yielded a modest shelf of books—Norm Clarke's book on theater, Lin Carter's *Notes on Tolkien,* Don Thompson and my own *All in Color for a Dime* and *The Comic*

Book Book, plus portions of James Blish's volumes of collected criticism.

It was a wonderful chapter in fan publishing, but it was only one chapter. Great fanzines preceded *Xero* and great fanzines followed it. Pat and I had a marvelous time with those ten numbered issues and assorted spin-offs.

When each issue was edited and designed and the stencils were cut and typed and mimeographed—we did invest in such a machine for ourselves—we would lay the pages out on our dining room table and invite a crew of volunteers to a collating party. There were Don Wollheim and Elsie Wollheim and Larry Ivie and bhob Stewart and Chris Steinbrunner and Steve Stiles, and I would act as drill sergeant as they marched around and around and around the table like caterpillars on the rim of a tea cup, assembling copy after copy after copy of the latest issue.

During this process Pat would be in the kitchen cooking up a huge pot of spaghetti. When the last copy was assembled and stapled the fanzines would go into cartons and everyone would sit down to a communal dinner.

Endless memories. Don Westlake had started his career writing both science fiction and mysteries. When he got fed up with meddling and/or incompetent science fiction editors he wrote an essay for *Xero* in effect resigning from the world of science fiction. When his agent heard about this he phoned me and pleaded with me to kill the piece, but it was too late, 300 copies had already gone into the mail.

"My god," Don's agent groaned, "he's killed himself."

Not hardly. Best-selling mystery writer, Oscar-winning screenwriter. And my dear friend until I learned of his sudden demise.

Mailing out those 300 fanzines. I was reluctant to get involved with the postal bureaucracy, so instead I would sneak out late at night and drop them into mailboxes all over Manhattan. Five copies here. Ten copies there. Until all 300 were mailed. I never heard from the postal inspectors, and as far as I know everybody got his copy.

Happy memories.

Precious memories.

Now it's somebody else's turn.

Edgar Rice Burroughs

AN ERB ADDICT GETS HIS FIX

THE FIRST CANAVERAL PRESS book that I saw hit me like a thunderbolt. It was *A Fighting Man of Mars*. I'd never seen a Burroughs science fiction book before. I'd been reintroduced to Burroughs by my wife, Pat. I'd last read a Big Little Book edition of *Tarzan and the Ant-Men* when I was eleven years old, had moved on to science fiction, and didn't look back—until Pat insisted that I was missing something good.

The year was 1959. As far as I knew, the only Burroughs books in print (at least in the US) were some Grosset Tarzans. I'd heard of Burroughs as a science fiction writer—more accurately, had read pleas for more Burroughs adventures in *Amazing Stories* when I was in high school—but I'd never actually laid eyes on a Burroughs science fiction novel.

And suddenly—there was a handsomely produced hardcover edition. I was working in the then-fledgling computer industry, and I sat down with the book—I recall, on a Friday night—and by Monday I was ready to head out on my lunch break and start searching for more.

Most Burroughs books were hard to find in the used book shops of Fourth Avenue, New York's legendary Book Row. So I was excited to learn that Canaveral had announced an ambitious program of Burroughs reprints. Every time a new release was scheduled I headed to my favorite bookstore, Stephen's Book Service on the Lower East Side. This establishment was run by Stephen Takacs, a classic bookman, forever gloomy and complaining that business had always been bad, was worse now, and was continuing to decline.

When a new release date arrived and the promised Burroughs books were not available at Stephen's Book Service, I made my annoyance felt. I had become addicted, there's no other term for what had happened to me, and like any other addict deprived of his fix, I became highly agitated.

Finally Stephen got tired of my complaints. "I can't do anything about it. The books are on order and they haven't arrived. If you want to complain, go complain to Canaveral. Their office is a five minute walk from here. It's at 63 Fourth Avenue."

So off I went.

Sixty-three Fourth Avenue was a four-story, nineteenth-century building. The sign over the doorway said, "Biblo and Tannen, Booksellers and Publishers." I entered and found myself in a wonderland of used books, ranging from battered reading copies to hundred-year-old treasures. I asked the man who greeted me if this building contained the offices of Canaveral Press.

He told me that Canaveral Press was a subsidiary of Biblo and Tannen and this was indeed the office of Canaveral Press.

That man was either Jack Biblo or Jack Tannen. They had been partners in the bookselling business since the 1920s, and like an old married couple they had come to look like each other. Each had dark, receding hair and a bushy moustache. Each wore a tweed jacket, plaid shirt, knit tie. Each wore horn-rimmed glasses.

Once we had introduced ourselves I voiced my complaint. The Burroughs books had been scheduled, they had been promised, I had taken the subway all the way downtown to buy copies from Stephen Takacs and he had told me that they were not available.

Wow, did I ever lay it on thick! No junkie pleading with his pusher ever put on a more impassioned show than I did.

Finally Jack—whichever of the two Jacks I was talking with—said, "I tell you what. We're doing our best but there are some things we can't control, such as the printer's and binder's schedule. But if you think you can do any better, how about you come and work for us?"

And that was how I got my job at Canaveral Press. I was just a kid—well, in my early twenties—and the two Jacks adopted me like a pair of doting uncles. Their office manager, the wonderful Alice Ryter, adopted me like a stern but loving aunt. Their close friend and sometime book scout, David Garfinkel, a dime novel scholar, missed no opportunity to regale me with stories of Old Sleuth, Young Sleuth, Baseball Joe, Buffalo Bill, and other heroes of his own boyhood, early in the twentieth century.

Working for Canaveral Press was the best job I ever had. I loved my work, I loved my co-workers, and I loved my surroundings: thousands and thousands of wondrous books!

The Canaveral edition of *Fighting Man* and most of the early Canaveral books were illustrated by Mahlon Blaine, a highly regarded artist of earlier decades. He'd fallen into obscurity in his old age; his career was resurrected by Jack Biblo and Jack Tannen, the owners of Canaveral Press. Burroughs fans generally disliked Blaine's interpretations. The fans had grown up on a tradition dating back to Hal Foster, Frank R. Paul, and J. Allen St. John. Art that was romantic in atmosphere and thoroughly realistic, representational, in execution.

Blaine's renderings were eccentric, often subtly erotic. Only Avram Davidson, writing in *The Magazine of Fantasy and Science Fiction,* suggested that the Blaine-illustrated books would someday be valued more for Blaine's drawings than for Burroughs' stories. When I met him, Mahlon Blaine had only one eye. I didn't get to know him well, regrettably, and never learned when or how he had lost an eye. I wonder how his monocular vision affected his work.

Illustration by Mahlon Blaine from
The Moon Men (Canaveral Press, 1962)

After Blaine, Canaveral issued one Burroughs book illustrated by Burroughs fan and comic book aficionado Larry Ivie.

And then came a miniature Golden Age.

Comics fans still revere the EC line of the 1950s. The science fiction and horror comics produced by this company—*Weird Science, Weird Fantasy, Vault of Horror, Crypt of Terror,* and finally *Incredible Science Fiction*—were arguably the best written and most skillfully illustrated comic books of all time.

But by now the EC line had disappeared, a victim of the Comics Code and politically-inspired censorship and self-censorship. The highly talented EC bullpen had scattered to the winds, but somehow—I don't know how this happened—half of these talented cartoonists wound up producing jacket designs and interior illustrations for Canaveral Press.

By this time I was working at Canaveral as an editor. Well, as *the* editor. It was a very small company. And here I was, with four of the artists whose work had thrilled me when I was a schoolboy—working for me! I tried not to look intimidated. I'm not sure how well I brought that off.

The most prominent of these artists was Frank Frazetta. He'd had a long history doing comic book art of a variety of themes, then moved on to painting scenes for hardcover book jackets and paperback covers. His work was spectacular. He was a master of color values, of design and anatomy. I think his greatest breakthrough was a portrait of Conan the Barbarian that he created for Lancer Books, where my friend Larry Shaw was editor.

There was nothing pretty about this Conan. He looked brutal, violent, like a killer.

Frank lived in Pennsylvania, so I didn't get to interact with him in person, save on occasions when he visited us at 63 Fourth Avenue in New York. He was thoroughly businesslike, and probably a bit shy. His work was always delivered on time and was always splendid, but he didn't care to socialize very much.

Roy Krenkel was a friend of Frazetta's, but a very different person. He was a grand eccentric. He lived with his aged parents and refused to install a telephone. If you wanted to speak with Roy you would jot down a note reminding him of your phone number, tape a dime to the page, and mail it to him.

Once he received your letter, if the weather was pleasant and if he was so inclined, he would walk to the nearest phone booth and call you. You'd set up an appointment, and maybe he would meet you as arranged. Or maybe not.

Roy was a perfectionist, and he would only deliver a piece when he was convinced that he'd got it right. He was particularly concerned with hands and feet. Apparently these are the most difficult part of the human figure for artists to portray. I wouldn't know: I'm strictly a word guy.

On one occasion I was taking lunch with Don Wollheim and Terry Carr of Ace Books. Don asked if I was planning to use Krenkel for future books. I told him I wasn't sure. I loved Roy's work (and I liked him as a person) but deadlines meant nothing to him and that made it very difficult to work with him. Still, he was so damned good! Every time a collector shows me a treasured copy of *Tales of Three Planets* with that spectacular Krenkel dust jacket I marvel at the achievement.

Another EC veteran was Al Williamson. Williamson had been born in South America—I believe in Chile—and moved to the US as a child. He was as handsome as a movie star and had a totally charming personality. Unlike the standoffish Frank Frazetta and the eccentric Roy Krenkel, Williamson was a gregarious yarn-spinner. He and his wife, Arlene, lived in a town north of New York City, not far from where Pat and I lived at the time. Arlene was similarly talented, and contributed some fine calligraphy to our Burroughs line.

Pat and I visited Al and Arlene from time to time; Al was a fan of vintage jazz and was especially proud of his collection of Woody Herman recordings. Many years later, after Al had blazed a brilliant career doing newspaper comic strips including Flash Gordon, I heard that he was very ill. I tried to renew contact. Arlene had died long before this, and Al had remarried. I had a warm conversation with Al's second wife, but Al wasn't up to speaking on the phone. His wife said that he was comfortable, though, and was busy listening to his Woody Herman collection.

Reed Crandall was a pal of Al Williamson's. Before moving upstate, Pat and I had lived in a Manhattan apartment. One evening Al dropped in on us and brought a friend—Reed Crandall. Reed was a versatile artist—as were all of the ex-EC crew—best known for Blackhawk comic book stories.

The Blackhawks were an international brigade of aviators who fought the Nazis during World War Two, and went on to battle Communist aggression in the Cold War. Reed was a careful researcher as well as a consummate craftsman. The Blackhawks flew authentic warplanes. I remember at one point they were flying Grumman F5F Skyrockets. Later Reed furnished them with a later model; I think these were F7F Tigercats.

Reed was a farm boy with roots in the Midwest. Unlike Al Williamson and Frank Frazetta who looked like matinee idols, and Roy Krenkel who sported a craggy, angular look, Reed Crandall was a rotund, jolly-looking individual. All he needed was a red suit and a white beard and he would have been a perfect Santa Claus.

Well, Canaveral Press is long gone now, and all of our artists—Mahlon Blaine, Larry Ivie, Frank Frazetta, Roy Krenkel, Al Williamson, Arlene Williamson, Reed Crandall—are gone as well. I miss them all.

~ ~ ~ ~ ~

CANAVERAL PRESS, Inc.

Affiliate of Biblo and Tannen, Inc.

63 Fourth Avenue

New York 3, N.Y.

THE ICEMAN COMETH

YA MAKIN' ME feel like one a them Neanderthal apes that they thaw out o' glaciers ever so often. Ya see stuff about it on the TV between wars and murders and politicians shouting at each other.

So what was it like in 1960, ya wanna know. Did we really travel by horse and buggy and cross the ocean in sailing ships? No, not quite. We even had cars and radios and a few TVs. They had one at the corner saloon near my house. Thirteen inches across and fuzzy black-and-white pitchers. Got two or three channels, depending on where Maria the bartender pointed the coat-hanger coming out of the top.

Dwight Eisenhower and Mao Tse-tung and Nikita Khrushchev played musical chairs to see who was top dog on the planet, ganging up two-on-one, shifting sides every couple a years.

Baseball teams kept moving around. Whatever happened to the Boston Braves, the Brooklyn Dodgers, the New York Giants, the Philadelphia Athletics, the Washington Senators, the St. Louis Browns? Danged if I know.

What the hell was happening to the world I'd been borneded into?

We had computers, that we did. They were the size of barns and cost millions of simoleons.

A bunch of malcontents dared to challenge the mighty National Football League and started the rival American Football League. The Super Bowl wasn't even a gleam in Broadway Joe Namath's eye.

Comics fandom got its start in 1960 and '61 with the appearance of three fanzines. The first of these was *Xero*. Originally planned as a science fiction fanzine, *Xero* carried a series of essays collectively titled *All in Color for a Dime* from its first issue. The editors were one of the few female fans of the era, Pat Lupoff, and her husband.

The others followed in short order. *Alter-Ego* was edited and published by Roy Thomas and Jerry Bails, and concentrated on superheroes. *Comic Art,* produced by Don and Maggie Thompson, took a broader view of the world of cartooning.

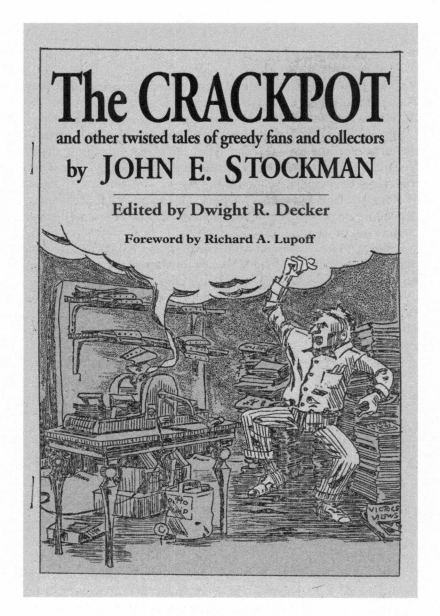

Fanzines in that era were typically produced by one of two systems. Mimeographs worked by forcing a thick, petroleum-based gunk through holes in a silk sheet coated with wax. Dittos were a development from the older hektograph system of jelly-based dye transfers.

You could tell which system a fan publisher used. Mimeographers walked around with a black ink residue under their fingernails. Ditto-users had purple hands.

High-end circulation for fanzines in that era was around 300. For most, the number was much smaller.

The first comic convention that I know of took place in a stuffy, rented meeting room in lower Manhattan. I don't know how many fans were present—at a guess, sixty. I entered the room quietly on a break from my day job, quietly stayed for about three quarters of an hour, then quietly exited and went back to my office.

My favorite source of older comics in that era was a store on New York's lower east side called The Memory Shop. It was run by a pleasant character named Mark Ricci. His pricing system for back issue comics was a dime a year. A five-year-old comic would set you back fifty cents. A twenty-year-old comic would cost you two bucks.

Not everybody wanted to take comics (or comics fandom) seriously. Pat and I received a postcard from a reader named Art Castillo. "All around you is a society seething, begging not only for a critical evaluation of its fundamentals but for a re-construction of those very fundamentals, and you people sit on your ass and discuss comic-books. What's wrong with you, anyway?"

He also accused us of Relativistic Dadaism, a phrase so charming that we made it the slogan of *Xero* for the rest of its run.

In fact there was a sort of proto-comics-fandom before that key year of 1960. As early as the 1940s there were the Captain Marvel Club, the Mary Marvel Club, the Junior Justice Society of America, the Supermen of America, the Buck Rogers Club, and certainly others. These "captive" fan clubs were created and operated by comic book publishers as a marketing device. The last and best of them was the EC Fan Addicts Club.

What made the new comics fandom of 1960 and thereafter different was the fact that it was created and operated (I won't say controlled!) by the fans themselves. Not by the publishers.

We've come a long way since then. I wonder how Art Castillo would react if he were plunged into the San Diego Convention Center in the midst of some 300,000 rabid comic book fans. I'm afraid his head would explode.

Burroughs fandom was another thing altogether. Edgar Rice Burroughs had been an immensely popular pulp author, and fans were collecting his books, magazines, and comics almost from the outset in 1912. Not long before Burroughs's death in 1950, a devoted fan named Vernell Coriell traveled from his home in the Midwest to California to meet the Great Man. Coriell wanted to start a fan club devoted to Burroughs and his works, and to publish a club journal.

Burroughs placed his blessing on Coriell's enterprise, and Coriell created the Burroughs Bibliophiles and their official magazine, *The Burroughs Bulletin,* and their newsletter, *The Gridley Wave.* Other fans followed suit: Camille "Caz" Cazedessus, with *ERB-dom* magazine and James V. Taurasi with *Barsoomian Times* newsletter.

Coriell was furious, insisting that his publications were the only legitimate, authentic, authorized Burroughs-related periodicals and that all others were poaching on his exclusive territory.

Enter John R. Stockman. In this man were united the three streams of fandom: Burroughs collecting, comics collecting, and fanzine publishing. Turn this man loose with a typewriter, a quire of mimeograph stencils, a couple of reams of twiltone mimeo paper, and a battered old A. B. Dick mimeo, and the result was little less than thermonuclear.

I never knew Stockman, alas, but the literary legacy he has left us, stories populated by fanatical collectors of comic books and Burroughsiana, are classic. I will leave it to others to try to understand "Mule" Stockman, to evaluate his unique contributions to the field, to place him in the history of memorable madmen.

Howard Browne

HOWARD BROWNE, PAUL PINE
AND THE HALO NOVELS

THE FIRST TIME I laid eyes on Howard Browne the calendar read April 15, 1988. It was Howard Browne's eightieth birthday. A group of Howard's friends and colleagues had arranged a surprise party for him at Green's Restaurant in San Francisco.

My own friend, Frank M. Robinson, had got me invited to the party. Frank had worked for the Ziff-Davis Publishing Company's pulp magazine group in the 1940s as a teenager just getting started in the publishing world. Now Frank was a revered elder statesman in the science fiction community in the San Francisco Bay Area. Among other things, he was known for the explosive guffaw that served him as a laugh.

The party was under way, people were exchanging small talk and topical jokes, waiting for the guest of honor to arrive. Somebody made a clever remark, Frank exploded with laughter, and from the hallway a thunderous bass voice roared, "That's Robinson the office boy!"

Howard Browne appeared in the doorway flanked by his wife, Doris, and his longtime pal Bill Nolan.

Browne was a huge man, well over six feet tall, broad-shouldered and heavy-set. He had dark hair, swept straight back from his wide forehead. He'd suffered from poor vision all his life, and wore thick-lensed spectacles. Although I got to meet him that day our encounter amounted to little more than a handshake and a "Happy birthday."

I knew who Howard Browne was. In my days as a science fiction fan in the 1950s I'd admired the spectacular job he did with a new Ziff-Davis magazine, *Fantastic.* For a while it was the most literate magazine in its field, as well as being lovingly designed and produced. I had the impression that Howard Browne, the editor, had put his heart and soul into that magazine. It was visually beautiful, printed on a superior grade of paper, with stories by writers well above the usual pulp standard. Nor were they all the usual suspects one would expect to find in a science fiction magazine. Browne had published Shirley Jackson, Cornell Woolrich, the enigmatic B. Traven, Truman Capote, E. M. Forster, Evelyn Waugh. He published new stories by them when he could get them; otherwise he would reprint classics.

Alas, the bean counters at Ziff-Davis weren't interested in publishing beautiful magazines filled with fine stories. They were interested in the bottom line, and *Fantastic* didn't bring in a bottom line that pleased them. The budget was cut and the magazine reverted to pulp adventure stories. It was still fun, but the sophisticated product that Browne had created was gone after just a handful of issues.

A decade later, in the 1960s, I was working for Canaveral Press in New York and acting as the posthumous editor for Edgar Rice Burroughs. I was working on a book about Burroughs as well, and spent months not only reading all of Burroughs's works but as many books as I could find that had seemingly influenced him or been influenced by him.

Two of the latter were *Warrior of the Dawn* and *The Return of Tharn*. While the eponymous character was a Cro-Magnon, these novels more nearly resembled Burroughs's Tarzan adventures than they did earlier cave man novels such as Richard Tooker's *Day of the Brown Horde* or Jack London's *Before Adam,* to mention only two of the many "caveman novels" published in the nineteenth and twentieth centuries.

Warrior of the Dawn first appeared in *Amazing Stories* in 1942, with a spectacular, eye-catching cover illustration. Four years would pass before it was published as a book—again with a fine dust jacket designed to grab the attention of any browser—by Reilly and Lee, a company better known for publishing many titles in the Wizard of Oz series.

Years later, when I got to know Howard Browne he told me the following story:

"I decided to write a book something like Burroughs's Tarzan novels. So I sat down with a stack of Tarzan books and copied out all the modifiers that Burroughs used, and kept track of how many times he used each one. When I'd finished I worked out the percentages for each adjective and adverb, and used the same ones in the same proportions in my Tharn stories and the readers seemed to like them. Once the first book was published I got a letter from a reader. It read, 'Dear Mr. Browne, Congratulations on *Warrior of the Dawn*. It's the best book I never wrote. Yours truly, Edgar Rice Burroughs.' "

~ ~ ~ ~ ~

Howard Browne was born in Omaha, Nebraska, in April, 1908 (sometimes reported as 1907). Raised in poverty in a broken home, he attended local public schools but was so bored he dropped out before completing high school. Dissatisfied with life in Nebraska he escaped into fantasy literature—Burroughs was a favorite—and sports, especially baseball. His weak vision prevented his playing, but he was an enthusiastic fan. Babe Ruth was his hero.

He hitch-hiked from Omaha to Chicago to see the Babe's Yankees play the Chicago White Sox. When he asked a local denizen which way to the ball park to see Ruth play, the Chicagoan informed him that he was in the wrong part of Chicago. He was on the North Side, where the Cubs played. The White Sox played on the South Side. Penniless, Browne walked the entire length of the city to see his idol perform.

But now that he was in Chicago he fell in love with the city and vowed not to return to Omaha. He had to earn a living, and soon obtained employment collecting payments for a furniture company. "I didn't know anything about the furniture business, and I couldn't see well," he told me decades later. "But the customers took one look at me and decided to pay what they owed."

Even though he was promoted to credit manager, he didn't find the job of collecting overdue payments for bedroom suites fulfilling, and after scouting around for another position, found himself employed by the Ziff-Davis Publishing Company. He was assigned to the company's burgeoning fiction magazine group. This included *Amazing Stories, Fantastic Adventures, Mammoth Mystery, Mammoth Detective,* and *Mammoth Adventures.* Editor-in-Chief of the group was Raymond A. Palmer, assisted by William Hamling and Howard Browne. Frank Robinson was, indeed, the office boy.

In later years, Robinson compiled one of the world's major pulp archives. He told me that he'd got his start by sneaking file copies of back issues out of the Ziff-Davis offices in the 1940s.

One of Browne's eventual claims to fame (or infamy) concerned the so-called Shaver Mystery. Part of Palmer's appeal to readers was the friendly, chatty atmosphere in the Ziff-Davis pulps. Palmer wrote informal editorials and ran lengthy columns of letters-to-the-editor. Part of Howard Browne's job was trolling the baskets full of letters from fans.

One day he opened a lengthy, semi-incoherent, hand-written letter from one Richard S. Shaver. The writer told a rambling story about an ancient civilization that was threatened by malign solar radiations. The godlike ancient Earthlings built a fleet of gigantic spaceships in which most of them left for safer planets, but a few instead retreated to caves from which they worked mischief on the surface dwellers of the present day.

The narrative didn't make much sense, the writing was at best semi-literate, and, furthermore, Shaver claimed that it was all true.

Browne dumped Shaver's letter in the wastebasket.

Palmer retrieved it. He looked it over, said something like, "Hmm, I think I can make something out of this." Ran a sheet into his typewriter, rewrote Shaver's screed, and scheduled it for *Amazing Stories*. The magazine's circulation zoomed, and to this day there are a few surviving Shaver Mystery cultists.

Howard Browne stayed at Ziff-Davis from 1941 to 1956 with breaks to write radio and motion picture scripts and novels. In later years it was rumored that he hated science fiction and only took the job of running *Amazing Stories* and *Fantastic Adventures* because they were bundled with *Mammoth Mystery* and *Mammoth Detective*. Palmer had left Z-D in 1949 to start a small publishing company of his own. Hamling followed shortly afterward. Browne, who had been working in Hollywood, was called back to take the top spot at the Z-D pulp group.

But later, when Ziff-Davis moved east, Browne found himself shuttling between New York and Los Angeles. Television was burgeoning, Hollywood beckoned, and before long Browne had become executive story consultant to 20th Century-Fox television studios. Not only that, he was story editor for series including *The Kraft Mystery Theater, The Virginian,* and *Longstreet*.

Along the way (and in later years) he worked as story editor and wrote screenplays for many television series, most notably *Perry Mason*. After more than half a century, dozens of TV episodes that Browne either wrote himself or supervised remain in the rerun rotation. He also scripted four feature films, most notably the screen biography *Capone*.

During his stays with Ziff-Davis he had also sold numerous stories to himself—a common practice in the pulp magazine field. Salaries were not very high, and many editors used their magazines as ATMs, usually using pseudonyms for their fiction, as publishers frowned upon the practice. Browne wrote dozens of detective stories for ZD's two crime pulps. For the science fiction pulps he wrote the serial that introduced his "Cro-Magnon Tarzan," Tharn, to the world. The first Tharn novel, *Warrior of the Dawn,* was published in 1943. The second, *The Return of Tharn,* followed in 1956. (The magazine version had been published in 1948.)

But while the two Tharn novels were quite good, Browne's heart and soul were in detective fiction. He was heavily influenced by Raymond Chandler's wisecracking, cynical picture of southern California. Browne created a Marlowe-esque private eye named Paul Pine, and kept him in familiar surroundings. For Browne, that meant Chicago.

The first Paul Pine novel, *Halo in Blood,* was published in 1946 under the pseudonym John Evans. The book starts with a Chandleresque problem. Pine's wealthy client disapproves of his daughter's fiancé. Pine is hired to break up the relationship by any means necessary. As the story proceeds several characters are revealed to be operating under false identities. Eventually, Pine succeeds in untangling a mare's nest of plots and subplots. The book holds up quite well despite a confusing tangle of actual and assumed identities.

After seventy years, *Halo in Blood* and the Paul Pine novels that followed are very much period pieces. To borrow a phrase from filmmaker Jacob Steingroot, everybody seems to live on alcohol and tobacco. Pine drives a Plymouth. From time to time we spot characters driving Nashes, LaSalles, or Packards. They don't make 'em any more.

Pine charges a surprisingly low rate for his services—$50 a day—and he pays his own expenses! In later books in the series, his daily rate increases and he starts charging clients for gas money. Even so, mid-century Chicago lives in these books. Anyone old enough to remember the 1940s and '50s will testify to this. Anyone younger need only take in a few of the wonderful gangster films of the era—including those written by Howard Browne.

The second Paul Pine mystery, *Halo for Satan,* came along in 1949. (A non-Pine novel, *If You Have Tears,* had been published in 1947.) Certainly featuring the most audacious McGuffin that I have encountered in seventy years of reading mysteries, *Halo for Satan* again evolves into a tangle of false identities. To this reader at least, it is the most fascinating of Browne's novels. Once drawn into the mystery, it is virtually impossible to lay the book down. There is also a remarkably nuanced treatment of a Chicago gang lord named Louis Antoni, obviously based on Al Capone.

Halo in Brass (1949) was the last of Browne's novels to carry a "Halo" title. Again, Pine enters the plot in a fairly conventional manner. A small-town couple's daughter, bored and frustrated by her limited lifestyle, has gone off to the big, wicked city of Chicago and has cut off communication with her parents. Worried that some ill fate has taken her, they hire the private detective to track her down and report back to them.

Like Browne himself, Pine is a longtime Chicago hand. Once on the trail of the missing daughter, Pine makes his way ever deeper into the demi-world of lesbianism and false identities. As author and critic Bill Pronzini has pointed out, the sexual theme of the book is daring for its era.

After *Halo in Brass* Browne temporarily abandoned Paul Pine. In the interval he published *Thin Air* (1954), a suspenseful novel that anticipated the "vanishing" theme of novels and films of later decades. This was followed by *The Return of Tharn* (1956), another skillfully executed excursion in the career of Browne's Tarzanic Cro-Magnon hero.

By the time Browne next returned to Paul Pine eight years had passed. There was no *Halo* in the title of the next book in the series. Browne had published the earliest Pine novels under the pseudonym John Evans. By now, however, he was writing under his own name, and the book was published under the evocative and serious sounding *The Taste of Ashes.* The year was 1957. Browne had ascended from the relatively modest house of Bobbs-Merrill and the even lesser realms of Mystery House and the fan-owned Grandon Company (for *The Return of Tharn)* to the prestigious publisher Simon and Schuster.

The Taste of Ashes had a more serious tone, combining the wisecracking, cynical Chandleresque mannerisms of the earlier Paul Pine capers with a darker and more pessimistic atmosphere typified by the works of James M. Cain. Critical response was positive. Pine is recruited by the widow of a murdered colleague to find his killer. There's a slight whiff of Hammett's *The Maltese Falcon* here, and the book is none the worse for that. As a formal mystery, *The Taste of* Ashes is nothing short of brilliant. To this day, major Browne scholar-critics Bill Pronzini and William F. Nolan have high praise for this book, with which I wholly concur.

In a sense, these four novels represent the essential Paul Pine. Howard Browne started a fifth Paul Pine novel, *The Paper Gun.* For some reason he never really finished the book. Allegedly, he'd written himself into a corner. He couldn't work out a satisfactory solution, and abandoned the project. The book was published by Dennis McMillan in 1985, and is included in the present Haffner omnibus. Who knows—it may go down as Howard Browne's version of Charles Dickens's *The Mystery of Edwin Drood.*

Browne's only short story featuring Paul Pine, "So Dark for April," (1966) is included here as lagniappe.

Aside from their often overcomplicated plots and confusing false identities, the Pine novels may be best remembered for the portrayal of Paul Pine and their many lesser characters. One Leona Sandmark, who could have stepped straight out of a Chandler novel, offers a description of Pine, to Pine, in *Halo in Blood.*

> "You've got a hard finish," she said slowly, not smiling now. "But I don't believe you are quite so hard underneath it. Perhaps the finish is there because you've seen too much of the wrong side of people. You go in for crisp speech and a complete lack of emotion. In a way you're playing a part . . . and it's not always an attractive part. Yet there's plenty of strength in you, and a kind of hard-bitten code of ethics. A woman could find a lot of things in you that no other man could give her." She flashed a sudden smile at me. "Besides, you're rather good-looking in the lean, battered sort of way that all sensible women find so attractive in a man."

As for those Chandleresque wisecracks, you'll find them scattered throughout the books like grains of ground pepper on a porterhouse steak. Here are a few that popped out as I reread the books recently:

"She stood up without creaking." (*Satan*)

"As a face it wouldn't start any wars but it would make coming home from one special." (*Brass*)

"Pretty soon a tree frog or two started rubbing their wings together, or whatever they do to make that high skirling note." (*Blood*)

"She moved a shoulder. Ethel Barrymore couldn't have done it better." (*Ashes*)

~ ~ ~ ~ ~

When he finally retired from the TV industry, Browne was recruited to join the faculty at the University of California, San Diego. He was an energetic man all his life. Retirement did not sit well with him, and he accepted the offer. He was a talented teacher. In one conversation with me he waxed sentimental about the apprentice novelists and screenwriters he had guided to success. Two that he mentioned were Paul W. Fairman and William P. McGivern.

In the last years of his life he continued to produce first-rate books: *Pork City* (1988) and *Scotch on the Rocks* (1991), as well as authorizing chapbooks retrieved from pulp-era magazine appearances, and an impressive collection of early short stories, *Incredible Ink* (1997).

The last time I saw Howard Browne was in the 1990s. With two associates I was producing a radio show about books and authors for station KPFA near my home in Berkeley, California. We had planned a trip to Southern California to record interviews with Ray Bradbury, Richard Matheson, and Howard Browne.

Browne welcomed us to his home in Carlsbad, a town near San Diego. He introduced us to his wife and daughter, then ushered us into his office. He sat behind his desk. A portrait of Jake Lingle hung above him. If you don't know who Jake Lingle was and you care to do a little research, you will encounter a fascinating character. A crusading crime reporter for the *Chicago Tribune*, Lingle was shot down in a railroad station on June 9, 1930. He was buried with honors as a fighter for honesty and decency. One Leo Brothers was arrested and convicted of Lingle's murder.

But it was odd that Lingle, whose salary from the *Trib* was very modest, could maintain both a comfortable home in the suburbs for his wife and children, and a luxurious hotel suite in the city for himself, and drive a fancy, top-of-the-line automobile, while living the high life with showgirls as his companions and frequenting Chicago's posh watering holes while Prohibition was in force.

Yes, it turned out that Lingle was playing a double game, crusading journalist in public, mob insider in secret. He apparently played the double-crosser once too often and paid the proverbial price. He fascinated Howard Browne. He may well have inspired some of the corrupt officials encountered by Paul Pine in the Halo novels. Browne's Chicago was dirty and corrupt, its police often as brutal as its mobsters. Yet, like the proverbial John who falls hopelessly in love with a prostitute, Browne was head over heels in love with Chicago.

Howard Browne was full of stories. One involved Mickey Spillane, who was at the peak of his sensational career as a hardboiled private eye writer when Browne was editing *Fantastic*. At the urging of the bean counters at Ziff-Davis, Browne had recruited Spillane to write a novelette for the new magazine. Before the story appeared in *Fantastic* Spillane gave an interview to *Life* magazine, proudly describing his new venture into science fiction.

In the meanwhile, Browne had read Spillane's manuscript and decided that it was simply unpublishable. So he wrote a whole new story and published it in the magazine under Spillane's by-line. When Spillane found out, he hit the ceiling. Browne soothed Spillane by saying that he couldn't run Spillane's original story because that been described in complete detail in the *Life* interview. The story is included in *Incredible Ink,* a collection of Browne's pulp-era fiction.

Reflecting back on his days at Ziff-Davis, Browne told the story of receiving a book-length detective story in the slush pile. The title was *The Cuckoo Clock.* Author was Milton K. Ozaki. Browne decided that he couldn't use it. It was too long to run in one issue of *Mammoth Mystery* or *Mammoth Detective*, and it was against house policy to run serials in the magazines. However, Ziff-Davis had a book division, so Browne stuck a buck slip on the manuscript and sent it to the mystery book editor.

Months passed before Browne heard back about *The Cuckoo Clock.* Then one morning he found a finished copy of the book on his desk with a note from the mystery book editor, thanking him for sending it over.

Browne got hold of the book editor and a conversation ensued in which Browne indicated that he was pleased that the book editor had liked the Ozaki novel.

"Liked it? I never read it. You recommended it, Howard, and I trust your judgment so I bought it."

"I never read it either. I only sent it over because I couldn't use it and I thought that maybe you could."

And Milton K. Ozaki went on to a long and prolific career as a mystery writer under both his own name and the pseudonym Robert O. Saber.

And then there was the following story, as told by Howard Browne:

"I was sitting in a bar in LA and looked over and recognized Raymond Chandler sitting near me. I introduced myself and told him that I'd written a series of mystery novels about a detective named Paul Pine, based on Chandler's private eye Philip Marlowe.

"Chandler turned around and held out his hand. He said, 'I want to shake your hand. I know a lot of writers have done the same thing but you're the first one who ever admitted it.' "

~ ~ ~ ~ ~

Now, wait a minute. Isn't that the same story that Browne told about Edgar Rice Burroughs and *Warrior of the Dawn?* What's going on here? Did he have two such similar experiences, one with Burroughs and one with Chandler?

Was he pulling a fast one, getting double use out of a single incident? Or was he just a trifle confused in his senior years? Maybe that kind of thing really did happen to him twice. Or only once. Or maybe he'd invented the whole thing.

~ ~ ~ ~ ~

Howard Browne died on October 28, 1999. He was very much a man of the Twentieth Century, and I don't think he would have liked the Twenty-First very much. I never got to know him nearly as well as I'd have liked to. He made an immense impression on me.

And as for the Paul Pine stories in this book—if you've read them before, at least not recently, I think you'll enjoy them more the second time around, and find a lot more depth in them than the first time. At least, that's been my experience. And if you've never read them before, you are in for a real treat. I guarantee it!

LIFE ON A BUCK-SLIP

IN A LIFETIME devoted to the world of books—as reader, writer, editor, and collector—it's been my good fortune to encounter an astonishing parade of fascinating characters. None more so than Howard Browne.

Born in Nebraska in 1908, Browne became an enthusiastic baseball fan as a youngster. When he heard that Babe Ruth's Yankees were going to visit Chicago to play the White Sox, Browne hitchhiked to Chicago just to see the Babe play baseball.

Not knowing Chicago's layout, he found himself on the wrong side of the city, and walked the entire length of Chicago in time to realize his ambition.

He also fell in love with the city, and settled there to stay. He worked at a number of pick-up jobs, including one as a collector of payments for furniture bought on the instalment plan.

Browne always had poor vision and wore coke-bottle spectacles, but he was also a huge, beefy individual with a booming voice that saw him through this perilous profession. Eventually he moved into the world of popular literature, landing an editing job at the Ziff-Davis Publishing Company. He worked for Ziff-Davis through a couple of tours of duty before settling in California as a screen-writer.

Along the way he wrote about a dozen books, most of them mysteries but also a couple of novels set in prehistoric times, plus several volumes of shorter fiction.

He was a great story-teller. Two of his stories—wait a minute now, these weren't published stories, they were yarns that he spun for me at our unfortunately few get-togethers—involved the classic encounter-in-a-bar set-up. Or maybe these were two versions of the same story. I guess I'll never know. Here they are:

The Paul Pine Story

Paul Pine was Howard Browne's private eye hero, featured in a series of detective novels. Browne was a great admirer of Raymond Chandler's hardboiled novels about PI Philip Marlowe. He admired Chandler so much that he wrote a series of novels (each with "Halo" in its title) about a detective named Paul Pine. The character resembled Marlowe, the plots were Chandleresque, and Browne used a writing style closely resembling Chandler's.

Shortly after one of the first Paul Pine novels was published, Browne stopped into a tavern in Los Angeles. He recognized Raymond Chandler bellied up to the bar. Never shy, Browne approached Chandler, introduced himself, and mentioned that he had written a novel in open imitation of Chandler.

Browne halfway expected Chandler to react angrily to this confession. Instead, Chandler turned toward Browne, stuck out his hand, and said, "I want to shake your hand, young man. Lots of writers have imitated me but you're the first one who ever admitted it."

~ ~ ~ ~ ~

The Tharn Story

While Howard Browne's true love as a pulp editor was a couple of detective magazines that he ran, he also edited a pair of science fiction magazines for Ziff-Davis. He was amazed at the fantastic popularity of the stories of Edgar Rice Burroughs.

So intrigued by ERB's success, Browne studied Burroughs' style. He kept a notebook. Reading a series of Burroughs novels he noted each adjective and adverb that Burroughs used, making a tic-mark every time he encountered it. Eventually he created a mathematical analysis of Burroughs's style. Based upon this he wrote two novels about a prehistoric adventurer named Tharn: *Warrior of the Dawn* and *The Return of Tharn*. Considering the similarity of the heroes' names, these might easily have passed for Tarzan novels. They were hugely popular in their time, and preserved hardcover copies are highly-sought by collectors today.

One afternoon shortly after *Warrior of the Dawn* was published Browne stopped into a tavern in Los Angeles. He noticed Edgar Rice Burroughs bellied up to the bar. Never shy, Browne approached Burroughs, introduced himself, and mentioned that he had written a novel called *Warrior of the Dawn* in open imitation of Burroughs.

Browne halfway expected Burroughs to react angrily to this confession. Instead, Burroughs turned toward Browne, stuck out his hand, and said, "I want to congratulate you, young man. I've read that book, and it's the best Edgar Rice Burroughs novel I never wrote."

~ ~ ~ ~ ~

Okay, take your pick. Howard Browne told me both of those stories. Was it just one incident, and did he change the story to suit his whim—or did both encounters take place?

~ ~ ~ ~ ~

But back in Chicago in his days as a pulp magazine editor at Ziff-Davis, Howard Browne of course received many manuscripts. His two crime pulps, *Mammoth Mystery* and *Mammoth Detective*, specialized in short stories. They packed hundreds of pages of them into each issue.

One manuscript that Browne received was for a detective yarn called *The Cuckoo Clock*. The author was a total unknown named Milton K. Ozaki. A cursory examination of the 'script revealed that it was a full-length novel.

Neither *Mammoth Mystery* nor *Mammoth Detective* ran novels. A novel was too long to fit into one issue, along with a generous supply of short stories, and Ziff-Davis had a policy against running serials. But Z-D had a book division as well, so Howard Browne stuck a buck-slip on the manuscript and shipped it over to the mystery editor in the book division.

He forgot all about the incident until the day he found a copy of *The Cuckoo Clock* in its bright brown and yellow dust jacket on his desk. There was a note attached thanking him for sending the manuscript over.

Browne made his way through the Ziff-Davis office warren until he found the mystery editor. "I'm glad you liked that Ozaki book," he told his colleague.

"Liked it," the mystery editor exclaimed, "I didn't like it. I didn't even read it. I published it on your recommendation."

"I didn't recommend it," Browned said, "I never read it. I just sent it to you because it was too long for me to use!"

I don't think Milton Ozaki ever knew about that incident. Once started on his career, he sent another manuscript to Ziff-Davis. This time the mystery editor read it, liked it, bought it, and published it. It was *A Fiend in Need.* From there Ozaki went on to write and sell dozens of mystery novels under his own name and the pseudonym of Robert O. Saber.

And it all happened because Howard Browne never read *The Cuckoo Clock.*

Baseball

A pitcher's worth a thousand words:
Star player Lupoff takes to the field in 2013

IN ANOTHER WORLD . . .

HERE'S WHAT IT was like when I was a kid. The world was in upheaval. We were fighting Hitler and Mussolini in Europe, Tojo and his minions in the Pacific. Joe Stalin was actually a good guy and FDR had been President since before I was born (or had any of my pals). My Uncle Eddie was in England repairing shot-up B-17s and I knew we were going to win, with him keeping 'em flying.

Yep, the world was in upheaval, but *my* world was stable. Superman and Captain Midnight were on the radio five nights each week, the Shadow and Jack Benny were there on Sunday. We saw a serial chapter at the local movie every Saturday, *Life* magazine and *The Saturday Evening Post* came in the mail every seven days but the kids were more interested in reading *Whiz* and *Action Comics*.

And we were all baseball fans. Sure, there were other sports, but baseball was every kid's passion, as least in my gang. And baseball was a rock solid institution. There were two leagues, eight teams in each, and after 154 games the two pennant winners met in the World Series. Thus it was and thus it had always been.

Just for the record:

NATIONAL LEAGUE: Boston Braves, New York Giants, Brooklyn Dodgers, Philadelphia Phillies, Pittsburgh Pirates, Chicago Cubs, Cincinnati Reds. St. Louis Cardinals.

AMERICAN LEAGUE: Boston Red Sox, New York Yankees, Philadelphia Athletics, Washington Senators, Cleveland Indians, Chicago White Sox, St. Louis Browns, Detroit Tigers.

Thus was it declared from on high, thus had it always been and thus would it always be.

Wow, if I'd only had a time telescope in 1945 and I'd been able to see the baseball world of 2015. What the heck are the Diamondbacks, Padres, Mariners, Orioles, Nationals, Mets, Rays, Rangers, Astros, Texans, Twins, Brewers, Angels, Blue Jays, Royals, Rockies, Marlins? Had I fallen into an alternate universe?

Here's what's weirder. If I pointed that time-telescope in the other direction I would have seen that not only had teams come and gone, whole leagues—several of them with a legitimate claim

79

to having been majors—had appeared and disappeared. They lie in
the dust now but they don't deserve to be forgotten. Their stars
were the Babe Ruths and the Walter Johnsons, the Sandy Koufax-
es and the Mickey Mantles of their days.

There's some dispute over whether the National Association of
Professional Base Ball Players was the first major league. Today's
MLB has yet to recognize the "NA" as a major league, but many
of its players and umpires are included in the standard major
league record books. Go figure.

Started in 1871, the NA had as many as 25 teams. The first
year, the pennant was won by the Philadelphia Athletics. The next
year—and every year from 1872 to 1875—the Boston Red Stockings won the pennant.

In 1876 a slimmed-down remnant of the lumbering NA was re-
organized by the National League. Six teams from the former NA
were joined by two independent clubs to form the National
League.

Professional baseball was off and running!

By 1882 the National League was well established, and fan
conduct was considered pretty straight-laced. A group of brewery
and distillery owners started a rival organization called the American Association. Blue-nosed National League owners at first
snubbed their rivals, calling them "The Beer and Whiskey
League."

It didn't take long for the owners to see the commercial appeal
of a grand play-off between the two league champions, and by
1884 they were playing an early version of the World Series. The
National League won the series in 1884 and 1885, but in 1886 the
upstart St. Louis Browns defeated the Chicago White Stockings
for the grand prize.

By the way, those St. Louis Browns later became the Cardinals
and the Chicago White Stockings became the Cubs. The present
Chicago White Sox came along later and the Browns became a
reincarnation of the old Baltimore Orioles. Go figure.

The championship series ranged in length from three games to
15.

In 1891 surviving teams of the American Association were
joined by the original Baltimore Orioles and Washington Senators,
plus now-defunct Louisville Colonels and the Cleveland Spiders
(now Indians) to create the American League.

Ever hear of the Players League, amigo? By the mid-1880s a
lot of the players felt that they were being exploited by the owners

so they formed a union called the Brotherhood of Professional Base Ball Players, walked out on their National League teams, and formed the Players League.

It only lasted for one season, 1890, but the quality of play was remarkably good. Teams were the Boston Reds, Brooklyn Ward's Wonders, New York Giants, Philadelphia Athletics, Pittsburgh Burghers, Cleveland Infants, and Buffalo Bisons. Boston won the pennant with a record of 81 wins and 48 losses. Roger Connor led the league with 14 home runs, Pete Browning—he of the infamous ruined Ad Gumbert no-hitter—was batting champion with a .373 average, and pitcher Mark Baldwin led the league with 34 wins.

Unfortunately the league was underfunded and went under after just one season. But 125 years later at least two of its franchises— the Giants and the Athletics—are still in operation, although in different cities.

The United States League came along in 1912. There were eight teams in the league, but its season was cut short, mainly by financial woes. The pennant winner in the truncated season was the Pittsburgh Filipinos (named in honor of their manager). Also in the league was the first of at least three incarnations of the Washington Senators. The owners tried again in 1913, but gave up partway through the season. However, several of the teams survived and joined the new Federal League, including the Filipinos.

The Federal League. It started as a minor league in 1913, declared itself a major league in 1914, and lasted for just two seasons. For the record, the Indianapolis Hoosiers won the pennant in 1914 and the Chicago Whales won in 1915. Other Federal League teams were the Baltimore Terrapins, Brooklyn Tip-Tops, Buffalo Blues, Kansas City Packers, Covington Blue Sox, Newark Peppers, Pittsburgh Rebels, and St. Louis Terriers. The Whales' stadium was later renamed Wrigley Field and is still in use.

Another oddity involved the Kansas City Packers, whose stadium was destroyed in a flood (in Kansas City!?) partway through the 1914 season. Undaunted, the Packers played out the rest of the season on the road. Their ballpark was rebuilt in time for the 1915 season.

Probably the most interesting player in the Federal League was Mordecai "Three Fingers" Brown. He lost part of his pitching hand in a farming accident, and further deformed what was left of the hand in a fall. The result was a weird spin on his pitches. His curve was reputedly unhittable. He was nearing the end of his Hall of Fame career with the Chicago Cubs when he pitched for the St. Louis Terriers.

But the Federal League, like the earlier Players League, couldn't compete successfully with the better established National and American Leagues, and disappeared after only two seasons.

The last serious attempt to start a third major league occurred in 1959, when Branch Rickey, its prospective President, announced the formation of the Continental League. The league was to start play in 1961. A longtime baseball executive, Rickey had had a short career as a major league catcher. He gave up 13 stolen bases in one game, a record that still stands.

Best known for signing Jackie Robinson to the Brooklyn Dodgers, Rickey's name and standing in the baseball world gave the Continental League a chance to succeed. MLB responded by starting the expansion that led, eventually, to the system of divisions and multi-tiered playoffs.

And that, in all likelihood, is the last we'll ever hear of any new major baseball leagues.

But that isn't the end of the story. We haven't even mentioned the Negro Leagues and baseball's role in first propping up the old Jim Crow system and then knocking it down. Nor have we mentioned the All-American Girls Professional Baseball League. Those are two great chapters in baseball history, and in fact they are intertwined. The Negro Leagues featured at least three female big leaguers: Toni Stone, Mamie Johnson, and Connie Morgan.

Here's your assignment, class: check out the history of the Negro Leagues and of the All-American Girls Baseball League. Write those chapters for yourself. You won't be sorry that you did!

Leland Brissie

THE A'S BIONIC PITCHER

IT WAS 1941 and Europe and Asia were ablaze with war but the United States, shielded by thousands of miles of ocean on either coast, dozed peacefully.

The Philadelphia Athletics' legendary founder-owner-manager Connie Mack was touring the backwoods of South Carolina and stopped to watch an industrial league game in the town of Ware Shoals. There was a sixteen-year-old kid on the mound, a rangy, six-foot-four left hander.

Speed guns were straight out of science fiction in those days, so nobody knows how fast the kid was throwing, but Connie Mack, a onetime catcher, was a talented judge of pitchers and he knew that this high school student had a blazing fastball.

Connie Mack was not the only talent scout to take note of this youngster. Records are neither complete nor totally reliable, but apparently as many as a dozen teams tried to recruit the kid.

Mr. Mack was ready to sign the youngster right then and there, but the kid's dad insisted that he finish high school before he turned pro. Even so, Mr. Mack offered to sponsor the young man's college career and invite him to A's training camp once he'd got his degree.

It seemed like a teenager's dream, but harsh reality intervened. Before the end of 1941 the United States was embroiled in World War Two. The youngster managed a brief stint at college, but before the end of 1942 he was a soldier in the United States Army.

His legal name was Leland Victor Brissie, but he was better-known as Lou. He was assigned to the Army's 88th Infantry Division in Italy. His unit became part of the grinding, difficult battle between American and German units, the Americans fighting their way up the "boot," the Germans resisting fiercely for every foot of territory.

On December 2, 1944, Lou Brissie's unit came under fire by a German artillery barrage. Lou was hit by shrapnel. Both his feet were shattered. Reporter Matt Schudel writing in *The Washington Post* said that Brissie's left tibia and shinbone were shattered into 30 pieces. "At the Army field hospital," Schudel wrote, "doctors told him that his leg would have to be amputated due to the severity of the injury."

But Brissie still dreamed of pitching for Mr. Mack. He talked the doctors into saving what was left of his leg. It took more than two years, 23 surgeries, and a metal brace on his leg, but Corporal Brissie, medals on his chest and Honorable Discharge papers in his hand, walked out of the hospital, got in touch with the Athletics, and told them that he was ready to sign that contract at last.

He spent most of the 1947 season pitching for an A's farm team in Savannah, Georgia. Despite his wounded legs and metal brace, he was a phenomenon, winning 23 games and losing only 5.

At the end of the season he was called up to the Athletics for the proverbial cup of coffee. He pitched in one game, against the Yankees in Yankee Stadium (which he lost) but by 1948 he was ready to roll.

He was the Athletics' starting pitcher on Opening Day at Fenway Park. Years later, in his autobiography, Ted Williams described their encounter.

"I hit a ball back to the box, a real shot, whack, like a rifle clap. Down he goes and everybody rushes out there, and I go over from first base with this awful feeling I've really hurt him. Here's this war hero, pitching a great game. He sees me in the crowd, looking down at him, my face like a haunt. He says, 'For crissakes, Williams, pull the damn ball.' "

And get this: Brissie got back up and threw a complete four-hitter, defeating the Red Sox 4-2. With two outs in the bottom of the ninth, who should come to bat again but Ted Williams, the Splendid Splinter. Brissie struck him out.

There were rumors that Brissie had only one leg. In fact that was nearly the case, but massive doses of the newly-invented antibiotic penicillin enabled him to fight off infection in his shattered legs, enabling his doctors to save both limbs. One can only imagine the pain he endured throughout his life.

In 1948 he started 25 games and compiled a record of 14 wins and 10 losses. A team photo from that year shows him towering over his teammates. And there in the front row is Mr. Cornelius McGillicuddy himself, stiff and upright in dark suit and tie and fedora.

Brissie's 1949 season was even better. He went 16 and 11 and made the American League All-Star squad, pitching 3 innings in Ebbets Field.

He was traded to Cleveland early in the 1951 season, and spent the next three years pitching for the Indians, mainly in relief, and retired after the 1953 season.

How much was Lou Brissie worth to the clubs he pitched for
between 1947 and 1953? It's hard to compare salaries of that period with the modern era of multi-millionaire athletes. In Brissie's
day, professional sports were a blue-collar profession. Most players held down off-season jobs as farm hands, coal miners, steel-
workers.

In 1947, Lou Brissie's first full year in the majors, he was paid
$2,400. The following year, Connie Mack doubled his salary to
$5,000. His peak salary was $17,000 with the Indians in 1952.

Well, what do you do when you "retire" at the age of 29? One
problem is, you don't know how long your retirement is going to
last. Considering the condition of Lou Brissie's legs—not only the
continual pain but also the constant danger of new and potentially
fatal infection—it would probably not have been very long. But in
fact, for Brissie it was fully sixty years.

He was surely eligible for a pension from Uncle Sam. Millions
of Americans had served honorably, and Brissie's wounds would
have entitled him to disability rights. Or he could have gone on the
rubber chicken circuit, giving speeches and picking up speaker's
fees all over the country.

But that wasn't Lou Brissie's way. He became involved in
American Legion youth baseball, and worked for the State of
South Carolina in a program that trained workers for new jobs.

Increasingly he toured veterans' hospitals, visiting wounded
and disabled ex-service members. His obituary in *The New York
Times* quoted an earlier interview, in which Brissie said that, "he
had been hesitant to speak about (his) war wounds, but had begun
to offer encouragement to the disabled. 'People with disabilities
have told me, "Because of you, I decided to try," he said. 'That
changes you.' "

Lou Brissie spent the rest of his life sharing his courage and de-
termination with his fellows. He passed on in 2013, at the age of
89, leaving a large family: his widow, children, grandchildren, and
great-grandchildren. He was a baseball hero and an American hero, and every A's fan can be proud of him.

~ ~ ~ ~ ~

Statistics and details of Lou Brissie's life were in part based on the Baseball Almanac, Wikipedia, and the *New York Times* obituary written by Richard Goldstein. Photographs generously provided by Ernie Montella and Mark R. Amos of the Philadelphia Athletics Historical Society <elmonte37@aol.com> <markbmos@aol.com>

1948 ATHLETICS

IN A ZONE

I'VE BEEN A steady reader and occasional contributor to my friend Christopher Weills' wonderful blog ever since he started publishing it. If you haven't seen a copy, and if you have even the most tangential interest in the world of sports, you ought to look it up.

A number of Christopher's contributors have written about the phenomenon called "being in a zone." Many athletes have attributed their peak performances to this mysterious condition.

A quarterback whose passes appear almost miraculously accurate in one game . . .

A basketball player who seemingly can't miss the hoop for part or all of one contest . . .

A batter to whom the baseball looks as big as a pumpkin as it floats leisurely up to the plate . . .

This is a real phenomenon. I've heard or seen enough examples of it to be convinced. And in fact I've experienced it myself. Further, it doesn't just take place for one game. You've heard of players (in whatever sport) having "a career year." The hitter whose batting average jumps thirty or forty or fifty points. The running back whose average yards-per-carry doubles. The miler who breaks four minutes and then goes out and does it again. Yes, they've each been in a zone for a full season.

As for your humble reporter, I was "in a zone" for two months in the summer of 1950. I was fifteen years of age, and a member of a baseball team so humble that we didn't even have a name, no less official standing of any sort. And uniforms? Don't make me laugh! We all just loved the game, loved playing, and wouldn't have swapped our battered mitts, muddy spikes and dinged-up bats for the world.

Everybody was busy with typical teenage-kid stuff, but we managed to play a fairly regular schedule of two games a week, Wednesday and Saturday afternoons. Our opponents were other kids a lot like ourselves. There were no official coaches or managers. We all self-selected our positions and lineups.

I swung a good bat and had a strong arm, but I was pretty slow afoot and not exactly an agile glove-man, so at various times I pitched, caught, or played right field. Mainly, I pitched. Typically, I took the mound (actually, a roughly circular patch of bare earth in the middle of the diamond) on Saturdays and either caught or played outfield on Wednesdays.

At the beginning of the season I had one pitch: a mediocre fastball with little or no movement on it. But we had a strong team and we won the first game I pitched. Don't ask me the score. Nobody wrote it down, and we're talking about a season sixty-four years ago.

But being a winning pitcher was really exciting, and I decided to work on my stuff every chance I got. First I managed to get my arm speed up. I have no idea how fast my so-called fastball actually was. Speed guns? I don't think they'd been invented yet. At least, none of us kids had ever heard of such a thing.

We talked baseball at every opportunity, memorized the rosters and stats of every team in the majors. Of course, that was easier to do in 1950. There were eight teams in the National League and eight teams in the American League, and they were in the cities where God had placed them and would stay there 'til the end of the world.

Once I was happy with my fastball, I discovered that I already had a change-up. Just throw the thing the same way, just not as hard. Wow! Now I was a two-speed pitcher.

So I started work on a breaking ball. I was a right-hander, and I could get a break on the ball by twisting my arm from elbow to fingertips as I released the ball. Twisting away from the center of my body produced a curve. Twisting toward my body produced a screwball.

Trouble was, throwing the screwball made my elbow ache for a couple of days after the throwing session, so I abandoned that. Still, I now had three pitches, and my team kept on winning the games I pitched.

By the last week in August, I'd started eight games, pitched eight complete games, and had a record of eight wins and no losses. The last game of the season was coming up and it was a Saturday game, meaning that it would be my turn to take the mound.

We were the home team and in the top of the first the other side went down one-two-three. I was focused on my pitching so I didn't keep close track of our own turns at bat. I think I got a couple of hits but I'm not sure. As I recall we ran up a fair number of runs.

As for the opposition, I struck out some batters—I have no idea how many—and got lots of ground balls. Lots and lots of ground balls. In fact, by the top of the ninth the other side had yet to get a base runner and our outfielders were suffering from terminal bore-dom. We did have an umpire who called balls and strikes and all other plays, but walks were almost unknown in our games. Every-body wanted to hit the ball.

I do remember that the first batter in the top of the ninth hit a routine grounder and our shortstop threw him out. The second bat-ter came to the plate. We actually had a home plate—talk about luxury! He was a right-handed batter and I had a feeling that he was going to swing late and hit a grounder to the right side of the infield for a scratch single.

That's what happened. Good-bye perfect game. Good-bye no-hitter.

The next batter came up and hit into a game-ending double play.

I think I read somewhere that the great Persian rug-makers al-ways made sure to include one false stitch in each of their crea-tions, lest they offend God by creating something perfect, for only God may create perfection.

I know that some ballplayers have thrown perfect games and the great Don Larsen of the Yankees even did it in the World Se-ries, pitching against the Brooklyn Dodgers in 1956. As far as I know God did not smite them down for their insolence. But I had a perfect season, nine wins and no losses, and an almost perfect game to end the streak.

That winter I was in a minor bicycle accident and I broke my pitching arm. We went to the hospital and the bone was set and they put my arm in a cast. It healed pretty well and I even tried out for my high school baseball team, but my elbow hurt so badly af-ter the first session that I had to give it up. I tried again when I got to college but it was obviously not going to work.

After that, I never pitched again. At least, not until I got to throw out the first pitch at an Oakland A's game in 2013.

Any time you want to talk about being in a zone—or if you ev-er encounter somebody who doubts that this is a real phenome-non—you just tell 'em about Dick Lupoff and his miracle summer of 1950.

THAT KID IN THE OUTFIELD

MY FATHER WAS a fan of the Brooklyn Dodgers, and I remember attending games with him before I even understood the game. (Does anyone ever completely understand baseball, with all its subtleties and complications?) Once in a great while he would trek reluctantly up to the Bronx to see a Yankee game. And when he was traveling he would catch a minor league or industrial league game, or buy a ticket (generally for 25 cents) to see a barnstorming team play some local aggregation.

At one time my brother and I were attending school in a small town in central New Jersey. Dad drove out there on a bright Sunday in springtime, picked us up in his maroon 1946 Hudson coupe, motored into Trenton, and bought us a couple of delicious steaks for lunch.

Then we headed to a rickety wooden ballpark where the Trenton Giants, a farm team of the then New York Giants, were playing. I don't know who their opponent was. My memory wants to say they were the great Yankee farm club, the Newark Bears, but I really don't know.

We sat in splintery pine stands and watched the contest. I don't recall paying very close attention to the game. At my early age I was more interested in popcorn or ice cream. But suddenly my father exclaimed, "Will you look at that! They've got a colored boy in the outfield!"

A colored boy.

Want to guess who that was?

Sure, you got it on the first try. And he really was a boy. A teenager. Willie Howard Mays.

I've tried to research that day, and all I can find on Willie Mays is that he played for the Birmingham Black Barons before signing with the Giants as a free agent in 1950. He made his debut with the Giants in 1951, apparently without ever playing in the minors.

Was it all a dream? Was that someone other than Willie Mays in the outfield, maybe Monte Irvin? You can search me. But it's my memory, and it's precious. I know I didn't make the whole thing up. If it wasn't Willie Mays, it should have been!

GONNA RATTLE THEM BONES

I DREAMED I heard Allie Reynolds' bone fragments rattling. It happened last night. I woke up and discovered that it was my tortoise-shell cat, Mina, playing with the venetian blinds, but I lay there gazing at the ceiling and seeing Yankee Stadium.

A stocky six-footer was on the mound for the home team, and every time he delivered a pitch I could hear that rattling sound. The pitcher was a fire-baller, and the opponents hardly stood a chance. I never got to see Reynolds pitch, and that's one of my chief regrets in three-quarters of a century as a baseball fan.

Reynolds was born in 1917 in Bethany, Oklahoma. His father was a preacher; his mother was a Creek Indian. Young Allie was a natural athlete. He exceeded in every sport he tried, especially if his role involved throwing. He was a quarterback at Oklahoma A&M. In springtime he was on the track-and-field team. He excelled at the javelin, and when the college's baseball coach, the legendary Hank Iba, saw him fling that spear, he managed to recruit Reynolds away from the track team and onto the pitcher's mound.

Drafted by the New York Giants football team, Reynolds opted instead to follow Hank Iba's advice and sign with the Cleveland Indians. After a lackluster minor league season in 1941, he went 18 and 7 in '42 and was called up by Cleveland for a cup of coffee at the end of the season.

World War Two was raging at the time, and Reynolds' draft board invited him in for a physical. They decided that he was too battered from his college football career and sent him back to the diamond. He never appeared in a minor league game again. In 1943 he started 21 games and relieved in 13.

Playing for the Indians until 1946, he recorded five-year won/lost totals of 51 wins and 36 losses. After the '46 season he was acquired by the Yankees for infielder Joe Gordon, allegedly at the urging of an outfielder named, oh, let me try and remember, right, Joe DiMaggio. I guess DiMaggio knew something about pitchers.

With the Yankees Reynolds went from strength to strength. In each of the next six seasons he racked up records of anywhere from 16 to 20 wins. In the final two years of his career, while his totals were smaller his effectiveness was, if anything, even greater.

In 1953 he went 13 and 7; in '54, 13 and 4. Not bad for a thirty-seven-year-old power pitcher.

Along the way he had injured his right arm and developed bone chips in his pitching elbow. According to the popular press of the era and legendary Yankees broadcaster Mel Allen, you could hear the bone chips rattling every time Reynolds unleashed one of his legendary fastballs. Fortunately the Yankees had one of baseball's first professional relief pitchers, Joe Page. Any time Allie Reynolds was in too much pain to finish a game, Joe Page was available—to the point where "Reynolds-Page" became a familiar entry in the box scores

Reynolds might have gone on pitching well into his forties, had a Yankees team bus not crashed *en route* to a game with the then-Philadelphia Athletics. Reynolds' back was injured but he went on to successful seasons in '53 and '54, before deciding he'd played enough baseball, and moved on to a second career as head of the AAA American Association.

During his playing career he was referred to in the press as the Superchief, a double reference to a famous streamliner train of the era and Reynolds' own Creek Indian heritage. In his personal life, and in baseball clubhouses, he preferred Allie.

His lifetime achievements were remarkable. His won-lost record was 182 and 107. He was selected for the American League All-Star team six times. He appeared in the World Series six times with the Yankees, both as a starter and reliever. He even batted a cumulative .308 in those series. He was the first American League pitcher to throw two no-hitters in the same season, 1951, once for the Yankees against his former team, the Indians, and once against the Boston Red Sox.

Here's a bit of baseball trivia for you: Allie Reynolds had a career base-stealing average of 1.000. Yep. One attempt, in the 1951 season. One successful steal. When he wasn't busy starting or relieving, he avoided boredom by performing as a pinch-runner. I am not making this up. As the late Al Smith used to say, "You could look it up."

Allie Reynolds is not in the Baseball Hall of Fame, and if that ain't a crime, Dillinger never robbed a bank.

Comics

A selection of novels by Kendell Foster Crossen

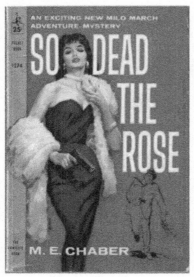

1960, cover art by Jerry Allison

1959, art by Richard M. Powers

1954, art by Richard M. Powers

1960, art by Robert Abbett

KENDELL AND MAGGA AND MILO AND ME

1. Venice, Florida, 1939

WHERE TO START? This is going to take a while, but trust me; to borrow a phrase from my longtime friend James Blish, the game will indeed be worth the candle.

With the country coming out of the Great Depression, my father became a successful businessman. He was able to buy a house in the Queens section of New York and to rent a winter cottage in the town of Venice, Florida. When the northern winter turned cold he would bundle up his family, of which I was the youngest member, furnish us with tickets on the Orange Blossom Special, and send us off to the sunnier climes of Florida's Gulf Coast. These experiences, indeed, furnish some of my earliest memories.

Venice boasted one main street in those days, its commercial establishments including a single drug store *cum* soda fountain *cum* newsstand.

One sunny afternoon in the winter of 1939-1940 my mother entrusted my older brother, Jerry, with a twenty-five cent piece, placed me in his charge, and sent us off to find entertainment. What an innocent era! Jerry was seven years old, I was four.

We selected a comic book to share communally and an ice cream cone for each of us. Jerry had chocolate, I had strawberry. The comic cost a dime and the ice cream cones were a nickel apiece. We sat side-by-side eating our ice cream and reading the comic book. Eventually we returned to our family's temporary home and dutifully returned the nickel change to our mother.

The comic book involved was the first issue of Fawcett Publications' *Whiz Comics*. Due to a legal problem it was marked *Number 2, February 1940*. There never was a *Whiz Comics Number 1*, except for a black-and-white so-called "ashcan edition" produced to secure copyright and never distributed to the public. This remains one of the many arcana of publishing history.

Hero of the lead feature in *Whiz Comics* was Captain Marvel, a superhero bearing a suspicious resemblance to Superman in the rival *Action Comics.*

Whiz Comics was an instant hit, and Captain Marvel not only equaled the rival Superman but eventually surpassed Superman in sales.

Now, here's where things get interesting. Since *Whiz Comics* was selling so well and Captain Marvel was such a popular figure—before long there was an excellent movie serial featuring Tom Tyler as the superhero—the editors at Fawcett, led by Ed Herron, decided to launch a spin-off feature meant to capture an even larger audience.

The result, as explained in later years by lead writer Otto Binder, called for devices to remind young readers of the connection. Thus, the character would wear a costume similar to that worn by Captain Marvel. His name would be Captain Marvel, Jr. And his magic phrase, rather than Captain Marvel's *Shazam,* was simply *Captain Marvel.* Thus, Binder said, "The kids would be reminded over and over that there was a Captain Marvel. It reinforced their buying loyalties."

The original Captain Marvel was drawn by C. C. Beck, a one-time sports cartoonist with a rollicking jolly style. Beck's approach was perfect for Captain Marvel, but Herron wanted to give Cap Junior a distinctive look. He chose an illustrator named Emmanuel Raboi, better known as Mac Raboy.

Raboy's style was slicker and more realistic than Beck's. While Beck's Captain Marvel could have earned a place on a professional football team, Raboy's Junior was slim, lithe, and far younger in appearance than Senior.

Introduced in *Whiz Comics* number 25, Junior was another instant hit for Fawcett. As a young child I didn't understand anything of the whole writing-drawing-editing-publishing process. I had no idea who Mac Raboy was. But I was instantly enthusiastic about Captain Marvel, Jr.

~ ~ ~ ~ ~

2. Trenton, New Jersey, 1944

Okay, here I was nine years old and totally addicted to comic books. On an allowance of fifty cents per week I learned the delivery schedule of new comics to the Main Street newsstand-*cum*-magazine and comic book emporium. Comics typically cost a dime in that era, and I had to parcel my treasury out to comics, Saturday matinees at the movies (twelve cents), and snack food. Not an easy task!

And one afternoon what should my wondering eyes behold but a new comic book featuring a new superhero drawn in the inimitable style that I had learned to associate with Captain Marvel, Jr. This character was portrayed flying through the air, his cape streaming behind him, and (most unusual in the superhero fraternity) a hood drawn over his head.

His tights were supplemented by gloves and floppy-topped boots. Unlike Captain Marvel, Jr., he was a full-grown man but he had the slim, graceful figure of a typical Raboy hero.

He was *The Green Lama—the Man Who Defeats Death!* At that age I had no idea what a lama was, but I was willing to sacrifice a candy bar and a single-scoop ice cream cone for this comic book.

The Green Lama's persona was patterned on Captain Marvel with a substantial tincture of the Shadow adding to the flavor. His secret identity was that of Jethro Dumont, wealthy Manhattan man-about town. He had spent a decade in Tibet, studying Lama-ism, and had returned to the United States to spread the peaceful doctrines of the Buddha.

No sooner had Jethro debarked from his ship when he wit-nessed a brutal gang battle and the slaying of an innocent child. The experience convinced him to devote his energies to fighting crime.

Hmmm. Something here of the young Bruce Wayne, don't you think?

Dumont utters the mystical phrase, *Om mani padme hum!* The words, now transliterated into Tibetan, echo eerily from a monas-tery high in the Himalayas and Jethro is transformed into that fly-ing superhero, the Green Lama!

Green Lama Comics lasted only eight issues, through 1944 and 1945. The lead stories dealt with a number of themes, as the Lama fought criminals on the mean streets of American cities, led flying attacks against the Axis hordes of World War Two, and delivered effective lectures on tolerance and equality.

In a 2009 reissue of the Green Lama comics, Chuck Rozanski offered the opinion that it was the message of tolerance that caused the failure of the comic. Rozanski suggests that distributors and potential readers in the states of the Old Confederacy effec-tively boycotted the comic in protest against its egalitarian inclu-siveness. This is Rozanski's interpretation, and in the context of Twenty-First Century political correctness it is not implausible. But I would argue that the small company behind the comic was underfinanced and outmarketed by the giants of DC Comics (Su-perman, Batman, Wonder Woman), Atlas Comics (Captain Amer-ica, Human Torch, Sub-Mariner), and Fawcett (Captain Marvel and many spin-offs and supporting features).

Even as this incarnation of the Green Lama disappeared from the newsstands, I was unaware that it was not the first incarnation of the character. Nowhere near!

~ ~ ~ ~ ~

3. Poughkeepsie, New York 1965

By this time I was working as a filmmaker for the nation's leading computer company. Yes, that one. I had a secondary career editing books for a small publisher in New York City. In that moonlight job for Canaveral Press I was assigned to edit a series of books by Edgar Rice Burroughs—a dream job for a kid who had somehow fallen into a trough and come up smelling like a rose.

Eventually I would write two books about ERB, *Edgar Rice Burroughs: Master of Adventure* and *Barsoom: Edgar Rice Burroughs and the Martian Vision.*

Much of my work involved research into the pulp magazines of earlier decades, and in due course I came across several copies of a magazine called *Double Detective.* Not the most famous or successful of the pulps, still *Double Detective* provided a solid package of entertaining fiction. And one of the issues I stumbled across featured a lead novel about the Green Lama—my old pal from the comics.

Of course the pulp version had actually preceded the comic book by years. Jethro Dumont was indeed the Lama's civilian counterpart. However, his flying tights were not present. Rather, he wore the dark green, fur-trimmed robes of a Tibetan lama. And Dumont had a *third* identity, that of Dr. Pali, who favored a pale green clergy suit. Dumont had inherited a fortune when his parents died in an automobile crash. He had then dropped out of Harvard, traveled to Tibet, studied Lamaism, and returned to New York. Here he made the usual array of contacts that such self-appointed crime fighters so often did.

A trio of examples:

The Shadow, mysterious amateur crime-fighter; real name originally Kent Allard, later (sometimes) Lamont Cranston.

Harry Vincent, depression-era would-be suicide, rescued to become the Shadow's key operative.

Moe "Shrevvy" Shrevnitz, the Shadow's personal cab-driver, saves Vincent's life and recruits him to work for the Shadow.

Burbank, the Shadow's radio operator and communications chief.

Margo Lane, Lamont Cranston's "faithful friend and companion," provides sex-appeal to the stories.

~ ~ ~ ~ ~

Doc Savage, "the Man of Bronze," magnificent physical specimen, brilliant scientist, all-around hero. Full name Clark Savage, Jr.

"Ham" Brooks, who looks like an ape.

"Monk" Mayfair.

"Johnny" Littlejohn, trained geologist and archaeologist.

"Renny" Renwick, mighty giant of a man.

"Long Tom" Roberts, electrical engineer.

Patricia Savage, Doc's cousin—a nice, safe female to add a little spice to the stories.

~ ~ ~ ~ ~

Captain Future, "Wizard of Science," "Man of Tomorrow," real name Curtis Newton.

Otho the android.

Grag the robot.

Simon Wright the living brain.

Ook and Eek, interplanetary pets.

Joan Randall, interplanetary police agent—she's lovely and in love with Curt, who fends off her advances.

~ ~ ~ ~ ~

And finally, our hero—

The Green Lama, consciously patterned upon the Shadow, on instructions from Kendell Foster Crossen's boss.

Gary Brown, ex-con and reformed citizen. We saw a lot of these guys in the pulps.

Dr. Harrison Valco, physician and scientist whose work with "radioactive salts" enhances Jethro Dumont's remarkable powers.

Ken Clayton and Jean Farrell, talented actors, sometime sweethearts and eventually married.

Tsarong, a Tibetan lama and sometime mentor, sometime assistant, to Jethro.

Evangel Stewart—the usual attractive female, sometime crimefighting associate of the Green Lama.

Theodore Harrin, a talented stage magician.

Magga—a mysterious woman who pops up at opportune moments to save the Green Lama's life and solve cases that have him baffled.

~ ~ ~ ~ ~

Jethro's group of associates is basically similar to the helpers of other pulp heroes, most notably the Shadow's band of operatives. Certainly Tsarong fits the mold of Kato, the chauffeur/assistant of that other multimedia crime-fighter, the Green Hornet, otherwise known as Britt Reid.

Theodore Harrin is a stage magician and stage magic plays a role in several Green Lama cases. Jethro Dumont is himself considerably adept at prestidigitation, as was Ken Crossen, as was told to me by his daughter, Kendra Crossen Burroughs.

Clearly, Ken Crossen had a playful side. As an editor at *Detective Fiction Weekly* and then at *Double Detective,* it was not uncommon in the pulp world for him to buy stories from himself. He wrote the Green Lama stories under the *nom de plume* Richard Foster and even inserted himself as a minor character in several of the stories.

For all the flirtatious conduct of Crossen's heroes—we'll come to this later, especially regarding insurance investigator Milo March—Crossen was ahead of his time regarding gender roles. The mysterious Magga, for example, knows all about the multiple identities of Jethro Dumont, Dr. Pali, and the Green Lama. But Jethro never learns the true identity of Magga. Among other things, she is adept at disguises. Whenever a mysterious character turns up to help Jethro out of a tight spot, you can bet that Magga is lurking behind the mask of the elderly harridan, gorgeous showgirl, or other player.

Maybe Magga was actually Evangel Stewart. Or maybe not. Crossen never tipped his hand.

For the most part, the Green Lama fought more or less ordinary criminals. The character was designed to compete with Street and Smith's The Shadow, who was primarily a crime-fighter rather than a superhero. The Green Lama did seem to have a limited super-power based on his body's ability to store an electrical charge and administer it to a foe. He probably picked this talent up during his decade-long stay in Tibet after leaving Harvard.

His friend, Dr. Valco, had developed a variety of "radioactive salts" which, when administered to Jethro, temporarily amplified his ability to administer electric shocks. Jethro was still a committed Buddhist and he did strive never to kill, and if possible to do no lasting harm to any conscious being.

Certainly a limitation on the effectiveness of a crime-fighter, amateur or otherwise. Thus, Jethro studied anatomy, especially the patterns and functions of the human nervous system. By applying pressure to key points in a foe, he could create temporary paralysis of an arm, a leg, or the power of speech. Facing a gang-lord's henchman, Jethro could touch him at key points rendering him selectively helpless.

This is only temporary, the Green Lama would explain, but by touching the crook again he could make it permanent. A highly persuasive tactic. It always worked, and the Lama kept his word and the paralysis did wear off—once the criminal had furnished the information the Lama needed.

A good many of the Lama's cases took place in the City of Cleveland, with which Crossen was obviously familiar. He also travelled to Hollywood, where a number of his adventures took place. Of particular note was a racket involving the kidnaping of infants and their return to their parents for a huge fee through a crooked adoption racket.

Like many heroes of the era in pulps, comics, and radio dramas, the Green Lama fought Nazis even before the U.S. officially entered the war. Kendra told me that her father was a "Hebrophile" and outspoken against all bigotry. In one comic the Green Lama teaches white American soldiers a lesson of tolerance toward their black brothers in arms.

Crossen wrote fourteen novels about the Green Lama. After three-quarters of a century they hold up admirably well. All fourteen have been collected and issued in three lovely omnibus volumes by Matthew Moring's Altus Press.

The first thirteen of these appeared in the magazine as it was originally published. There was a gap between the thirteenth and fourteenth issues containing Green Lama novels, and when the fourteenth was issued it was under the aegis of a new publisher. There was a new cover design, and the emphasis of the magazine was changed from standard detective fiction to so-called "weird menace," emphasizing voyeuristic sex and leering sadism. Clearly there was no place for a non-violent Buddhist superhero in the revamped *Double Detective*, and both the Green Lama and *Double Detective* promptly disappeared from the newsstands.

~ ~ ~ ~ ~

4. Jamaica, New York, 1944

As a fictional creation, the Green Lama has been durable as well as versatile. Okay, we're not talking Sherlock Holmes here, or Tarzan of the Apes, or even Superman. But the Lama has had a long run, and he's still with us.

We were living in a section of the Borough of Queens and I was sitting in a little workroom in the basement of our house, building a model battleship, when my older brother, Jerry, walked in. He'd been at a birthday party. There was a contest there and he'd won a prize, which he proudly displayed. It was, appropriately, a copy of *Prize Comics*.

This was one of the so-called anthology comics popular in the era. Patterned on the variety pulps like *Argosy* or *Blue Book,* there might be one story devoted to a superhero, another to a cowboy, another to a magician, and so on. At the age of nine I was addicted to superheroes, and when Jerry had finished reading his copy of *Prize Comics* and loaned it to me, I hit on the costumed heroes in the comic. There was the Owl. He wore a standard superhero suit—purple tights and a cape, plus an owl mask, as best I remember—but this was a very long time ago. And there were Yank and Doodle, the Yankee Doodle Twins, a pair of adolescent brothers who wore patriotic patterned tights.

There was also a feature about the Green Lama. It may well have been drawn by the same Mac Raboy who would later draw the "flying" Green Lama. In this version the Lama wore a baggy, hooded robe and battled bank robbers and other such baddies, and I found the Owl and Yank and Doodle the Yankee Doodle Twins more interesting. In later years I learned that this depiction of the Lama was more in keeping with the attractive paintings on the covers of *Double Detective*.

Much of the material in *Prize Comics* was created in a comics studio in New York. The great Otto Binder did the lion's share of the writing with his brother Jack providing illustrations, but the eccentric, talented Richard Briefer both wrote and drew a monthly adventure of Frankenstein. A minor text box explained that Frankenstein was the name of the monster's creator, not the name of the monster. But . . .

From month to month the monster smashed dams, brought down airliners, and generally wreaked havoc. His chief foe was a tights-wearing but otherwise mundane crime-fighter named Bulldog Denny. But in at least one case a superhero team consisting of Denny, the Owl, Yank and Doodle, and the Green Lama fought the monster to a standstill.

You can't keep a good superhero down, and after the pulp magazine version and the *Prize Comics* series came to an end, the new *Green Lama Comics* made its debut. The comic only ran for eight issues, but they have been lovingly collected into two volumes by Dark Horse Books. Unquestionably, the renderings by Mac Raboy represent him at his best. Eventually he would take over the Flash Gordon Sunday page, and continue the superb work of Alex Raymond.

Ken Crossen was obviously a man of conscience, and he used the pages of the Green Lama comic to advance a message of tolerance and acceptance. On the face of it, an unarguable position. But while the artwork was absolutely gorgeous, the stories themselves and the speeches attributed to the Green Lama come across as preachy even today; they almost surely did so in the 1940s. Comic book readers didn't want lectures on sociology, they wanted action-filled adventure stories.

There was even a Green Lama radio series patterned closely on *The Shadow*. Jethro Dumont was played by the astonishingly talented Paul Frees. Frees did a spot-on imitation of Orson Welles, who had played Lamont Cranston, the secret identity of the Shadow in the radio incarnation of that mystery man.

Round and round the carousel goes!

A handful of Green Lama radio episodes survive and are readily available over the internet. Crossen reportedly did not write the scripts, but he supervised the productions, and some of the storylines do echo the plots of Crossen's pulp novels.

~ ~ ~ ~ ~

5. Northern California, 2015

Over the past half century or so I've written a good deal about the comics, and seem to have attained the status of elder statesman (or maybe living fossil) in the comics industry. There's an establishment called Escapist Comics not far from my home, and I enjoy dropping in to see what's new and to chat with a couple of friends on the staff.

When I caught a glimpse of the Dark Horse collections I was reminded of how much I enjoyed Mac Raboy's work and Ken Crossen's writing. I knew that Raboy had gone from strength to strength, finally adding his touches to the Flash Gordon page. But what had Ken Crossen done after the Green Lama ceased publication? For that matter, what had be done *before* creating the Green Lama?

I found a good deal about him, starting with the good old reliable internet. I also had the great good fortune of being put in touch with Kendra Crossen Burroughs. Turns out that Ken Crossen had a long, prolific, and versatile career after the Green Lama. He worked in radio, television, and motion pictures. And he wrote dozens of books.

The greatest number of them featured an insurance investigator named Milo March. Crossen had done this work himself at one time, according to Kendra Crossen Burroughs, and he returned to it often in his fiction. He even created an interplanetary insurance man, one Manning Draco, for a series of clever, comedic capers in *Thrilling Wonder Stories.*

Crossen had a penchant for oddly named amateur or semi-professional crime-solvers pursuing unusual professions in their non-detecting hours. Jethro Dumont had of course been the archetypical millionaire playboy *à la* Lamont Cranston or Bruce Wayne, but more often Crossen went for something a little more distinctive.

Or a lot more.

Vide, Mortimer Death, Undertaker Detective. Pulp scholar and historian Monte Herridge uncovered this character and has my gratitude for doing so. As far as I know, Herridge has located four Mortimer Death stories, all published in *Detective Fiction Weekly* in 1940 and 1941. Typically, Mortimer Death starts off by helping the official police investigating a recent murder case. Eventually the police are baffled and Mortimer solves the crime.

Of greatest interest is "Prest-o Change-o Murder." The victim in this story is a magician—one of Crossen's favorite tropes.

All four Mortimer Death stories appeared in *DFW* under the by-line "Bennett Barley." Other pseudonyms used by Crossen included Richard Foster, Christopher Monig, and Clay Richards. Another was M. E. Chaber, a transliteration from Hebrew, meaning maker or creator or, loosely translated, "writer."

But to get back to good old Milo March. This fellow had been an army officer assigned to duty with the OSS (Office of Strategic Services), the World War Two predecessor of the later CIA (Central Intelligence Agency). Bet you already knew that, didn't you? In this capacity he was widely traveled and was an expert linguist, fluent in many languages.

At the end of war he was not officially discharged from the OSS but released from active duty and placed in the army reserves. Most of the time, then, he operated a one-man insurance investigation firm (sometimes with a female secretary) taking cases on special assignment from commercial insurance companies.

In a typical case he would be invited to the offices of a nearby insurance firm and told of a very large and highly suspicious claim. Often these would involve travel to remote locations. Hong Kong was a favorite. There Milo would make contacts, most often with a beautiful and sexually provocative young woman, through whom he would make the connections necessary to infiltrate the local underworld.

There is a remarkable sense of presence and of time in these books. Hong Kong was then a British colony. The mainland—"Red China"—was regarded as a mysterious and dangerous place. Smuggling of anything from machine tools to ancient art treasures between Hong Kong and mainland China was a major, if clandestine and strictly illegal, industry.

Milo was clearly a garrulous and congenial fellow with a real talent for forming friendships. Wherever he traveled in pursuit of his assignments he would enlist a local surrogate. This might be a taxi driver, a hotel staff member, even a potentially disaffected member of the local underground.

During his stays Milo would drink an immense amount of alcohol and smoke uncounted cigarettes. He was also something of a gourmet, and Crossen delighted in describing Milo's meals. He liked to rent a car whenever that was possible. His first preference would always be a white Cadillac convertible.

He liked to push people psychologically. This would begin with his initial meeting in each insurance case with a local executive of the company hiring him. He would arrive for his first meeting, ogle the invariably nubile receptionist, issue financial demands to the executive who'd called him in, and walk out with everything he wanted. In the earliest cases his fee was $50 a day, and Milo would pay his own expenses. As his career blossomed his daily fees increased, he demanded and received a generous expense account, and he would receive a cash advance before ever setting out on his journey.

The cases are breezy and thoroughly readable, perfect reading while sitting in an airliner or reclining on a beach chair or before turning off the light in bed. The incredible amount of booze that Milo consumes, the uncounted cigarettes that he smokes, and the unending parade of gorgeous and readily available women he romances give a vivid period feel to these books.

Did insurance investigators really live that way in the mid-Twentieth Century, or was this a sort of Mickey Spillane—John D. MacDonald—Ian Fleming fantasy? I wouldn't know for sure, but I suspect that the latter is the case. Is it the fantasy that aficionados of PI novels enjoy today, the fantasy that writers of such books spin for the amusement of their readers? I think not. I'm sure that the changing years have brought about changing fantasies, but fantasies are with us always.

But remember, Milo March was still a reserve officer in the US Army and subject to recall for duty as a CIA spook. Whenever he received such a summons he would confront his old boss and sass him mercilessly. The general would ask Milo whether he preferred to be recalled, officially, to active duty in the army . . . or work as a temporary civilian employee.

Invariably Milo would choose the latter because the general couldn't then order his court martial for any infraction, starting with sassing him off.

These cases, more James Bond than Mike Hammer, involved sending Milo behind the Iron Curtain, into the German Democratic Republic or into the Soviet Union itself. In the latter case, a CIA mole was threatened with exposure. It was Milo's job to find him and spirit him out of the USSR, through the Iron Curtain and safely back to the West. As might be expected, Milo becomes involved with a lovely and more than willing Soviet beauty, vast amounts of vodka are consumed, there's considerable skullduggery involving illegal currency exchanges, and Milo comes home, mission accomplished.

The most noteworthy of the two dozen Milo March novels is *The Splintered Man* (1955). In this novel Milo is "invited" to a meeting with military brass and eventually confronts Lieutenant General Sam Roberts, a onetime comrade is the OSS during World War Two.

As Roberts explains, an important research scientist has disappeared into the GDR. Was he kidnapped? Was he lured into East Germany and prevented from leaving? Did he defect voluntarily? After considerable discussion—Milo is not eager to take this job!—Milo agrees to investigate. Best case, he'll locate the scientist and bring him back to the West. Worst case—you can imagine.

After considerable travail, Milo finds the scientist. He's working in a joint Soviet / East German research facility, experimenting with a drug called *lysergic acid diethylamide.* Yes, it was LSD. Milo is captured and brought into the experimental program. Knowledgeable readers have commented that Milo's experiences with LSD are quite accurately described, although Kendra Crossen Burroughs has told me that her father never actually used the substance.

The Splintered Man is the one Milo March novel I would recommend to anyone curious about this series and about Kendell Crossen's work. It has a more serious tone than most of the other March novels. Aside from the LSD theme, Crossen delivers himself (speaking through March) of impassioned views on the Holocaust and possible Nazi revanchism. This is a remarkable book, especially for its day.

In 1967 Crossen published his second novel on this theme, *The Acid Nightmare.* Packaged as a "YA" (young adult) novel, this is actually no different in tone from Crossen's adult novels, except for its cast of characters, most of whom are teenagers or twenty-somethings. Two acid experiences are described in detail. The book is worth reading, but between this and *The Splintered Man,* the latter is more powerful and historically more important.

Oddly, *The Acid Nightmare* carries the M. E. Chaber by-line on both dust jacket and title page, but the copyright is attributed to Crossen. I have no idea which name is used in any library that might still have a copy.

~ ~ ~ ~ ~

6. Northern California, 2016

There's so much to say about Crossen, a man who created a body of such breadth and depth, that I hardly know where to stop. For instance, I know I mentioned the Manning Draco science fiction stories. Crossen also edited a couple of very good science fiction anthologies. You can hunt 'em up in a local used book store, or search for them on the internet.

He also wrote two science fiction novels, *Year of Consent* and *The Rest Must Die*. The former is a near-future dystopia, somewhat in the manner of *1984*. The latter (written as Richard Foster) takes place in New York following a nuclear attack. Survivors trapped in a subway station must find a way to survive. Anyone familiar with the noises, sounds, and odors of a New York subway can imagine the sensations this book evokes.

Both novels are accessible and intelligently executed, but not of exceptional note.

Crossen's work in comics brought him into partnership with Horace Gold, creating story lines for Captain Marvel, Superman, and Batman. He was editor of *Captain Marvel, Jr.,* for which Mac Raboy did much of his best work. Later, of course, Raboy would draw brilliant covers and execute interior stories for Crossen's *Green Lama Comics.*

He contributed to numerous radio and television series. He wrote radio and television scripts for *Suspense, Molle Mystery Theater, Find that Clue, The Falcon,* and *The Kate Smith Show.*

Born July 25, 1910, in Ohio, Crossen died November 29, 1981. For several decades his works were almost all out of print, but a significant Crossen revival is under way. Matthew Moring's three-volume Altus reissue of the Green Lama pulps are a major achievement in the field of pulp history. These include reproductions of the 1940s illustrations by V. E. Pyle, and they are splendid. The two-volume Dark Horse reissue of the Greene Lama comics shows off the Raboy interpretation at its best.

Despite some controversy over the copyright of the comic book character, new Green Lama stories in both text and graphic form continue to appear. Several Green Lama radio shows and audio books are available for download or as CDs.

Altus has also reissued a two volume set of Crossen's Manning Draco stories, and has announced plans to reissue the Milo March novels as trade paperback books.

Most exciting, Kendra Crossen Burroughs has told me that there was one more Milo March manuscript in inventory when the series was cancelled. Reason: disagreement between Crossen and his publisher over politics. Not surprisingly to anyone who has read much of Crossen's work, he was distinctly progressive in his views. Apparently his publisher was not.

With Milo coming back from Altus, we can hope to see that final novel in print at last, all these years after the author's demise. What a celebration that will bring!

~ ~ ~ ~ ~

MY FAVORITE CAPTAIN MARVEL STORY

WHAT AN ASSIGNMENT! Somebody once asked Ludwig van Beethoven which of his symphonies was his favorite, and the great composer responded, "Which of your children is your favorite?" When Paul Hamerlinck asked me to contribute a little essay on my favorite Captain Marvel story, I think I knew how Ludwig felt!

Was it the very first Captain Marvel story? I read it in a drugstore in Venice, Florida, when I was five years old. I can still see some of C. C. Beck's wonderful panels after seventy-five years! There was the great "Monster Society of Evil" serial. Oh, that cliff-hanger with Billy Batson frozen in a giant ice cube, unable to say the magic word. There was the incredible struggle between Captain Marvel and Mr. Atom. And the one in which the Fates who control the world got their yarn tangled and 1942 turned into 1492. And no way I could forget the terrible incident in which the evil Captain Nazi knocked Freddy Freeman out of a rowboat and nearly killed him—and Captain Marvel rescued the boy who would shortly become Captain Marvel Junior!

But of these all, I wound up with "Captain Marvel Battles the Giant Earth Dreamer," that appeared in *Captain Marvel Adventures* #52, dated January 18, 1946. The comic was so popular by then that it was published every two weeks.

I was wandering through a "five-and-ten" in Jamaica, New York. I was approaching my eleventh birthday. I had a couple of dollars in my pocket, including a counterfeit dollar bill that someone had passed to me, and I decided to risk time in a federal prison by spending the phony dollar instead of turning it in at the nearest FBI office. Oh, and I got away with it!

The cover illustration on the issue showed Captain Marvel delivering a punch to a startled individual with pop eyes, shaggy hair, and a scraggly beard. This was long before the hippy era; such hirsute adornment in those days was generally attributed to hermits or farmers, and the individual on the receiving end of Captain Marvel's sock was clearly the latter.

Inside the comic book, this was the lead story written by the great Otto Oscar Binder and illustrated (probably) by C. C. Beck. Unless it was done by Peter Costanza.

The story opens with Billy Batson reading a news story about a Professor Plato Q. Thinkler, who believes that our entire universe is the product of a dream by a giant dozing in a fourth dimensional mega-universe. Just as the scale of the mega-universe is far larger than ours, so is its time-dimension, and the giant's nap of a few hours has lasted for 10,000 years of "our" time.

Captain Marvel visits Professor Thinkler, who warns him that the giant earth-dreamer may wake up at any moment, which event would spell the end of our universe. It would be painless, Thinkler warns Captain Marvel. Just—poof!—and we'll be gone.

In order to save the universe—now there's a tall order for you—Captain Marvel tries to wish himself into the mega-universe. And since this is all a dream, anything can happen—and it does!

Captain Marvel tries various methods of getting the giant dreamer to sleep soundly, and when he succeeds (by knocking a tree onto him) our universe is guaranteed another 10,000 years. Cap then wishes himself back to Professor Thinkler's laboratory.

The Professor explains that he has improved on his theory. He tells captain Marvel that he—Thinkler—had dreamed up the giant, who in turn had dreamed up our universe.

And in the end, Billy Batson wakes up in his own bed, having dreamed up Professor Thinkler. Oh, it was enough to make a ten-year-old's mind spin. I still love it.

WHEN IS A PULP NOT A PULP?

IT'S NO SECRET that I grew up reading comic books. Okay, and listening to adventure stories on the radio and seeing Saturday afternoon serials at the movies. Eventually I graduated to pulp fiction, and quickly realized that most of the comics and radio shows and chapter plays I loved—detective stories, swinging teen-agers, funny animals, and above all superheroes—were really just pulp fiction in sound and pictures.

My favorite characters were Captain Marvel and assorted spin-offs of that great series, and my favorite publisher was Fawcett. But I was omnivorous. I would read all the stories in *Captain Marvel Adventures,* but I would also read the back-up features, behind Captain Marvel, in *Whiz Comics.* And similarly with *Master Comics* (backing up Captain Marvel, Jr.) and *Wow Comics* (backing up Mary Marvel).

And a lot of those back-up features were great fun. Ibis the Invincible, Commando Yank, Spy Smasher, Golden Arrow, Bulletman, Mr. Scarlet, Radar the International Policeman, Nyoka the Jungle Girl—happy memories! And then there was Lance O'Casey. Fawcett comics seldom carried by-lines, but I think that this feature was usually written by the great Otto Binder and nicely illustrated (or so I've heard) by the little-known but talented Harry Anderson.

O'Casey sailed the waters of the South Pacific encountering modern-day pirates, lost cities, giant creatures and—remember, this was wartime—the Japanese navy. He wore a striped tee-shirt and white duck trousers and a captain's cap on his bright red hair. No way could his appeal overshadow that of the Big Red Cheese, but the stories were reliably clever and colorful and I always enjoyed them.

A few years ago when I was asked to create a pulp-type figure, Lance O'Casey came to mind. I didn't want to pull him out of the half-century-old pages of *Whiz Comics* but I wanted to create a similar character as homage to this character who was always good if not great.

Problem was, O'Casey never had much of an origin story—the comics version of a creation myth. So I decided to write one for my seafaring adventurer, Seamus "Splash" Shanahan. I won't repeat it here, it's all in "The Secret of the Red Robe Men." It's designed to give the character more depth, more of an internal life, and more motivation for his chosen lifestyle. One difference was the time-frame. Lance O'Casey's adventures took place in the 1940s; Splash Shanahan's took place in 1928—with a further back story to 1918!

The Red Robe Men themselves are real. I learned about them from a fascinating book, *1421: The Year that China Discovered the World,* by Gavin Menzies. You might want to scout up a copy for a fascinating read.

I had a grand time adventuring with Splash Shanahan, so grand that I wrote another story about him, called "Tangaroa's Eye." You'll see it in the next issue of *Pulp Adventures.* And now that I'm thinking about Splash, I have a feeling that more of his voyages may well be on their way.

THE AICFAD STYLE SHEET

[Half a Century Later: Once the *All in Color for a Dime* series got rolling, we found that enthusiasm was high but some of our would-be contributors were floundering as to how to go about writing the kind of essay we wanted. So we made up the following style sheet for our writers. In Hollywood I guess they would call it the series Bible. In the course of keying this in, I reread it for the first time since it was published in *Xero* for January, 1961. I was amazed at how well it holds up. – RAL.]

A GRATIFYING NUMBER of people have offered to contribute articles to the "All in Color for a Dime" series of articles on comic books. Some would-be contributors may have been scared off, however, because they're not sure as to just what is wanted in these articles. Worse, a couple of hardy souls went to the trouble of researching and writing articles intended for the series, only to have them bounced because they just did not tell the story that is wanted.

So this style sheet is presented, not as a strait jacket—express *your* ideas as *you* see fit—but as a checklist. The material listed should be the minimum *factual* content of your article about the Purple Zombie or whomever you select to write about. The evaluative, analytic, opinion-type stuff is strictly up to you.

I. ORIGIN. Where did this guy come from? What is the source of his powers (if any), the motivation of his actions, etc.? Was he supernatural, or an alien from another world, or a half-human from beneath the sea, or an android? Or was he an ordinary human being?

II. DESCRIPTION. What did your hero look like? How did he dress? If he had an alter-ego (most did) how did *he* look, dress, etc.?

III. POWERS / DEVICES / SETTING. What super-normal powers, if any, did he have? What special gadgets or devices did he use? Was there an unusual setting or element in the setting of the tales?

IV.   OTHER CHARACTERS. Who beside the hero was a significant member of the cast? Did the hero have a side-kick, comic-relief character, girlfriend, mentor, continuing foe, police contact? Were there any other noteworthy characters in the stories? If there were, describe their appearance, character and role.

V.   PUBLISHING HISTORY. Who were the authors, editors, artists, publishers of the series? In what comic books did the strip appear? Was it ever in other media, such as newspaper comics, movie serials or full-length films, radio or television, Little Books or other publications? When?

VI.   STORY CONTENT. Reconstruct, to the best of your ability, one or more of the best or most important stories in the series.

VII.   CHARACTER CROSSOVER. Did heroes or other characters from other strips ever turn up in this one? Did the hero or any character from this series ever enter another strip?

   In short, paraphrasing Don Thompson: Pretend that you have a friend who is an intelligent, educated person, except that he never even *heard* of the Green Turtle. You are a real fan of the Turtle and are going to tell your friend all about him. That's what your article should be like.

   Well, let me say one more thing: this page is intended to help people write articles for the series, not to scare them off. If you are interested but doubtful about doing an article, be assured that I will do all I can to help you out. As I've said before almost to the limits of others' listening endurance, I want this series to be really worthwhile, not just casual nostalgia *à la Playboy*. All I can do to help contributors, I will do.

CRASHING COMETS, BLASTING ROCKETS, BLAZING RAY GUNS, HIDEOUS MONSTERS AND GORGEOUS, GORGEOUS, GORGEOUS WOMEN

WHEN I WAS five years old my mother (Sylvia) used to take me with her to visit her sister (my Aunt Marion). She would drive us to a subway station and take my hand as we descended the steps into the darkened, mysterious world below the earth.

At the end of our ride we would re-emerge into the sunlight and walk to the apartment building where Aunt Marion lived with her husband, Sam. (Yes, I had an Uncle Sam, actually and literally.) The two sisters would sit at the kitchen table drinking coffee and smoking cigarettes and talking about matters that were totally incomprehensible to me.

Soon my Uncle Sam would take me by the hand and we would descend in the building's elevator. Leaving the lobby we would walk to a neighborhood drug store where Uncle Sam would buy us chocolate ice cream sodas, and after we had consumed them he would buy a comic book for me. As I remember, my uncle chose the comics, and the comics he chose always featured beautiful ladies in tight-fitting leopard-skin costumes, posing in jungle settings.

I realized in later years that these were probably either *Jumbo Comics* or *Jungle Comics,* both published by the oddly named Love Romances Publishing Company under the label of Fiction House. Good old Fiction House and its bull's-eye cover symbol.

Fiction House itself dated from the 1920s, when it started a wide-ranging line of pulp magazines. By the late 1930s the company expanded into the burgeoning comic book field. With an established family of pulps, it was natural that a line of comics would run in parallel with the pulp magazines—*Jungle Stories* and *Jungle Comics, Wings Stories* and *Wings Comics,* and—of immediate concern—*Planet Stories* and *Planet Comics.*

Based on its appearance, *Planet Stories* was the pulpiest of pulp science fiction magazines. Issue after issue featured cover paintings of the classic BEM / Babe / Bum triad. Yes, an alien Bug-Eyed Monster, a gorgeous scantily-clad human female, and a ray-gun toting spaceman. Pure space opera, yet if one goes beyond the package, *Planet Stories* contained first-rate science fiction by such luminaries as Poul Anderson, Isaac Asimov, Leigh Brackett, Ray

119

Bradbury, Theodore Sturgeon, and even the now-revered Philip K. Dick.

When the pulp *Planet Stories'* comic book sibling, *Planet Comics*, came along, an historically-minded scholar might expect to find those issues filled with wild interplanetary romances and space operas, a glorious mixture of Edgar Rice Burroughs and Edward Elmer "Doc" Smith.

Alas, such was not the case. Album reprints of the early *Planet Comics* in the PS series reveal a disappointing array of simplistic plotlines and almost childishly crude artwork.

There were a few rather feeble attempts at superheroes. There was the Red Comet. There was no explanation of his name or origin, at least that I know of. He was just there. His super power was the ability to change his size. Confronted by an army of enemies he could turn into a giant and stomp them to death. Of course a Red Comet blown up to 100 times his normal size would, presumably, have only his original mass, making him as insubstantial as a child's balloon, but such scientific trivialities were no obstacle to the plotters of these stories. And there was Amazona, Mighty Woman. I had some trouble understanding Amazona. Not sure what her powers were or whence they came. I guess she was mighty.

Aside from those really uncharismatic superheroes, there were some smashing space battles reminiscent of the earliest 'prentice work of Edmond Hamilton in the *Science Wonder Stories* and *Weird Tales* of a decade earlier. For all that those earliest issues of *Planet Comics* are of historic interest, they make for disappointing reading. One bright spot was their covers, always filled with colorful action, exotic settings, and classic BEM / Babe / Bum triads. Initially the work of the young Will Eisner, these covers alone promised far better things to come.

The target audience of the Fiction House pulp line was likely single males in their teens to early twenties. I'm guessing at that, I'll admit, but surely those covers would have caught their eyes and the stories in the magazines offered an array of dramatic characters and fast-paced action in a variety of exotic settings.

Most early comic books—and for that matter, most of those published to this day—were aimed at several clearly identifiable age groups. Funny animals and fairy tale comics were aimed at small children, little beyond the toddler stage. Superheroes were expected to appeal to ten-to-twelve-year-olds. Once in high school, it was assumed, most readers would graduate to pulp magazines and / or "real books."

The executives at Fiction House worked a variation on that strategy. By featuring a never-ending parade of gorgeous women in form-fitting costumes and provocative postures, they realized that they could keep their post-superhero readers. No fifteen-to-seventeen-year-old male, his ductless glands pumping out a daily rush of testosterone, could resist the wiles of those gorgeous females featured in the Fiction House comics.

Even the eyes of my relatively mature Uncle Sam gleamed at the shapely gams and bosoms of those jungle queens. Edgar Rice Burroughs' Tarzan might be the king of the jungle in hardbound novels but Will Eisner's Sheena was the queen of the comic books and the dreams of hundreds of thousands of adolescent readers.

If the writers and artists producing the very early issues of *Planet Comics* were essentially clueless as to how to produce a valid science fiction story, they either learned their craft in short order, or were replaced by creators who understood the field. I'm only guessing here, but I suspect that *Planet Comics* regulars were handed copies of *Planet Stories* and told to take them home and read and learn.

This eighth volume of the collected *Planet Comics* contains the thirtieth through thirty-fifth issues, as they appeared on a bimonthly schedule between May, 1944, and March, 1945. Five years into its run, *Planet Comics* had evolved into the best written and best illustrated science fiction comic in existence, not to be equaled until EC Comics' *Weird Science* and *Weird Fantasy*, which eventually morphed into *Weird Science-Fantasy* and then *Incredible Science Fiction*—the first attempt to publish a real science fiction magazine in comic book form.

Certainly the premiere feature of the more evolved *Planet Comics* was "The Lost World," an apparently open-ended narrative set in a near-future Earth that has been devastated by the invading Volta men. Humanoid beings with green visages and deeply wrinkled, desiccated skin, the Volta men wear coal-shovel helmets patterned on those of World War II Nazi troops, topped with spikes like those of World War I German soldiers. The Volta men wear plain uniforms also vaguely suggestive of Hitler's armies, and seem to have no particular motivation save the total annihilation of the human species.

One oddity is that there were apparently no Volta *women*. I don't have all of the instalments of "The Lost World" before me—

I look forward to reading the rest of them in due course—but in the episodes I've read, the Volta invaders are apparently all males. Perhaps they were an advance party, sent to conquer Earth and prepare the way for a full-scale colonization. And while we see the horrors of the Volta conquest of Earth, I would have thought (as a sometime science fiction writer myself) that the home world of the Volta men had potential for some strong plot lines.

But then, I suppose there's little point in applying the *coulda-shoulda-woulda* yardstick to stories written three quarters of a century ago.

Fighting the Volta men are skilled archer Hunt Bowman, his gorgeous companion Lyssa, and their faithful canine companion. At times the story line suggests that Hunt and Lyssa are the only humans left alive, but in fact they frequently encounter other survivors. If "The Lost World" has a weakness, it is the apparent absence of an overall story arc. Each instalment follows a familiar pattern as the Volta men strive to capture or kill Hunt and Lyssa, while the two humans fight back, Hunt's astonishingly accurate talents as archer proving deadly effective.

The scripts for "The Lost World" were by-lined by one Thorncliffe Herrick. Alas, I have been unable to learn anything about this writer. Even the thoroughly researched and authoritative Miller / Contento index has no listing for him. My guess is that Herrick was either a pseudonym or a house name used by a variety of authors. Possibly the editors of *Planet Comics* wrote the stories themselves—not an unknown practice in the comics industry.

I'm going to cheat a little and look ahead of the issues of *Planet Comics* included in this volume. I guess I couldn't help myself. If this calls for a spoiler alert, just skip ahead a paragraph or two and we'll get back together.

The "Lost World" feature, once it got going, ran in *Planet Comics* through issue 70. The characters evolved. The story line was not consistent. Did the events take place in the 28th Century or the 34th or in some other era? Was Lyssa originally from Earth or had she been brought here by the Volta men after they'd conquered her home world? Were she and Hunt Bowman really the only survivors of humanity? (Obviously they weren't!) And why and how had the Volta men evolved from blobby pale humanoids into wrinkly-skinned green quasi-Nazis? And for that matter, why did they originally speak standard English only to have their verbal patterns degenerate into the stilted pseudo-Latinesque constructions of later episodes?

Don't look for answers to these questions, amici. For the adventures of Hunt and Lyssa simply disappeared with *Planet Comics* issue 71. "The Lost World" and most of the other continuing features in *Planet Comics* just stopped. Maybe they were kidnaped by aliens. Suddenly, *Planet Comics* became an anthology comic book, a collection of single stories in each issue with few if any continuing characters or protracted story lines.

The "new" *Planet Comics* didn't get better. It didn't get worse. It just became—different. As far as I can determine—I might be wrong!—there was no explanation, no editorial statement, no "message to the readers." Just—*Planet* 70 was the old version and *Planet* 71 was the new version.

One feature hung on for a single issue of the new *Planet*— "Space Rangers," featuring Flint Baker and Reef Ryan. *Planet Comics* issue 73 was the last published. It was dated winter, 1953.

A number of editors came and went at both the pulp and the comics sides of Fiction House. During the 1944-45 period we're considering, Paul Payne was listed as editor of *Planet Comics;* Jack Byrne was managing editor, and Thurman T. Scott as business manager. For many years Jerry Iger, onetime partner of Will Eisner, was credited as art editor. Certainly the Eisner-Iger style was present in *Planet* from the first issue to the last.

Well, like the poet Walt Whitman, I contradict myself. Since I wrote the above I've researched those earlier issues of *Planet Comics,* and studied the earliest instalments of "The Lost World." Initially, to my surprise, Lyssa arrives in Earth as a prisoner of the Volta men. We learn that she is a native of another planet, previously conquered by the Voltas.

Why they have brought her to Earth isn't quite clear—at least not to me, but by this time my head was spinning and I might well have missed something. There's some interplanetary derring-do between Earth and Lyssa's home planet, but eventually she winds up on Earth, partnering up with Hunt, and the plotline goes on from there. And it turns out that the Volta men didn't destroy human civilization after all. Rather, incessant human-against-human war had accomplished this trick before the aliens ever landed.

Also to my surprise, the Voltas weren't originally those wrinkled green-complexioned horrors that I grew up fearing. At first they looked more like pale, pasty-skinned, bald-pated humans. Why and how they turned green and wrinkly, I haven't discovered yet, but maybe I will. They also seem to speak regular, colloquial English in the early instalments. Eventually their speech deteriorates into a weird pseudo-Teutonic patois. My dear friend Dick Ellington thought it was more Latin-based than German. He may have been right, but I grew up fearing Hitler's brutal storm troopers, not Caesar's conquering legions.

"The Lost World" was generally the lead story in *Planet Comics,* and most frequently was featured on the cover. The backing features were often entertaining, even if they lacked the depth and fine craftsmanship that went into "The Lost World."

"Mars, God of War," was another example of "frustration drama" (and was also credited to the elusive Mr. Herrick). In each instalment the legendary deity appears as a ghostly image, decides to take a hand in human affairs, and provokes an episode of violence and destruction only to retreat, vanquished, vowing to return another day.

Puzzled me when I was a kid. Puzzles me now.

"Norge Benson" (by Olaf Bjorn, sometimes Olaf Bjornson) was a wonderfully lighthearted adventure strip featuring an interplanetary explorer, his gorgeous girlfriend (of course), his pet polar bear cub, and occasionally a very cute baby mammoth.

Other ongoing features included "Space Rangers," "Star Pirate," and "Gale Allen and the Girl Squadron." All were more-or-less standard model space operas, written and executed with a good degree of talent. "Gale Allen" bears particular note, certainly deserving of an honored position in the annals of feminist comics, along with Eisner's Sheena, Binder's Mary Marvel, Marston and Peter's Wonder Woman, and the slickly executed Miss Fury, created by Tarpe Mills.

Gale Allen and her female troupers piloted space ships and fought aliens with the best of their male counterparts, all the while, of course, displaying their feminine charms to maximum advantage.

Just as the earliest issues of *Planet Comics* leaned toward simplistic story lines which evolved into more complex and sophisticated plots, the early illustrations in the magazine also improved dramatically with passing time. A roll-call of artists who contributed cover illustrations and story work is astonishing.

The early Joe Kubert, who went on to create Hawkman for DC Comics as well as DC's classic war comics, was one of them. Graham Ingels, before going on to draw EC horror comics as "Ghastly Graham Ingels," honed his skill on the Volta men of "The Lost World." George Tuska went from "Star Pirate" to Captain Marvel, Iron Man, and Lev Gleason's notorious *Crime Does*

Not Pay. Lee Elias, a talented disciple of the great Milton Caniff, did fine work on "Space Rangers." Murphy Anderson, another versatile stalwart in later years, producing some of DC's finest superhero features, polished his talents on "Star Pirate" and on *Planet Comics'* pseudo-documentary feature, "Life on Other Worlds."

Equally as remarkable were the hugely talented female artists who got to work for Fiction House. *Planet Comics* alone featured the work of Lily Renee and "the two Frans" (Dietrick and Hopper, and more about "them" in just a moment) on a variety of its ongoing features, and they turned out cover art and narrative pages every bit as good as their male compatriots. It should perhaps, in this modern enlightened era, be unnecessary to discuss the gender of these splendid artists. After all, talent is talent, good work is good work.

But in the 1940s attitudes were very different, and a "girl" (!) comic book artist was about as common as a female bomber pilot ferrying a B-17 from its factory in the US to an Eighth Air Force base in England. Come to think of it, there were such pilots during the Second World War, but that's a topic for another essay.

Remind me, will you?

Back to *Planet Comics.* Lily Renee's beautifully crafted work appeared across the Fiction House line, including *Fight Comics* and *Rangers Comics* as well as *Planet.* A European-born holocaust survivor, Renee took over *Planet's* top feature, "The Lost World." Cartoon scholar Trina Robbins has devoted an entire book to her.

Fran Dietrick aka Fran Hopper was another Fiction House regular, appearing in *Planet Comics* and *Jungle Comics* as well as non-Fiction House periodicals like *Dime Comics* and *Phantom Lady.* For *Planet* she created Mysta of the Moon, an ongoing, beautifully drawn feature that morphed out of the puzzling "Mars, God of War." As Fran Dietrick she did marvelous work on "Norge Benson," as well as cover art for *Planet Comics.* Confusion over whether the Frans were one person or two was resolved by Trina Robbins, who interviewed the artist and determined that Dietrick was her maiden name and Hopper was her married name.

I'm afraid I've rambled on far too long about these few issues of *Planet Comics* and the talented creators responsible for them, the unsung writers (who *were* they, really?) and the grand, talented artists who drew them. If you're still with me, gentle reader, I thank you most profoundly for your patience, and will urge you, now, to proceed to a series of comic book science fiction at the peak of its brilliance.

As for me, I can only try to relive those wonderful expeditions when I was five years old and my Uncle Sam took me to buy an ice cream soda and a comic book.

THE COMIC-BOOK BOOK

Edited by
DON THOMPSON AND DICK LUPOFF

RECALLS THE GREAT COMIC-BOOK FEATURES OF THE PAST

ZOWIE!

AWK!

!!!

AARGH..!

HMMM!

CONTINUED

THE PROPWASH PATROL

WE WERE AIR-MINDED in those days. Those days were the days and years of World War II, the last war, I think, that ever got a "good press" in this country. Korea got a mixed press; at first it was a clear-cut and generous response to aggression but as the fighting dragged on inconclusively, casualty reports poured in weekly, political wrangling arose over so-called no-win policies, Truman fired MacArthur, truce talks went on and on and on at Panmunjom . . . we got tired of Korea. And Vietnam, of course, has been an unmitigated disaster from anyone's viewpoint.

But World War II . . .

Maybe it was just because I was a small boy at the time, or maybe it was at least in part because we had something pretty close to a controlled press, with the OWI—the Office of War Information—feeding coverage to the media and military cameramen providing "official" footage to the newsreels.

But mainly I think it was because the American people really *believed* in the war effort, we believed that the world was divided into two great warring forces, one good and one evil, and of course our side was the side of good. The "gray areas" that make it so hard to tell the good guys from the bad guys any more were . . . well, not quite *absent* 30 years ago, so much as conveniently brushed aside, overlooked.

The good guys were America, Britain, France, China, Russia. The bad guys were Germany, Japan, and their agents, dupes, and collaborators. About the only country to receive equivocal treatment was Italy—somehow we felt that the Italians had been led into war on the wrong side by a vain and foolish dictator, and would gladly have opted out of the Axis cause at the first opportunity (which of course they did).

This world-view was both reflected and reinforced by movies, press, radio, and—for us kids—the comics. We thrilled equally to the news and to fictionalized narrations. Our heads were filled with exhilarating visions of heroic marines storming ashore on lush, sandy, rocky islets in the Pacific, rooting out fanatical subhuman Japanese defenders with bomb, bullet, flamethrower, and bare fists.

We imagined ourselves, faces and hands darkened with lampblack, dogtags taped together to avoid sound, parachuting silently into occupied France to make clandestine contact with daring *maquis* and assist them in sabotaging Nazi installations, preparing for the great day of liberation that lay ahead.

But above all we dreamed by day and by night of soaring high over the war zones in sleek sky-chariots, mighty engines roaring as they hauled us into single duel with the enemy: P-47 versus Messerschmitt 109, Lockheed Lightning versus Focke-Wulf 190, Grumman Wildcat versus infamous "Jap Zero." The only rivals for our affection that those zooming fighter planes encountered were the mighty bombing craft, the Boeing B-17 Flying Fortress, the Consolidated B-24 Liberator, the carrier-borne Grumman Avenger torpedo-bomber (skimming low over the warm Pacific swells to deliver a load of deadly steel fish against a Japanese destroyer flotilla . . .), and finally the mighty B-29 Superfortress, rising from steel-mat runways on Saipan to make firebomb runs against paper-walled Japanese cities until finally the *Enola Gay* . . .

We flew with Jimmy Doolittle in his B-25s and floated with him on his life-raft afterwards, we rose with Richard Bong and Pappy Boyington to dogfight and glory.

Of course I was a small boy.

On the home front there were things to do beside dream of combat. We saved our dimes to buy War Savings Stamps, carried ration coupons and tokens along with the dollars our mothers gave us when we went to the grocery store for food (grocery store, right? not yet supermarket) We did our bit in wartime scrap-metal campaigns, reminded Mom to save that bacon grease and turn it in, collected newspapers for paper drives.

Sometimes we even gave comic books—speak of childhood trauma!

But most of all we trained ourselves to be aircraft spotters. In my house, at least, we bought aviation magazines and books at every opportunity; pictures of warplanes were clipped and hung on bedroom walls as if they were pin-ups of Betty Grable or Marlene Dietrich.

I remember that my personal treasure chest was divided into sections: one for comic books; one for bubble gum cards, "send-away" premiums, and the like; and one for the paraphernalia that reflected my personal air-mindedness. In the last category were balsa-wood scale models, a wall-chart of aircraft silhouettes (courtesy the Aluminum Company of America), *The Aircraft Spotter's Handbook*—thumb-indexed, publisher I'm afraid long since forgotten—and *Know Your War Planes*, a beautifully printed 44-page booklet featuring "26 American fighting planes in action painted by William Heaslip and 96 authentic silhouettes of warplanes of the world—American, British, Russian, German, Italian, Japanese."

Know Your War Planes was published in 1943 and found its way into my hands while still hot off the press. A notice inside the back cover says that "Additional copies may be obtained for $.10 each (stamps or coin) from the Coca-Cola Company, Department WP, Box 1734, No. 1, Atlanta, Georgia, U.S.A." I still have that little book.

I think I'll send for a fresh copy this afternoon.

It was inevitable that "air-mindedness" find its way into the comics, and in fact it did so before the United States ever entered World War II; before, in fact, the war broke out in Europe.

There's substantial disagreement over the parentage of the comic book. Comic specialists like Bill Blackbeard and Maurice Horn maintain that the comic book is basically a mutation—and not a very desirable one—of the (newspaper) comic *strip.* Those who support this position point to the obvious similarity of format—panel-breakdown, graphic narrative techniques, dialog in speech balloons, and so on—and to the undeniable historical fact that most early comic books were mere compendiums of newspaper strips, which gave way to new material only as the supply of reprintable newspaper comics began to run out.

Others, though, such as Jim Steranko, suggest that the real parent of the comic book was the pulp fiction magazine wherein cavorted cowboys and athletes, aviators and detectives, seafaring men and soldiers of fortune, as well as war; and, yes, even superheroes, long before the comic book was so much as a gleam in the eye of the late Mr. M. C. Gaines.

Aviation adventure was one of the staple categories of pulp magazines, with titles ranging from *A* to *Z.* (Literally—from *Air Wonder,* a kind of hybrid aviation/science-fiction magazine founded by Hugo Gernsback, to *Zeppelin Stories,* the content of which should be obvious.)

In addition to these (relatively) conventional pulp magazines, which featured a mélange of yarns grouped around the general theme indicated in their titles, there were the "single-character" pulps that appeared month after month featuring the same hero in an open-ended series of exploits. The best-known of these were *The Shadow, Doc Savage,* and (in the science-fiction realm) *Captain Future.* But in all there were scores.

In the aviation field they included *Bill Barnes, G-8* (recently resurrected as a paperback book series), *Dusty Ayres, Tailspin Tommy* (who made it also to screen and comic-book page), and *Terrence X. O'Leary* (the *X* stood for X-cellent).

Most of these magazines concentrated their attention on fictionalized exploits of imaginary heroes of the *First* World War. The skies over France and the earth-bound adventures of temporarily grounded aviators trapped behind German lines offered fertile territory for authors' imaginations, but by the time the War to Make the World Safe for Democracy had receded two decades into the past, the writers may well have wondered if they were not mining a played-out vein.

O'Leary turned for several issues into a space-action magazine; others cast about for new skies to conquer, and the gathering clouds of the approaching War to End Wars offered silver linings.

The Fiction House pulp line—*Jungle Stories, Fight Stories,* etc.—was far from unique in maintaining a series of comic books at the same time that the pulps were going along vigorously. Fawcett, Dell, and Standard (Pines) Publications all did the same, as did the giant Street & Smith firm with its hugely successful Shadow and other characters. But Fiction House maintained the closest correspondence between its parallel pulp and comic series, at times running not merely the same characters but even the same covers on *Planet Stories* and *Planet Comics,* and *Rangers* (of Freedom) magazine and *Rangers* (of Freedom) comics.

Fiction House also published a *Wings* magazine devoted to aerial adventures of World War II, and matched it with *Wings Comics,* to which I shall return shortly.

For the "air-mindedness" that swept the nation—and the comic books—was not limited to what we usually think of as aviation strips. It seemed that *everybody* was flying in the comics, and not just the outright superheroes either—Spy Smasher had his marvelous Gyro-sub, Batman the Batplane, Wonder Woman her odd transparent robot plane; while Hawkman flew with the aid of artificial wings and nth-metal belt, Bulletman with the assistance of his gravity helmet, Starman with that of his Star-rod, Ibis courtesy of his magical Ibistick, and so on.

But the three great aviation comics that flourished during the war (and for some years after) were Fiction House's *Wings Comics,* Hillman Publications' *Air Fighters* (later *Airboy) Comics,* and Quality Comics' *Military* (later *Modern) Comics,* whose bellwether feature, *Blackhawk,* survived in the comic books until (relatively speaking) just yesterday.

These were the great three, and of them the first, if not the greatest, was *Wings Comics.*

The publication began a year and a half before the United States entered World War II; its first issue was dated September, 1940, suggesting that the outbreak of war in Europe the previous September provided the inspiration for *Wings.* The Luftwaffe's deadly gull-winged Junkers 87 Stuka dive-bomber did a lot to make the world aware of the role aviation would play in the new war, and the waters of the English Channel already reflected the images of the Heinkel and Dornier bombers that, along with their fighter escorts, would face defending Spitfires and Hurricanes in the impending Battle of Britain.

With the United States strictly speaking at peace and theoretically neutral regarding the war, there was a small problem in getting *American* heroes into those flaming skies, but the staff of publisher T. T. Scott (and the Iger-Eisner studio, to which much of Fiction House's creative work was farmed out) found inspiration in several real-world practices of the period. There were Americans who had traveled to Canada, there to apply at British recruiting offices with the end result personified in the "Yankee Flier in the RAF" phenomenon. Simultaneously, General Claire Chennault was leading the famous Flying Tigers, the American Volunteer Group of fliers who piloted Curtiss P-40 Warhawks against the Japanese invaders of China.

All of this information, I confess, is largely the product of latter-day research on my part. I didn't really get into *Wings Comics* until after the United States entered the war, and then I did so largely through the hand-me-down enthusiasm of my older brother.

But the jingoism and uncritical pro-war and pro-aviation attitudes of the time are clearly visible in surviving copies of the old comics that my brother handed down to me in later years.

Once the United States got into the war there was undisguised gloating on the part of publishers of war-flavored comics and pulps. Let me quote here an editorial from the oldest copy of *Wings* I've been able to dredge up, the September, 1942, edition:

Wings Salutes You!

Wings celebrates its second birthday . . . its second year of success.

For this we want to thank our vast audience . . . thank you particularly for your enthusiasm and your loyal support of *Wings* in its reckless infancy before the U.S. entered the war.

In those days loudmouths insisted that Hitler, Mussolini and the Japs were nice guys . . . merely misunderstood. We could get along with the Axis, do business with it, they were fond of claiming . . . on Axis terms of course!

They called *Wings* "warmonger" and "alarmist" because, long before Pearl Harbor, it chose to dramatize and glorify the Yank aces . . . those dauntless, unconquerable chips off the old block who had rushed to join the R.A.F. in high battle, or who volunteered with Canadian war-birds, or with Chiang Kai-shek's lean squadrons.

To those who stuck by *Wings* through thick and thin we offer our heart-felt thanks.

Once again *Wings* reminds the world that Yank love of adventure and freedom and Yank hatred of tyranny and brute aggression will live as long as there is an America. These qualities are part and parcel of America. This gallant spirit is what made our country great, and will make it greater.

Carping critics or not, *Wings Comics* will continue to glorify the freedom-loving, devil-may-care Yank spirit that sparks America's swift-growing air fleets across five oceans and as many continents.

Keep 'em flying!
The Editor

Skull Squad, (the lead feature in that 20 year old issue of *Wings Comics,* was about a kind of hero team of the same name, a trio of RAF fliers assembled before U.S. entry into the war: Jimmy Jones, American; Sandy MacGregor, Scotsman; and Kent Douglas, Englishman. Its structure was simple, and typical of the *Wings Comics* approach to air-war fiction.

There was little characterization, almost no motivation (hell, there was a *war* going on, it was just us against them, that's all!), very little background, and hardly even a plot. Just action! Kent arranges with a commando-forces captain to raid German shore batteries in France preparatory to a commando raid. (The purpose of the raid is to free commandos captured on an earlier raid.)

Shortly after, red-haired Sandy MacGregor gives the American Jimmy the good news about the impending action (all of these guys are just aching for a fight, there's nothing they love more than fighting, there's nothing they dig more than killing, but it's all right because they're good guys killing bad guys), and the only one let down is Lisbeth, the pretty canteen girl, who wants to come along but is told she has to stay in England.

Following this the Skull Squad take off in their blood-red attack bomber. (I think it's a Douglas A-20 Boston, but the details are not too clear in *Wings.)* They spot the commando boat in the Channel, about to be sunk by a German patrol boat, so the Skull Squad sink the Nazi boat with bombs—only to be signaled by the commandos to land on the French beach!

The Skull Squad do so, and the commandos come ashore with a stowaway "spy." "We don't know how he got on!" the commando leader says, "But he insists he knows you chaps! Here he is! Recognize him?"

"By Jove! It's Lisbeth!" Kent exclaims, only to be hushed by one of the other Skull Squadders ("Shh! Don't tell the captain!"); of course they take Lisbeth along with them; soon they get involved in a battle with a flight of Messerschmitts above the very area where the commandos are carrying out their successful raid on the prison in which their comrades are held.

Kent, Jimmy, and Sandy, with Lisbeth in tow, outfly and outshoot the Messerschmitts until finally one of the German planes collides with the Douglas. Kent and Sandy parachute safely; Jimmy gives his chute to Lisbeth, crawls onto the Messerschmitt, takes the chute from its dead pilot, and jumps. They all land safely, join the commandos, who have now freed their comrades, and everyone sails happily home to England.

Suicide Smith is the second feature in the book (he carried the sobriquet "Blitzkrieg Buster" at this point in his career) and is both better written and better drawn than *Skull Squad.* We meet Suicide just climbing out of his trim monoplane (we see only part of the plane—it might be either an AT-6 Texan trainer converted for personal transportation or a Douglas Dauntless torpedo-bomber similarly adapted) to report to Major Olsen, who quickly involves him in a spy plot centered around Frisco Flo, a gorgeous redhead.

As the airplanes that were featured on the excellently drawn covers of *Wings* and in the stories provided considerable appeal for us air-minded American lads in the forties, the likes of Frisco Flo and Lisbeth the canteen girl presumably appealed to our older brothers. Flo is a breath-taking siren. Her auburn-rich red hair flows to her shoulders in sensuous-looking waves; she wears a floor-length yellow dress cut all the way to the sternum at the top and slashed well up to the thigh at the bottom. The artist (anonymous, but with the style of the Eisner school—perhaps Lou Fine) lovingly shades every line and curve of Flo's generous bosom and graceful hips. She stands usually with one hand on her hip and her dress clings so that even her navel is clearly delineated!

Caught in a nest of Japanese agents, Flo talks her way out of hot water by claiming to have been their prisoner; she slugs a sergeant and puts on his flying suit, then steals his plane (it's a Douglas TBD Devastator), picks up Suicide Smith as passenger, gets entangled with a trio of Japanese fighters off the coast of Mexico, gets shot down, shares a parachute jump with Smith into the Pacific, gets picked up by a Japanese patrol boat and taken to a small island where she sells Smith to the Japanese for 1,000 yen. While the Nips show Smith their giant dirigible (that will "soar above stratosphere, dropping hundreds of bombs") we're treated to some lingerie-art shots of Flo putting on a different yellow dress.

Enter now a Nazi liaison officer, Count Von Muck. Puffing cigar smoke from one corner of his mouth, the fat, monocled Von Muck growls: "Fraulein Flo, you work for low stakes. To get Smith aboard mein U-boat, I vould pay ten time dot sum."

Flo's response is a single word, "So!" She promptly feeds the Japanese guard captain drugged sake (we get some neat garter-art as she sits on his desk), stabs the Japanese turnkey, and takes Smith at gun-point to Von Muck's submarine. Von Muck repays Flo's treachery with treachery of his own: "Aha! Thank you, Fraulein Flo! I vill take Schmidt back to Bremen. Our gestapo vill make him reveal his anti-blitz tactics, but I haf no marks for you. Der Japs vill pay you for your treason."

"Why you double crossing pig!" Flo replies. Can't blame her for being peeved, I guess, but all these nasties are just waiting for a chance to sell each other out.

At this point the Japanese super-dirigible just happens to be passing overhead. Coincidence played a huge part in these stories, as you may already have begun to notice. Smith grabs a trailing rope and climbs from the submarine to the dirigible, taking Frisco Flo with him. They get into a fight with the Japanese crew, killing several, but "Suicide finally goes down before superior numbers." (Our heroes were *never* defeated in fair and equal combat—they were sometimes felled by treacherous blows from behind,

drugged, hypnotized, etc., etc., and fairly often put down by superior numbers, but *never* whupped fair'n'square, never-never-
never.)

Suicide is lashed to a bomb but Flo plays her trump card when
the Japs threaten her with similar treatment. "Under orders from
Vice Admiral Tojura I discovered the secret West Coast arsenal
and tattooed its location in special code. You cannot read
it . . . and if you kill me it will be destroyed!"

Now where is this tattoo? On her thigh, of course, providing the
artist an excuse for three more luscious garter shots.

Stalemate—until, "several miles off the Golden Gate" the Japanese prepare to launch a small airplane to "direct our aim by radio!" Flo flips a guard with a jiu-jitsu trick, grabs his gun, frees
Smith, seizes the patrol plane, and the two of them take off!
"Wriggle into one of the chutes, Flo," rasps the blond and stern-
faced Smith in heroic low-angle close-up. "I'm going to ram that
flying sausage!" Smith and Flo do the twin-chute thing again, the
plane and the dirigible go down in flames, and we fade out on a
scene back in Major Olsen's office with Olsen, Smith, the slugged
sergeant, and Flo all making accusations of one another. Flo has
her hand on her hip as usual, and I have a feeling that she talked
her way out of it again. But I expect I'll never know for sure.

Actually it was a helluva good action story (credited to Capt. A.
E. Carruthers, who almost certainly never existed), very nicely
drawn, with plenty of good shots of aircraft (if that was your thing;
in 1942 it was mine), nicely delineated human figures (those of
Smith, Count Von Muck, and even the bit-players and sword-
carriers as well as the cheesecakey Frisco Flo), and all of those
fights, captures, escapes, chases, and confrontations packed into
just eight pages.

As a work of fiction, I think it would have been a whole lot better if "Captain Carruthers" had stretched out, devoted some space
to characterization, and saved up his action for climax situations in
the story, instead of running at full-speed from start to finish. But
as a pure action yarn, this Suicide Smith adventure can't be fault-
ed; *Wings* wasn't the kind of comic you'd curl up with on a rainy
afternoon, I guess, but it *was* one that you could fold in half and
shove in your pocket, and read for five minutes when you got a
break. As such it was the kind of comic that a soldier might read—
not a combat trooper, who lived daily with the violence and death
that filled *Wings,* but a basic trainee or a desk-bound rear echelon
type could really get off on *Wings.*

There were several other features in the comic that deserve attention, especially since the lineup of features didn't change a whole lot in the magazine's long career. (It lasted for 124 issues, all the way from 1940 to 1954, and the changes that it underwent in those latter years we'll get to in a little while, too.)

But back in 1942, *Suicide Smith* was followed by a flat-out combat feature called "Suicide Squeeze" by "Capt. Derek West"; there wasn't really much of interest in the story, which just dealt with a series of dogfights between Navy Wildcats and Japanese Zeros, ending with the destruction of a Japanese super-bomber. What is interesting is the format—a series of balloonless drawings with all dialog and narration set in separate, accompanying panels. To the eye accustomed to the usual comic-book format, the drawings look strangely stylized and formal, clean and graceful but somehow remote. Speech balloons seem to lure us right into the panel, while the separated narration draws the eye *away* from the picture.

That, for what it's worth, and with due respect to Prince Valiant, Flash Gordon, and their respective creators, is my view.

The closest thing to a title-feature in *Wings Comics* was, of course, the story about Captain Wings himself, who originated in *Wings'* sixteenth issue. (In smaller type he shared his billing with the "Hell-Diver Squadron.") Again the art was anonymous but admirable, with the viewpoint cutting between ground and air, between "camera-angles," and between long, medium, and close-up shots in fine cinematic style.

For once there was an attempt to characterize and motivate the leading player of a series—most of the *Wings* crew were just good guys fighting bad guys, but not so Captain Wings. His real name was Boggs, and he was a sort of desk-bound CO of a fighter squadron stationed in Australia. Day by day he would send his men off to fight the Japanese, and day by day they would return with word of casualties, ever more resentful of their "ground officer" who sat safely at base while they flew to their deaths one by one.

Boggs sends his men back into the sky again and again, until they are near open rebellion. "Link," Boggs says, "You're squadron leader. Keep in touch with me! I'll relay orders!"

As Link climbs into his Curtiss SB2C he bitterly retorts: "That's it! You'll sit here and order men to their death! I've heard that you once flew in the R.A.F. and were called Captain Wings! Bet you started the rumors yourself!"

A few hours later, a ground-based radio operator turns to the nattily uniformed Boggs and quotes a message just coming over his earphones: "Hell-Diver Squadron reporting . . . Jap beachhead established . . . three Hell-Divers been knocked down . . . Is Captain Boggs cleaning his finger nails? Call you later . . . Link!"

Too much for Boggs! "Poor devils!" he exclaims, "I'm going!" He climbs into flying gear and climbs aboard the only plane left— a Curtiss JN-4 Jenny, a World War I trainer! He flies to the beach where his men are offering air-support to defenders against a Japanese landing column, finds a flight of Japanese Naka 97 fighters, and heads straight at its leader.

"The American flying that strange craft seems determined to crash me! I had best yield!" says the Japanese commander. (He must have been educated in the United States to speak English so well—most likely he attended Yale and/or Berkeley.)

As the Japanese pulls away, Captain Wings, in close-up, remarks: "That yellow devil's nerve cracked! Now the formation is broken, we'll have more of a chance!"

But, forced to fight such a rickety old plane, Wings blacks out in a power-dive, crashes at an enemy base, and after a fist fight with a German pilot (obviously on exchange duty with the Japanese air arm) is knocked unconscious. Well, he was still groggy from that blackout or he couldn't have been beaten by a single Nazi.

Wings is carried into a Japanese aid station, where Jerry Austin, an American nurse, has been forced to work. A fiendish Japanese doctor injects a hypnotic drug in him (this sequence is interspersed with numerous leg-art shots of Nurse Austin), and Wings is sent up with a flight of Japanese planes to attack the American base!

Jerry stabs a Japanese doctor with a stolen scalpel (we saw her conceal it in the top of her stocking) and rides with Wings, whom she clouts with a fire extinguisher in the cabin of "his" Jap plane.

Stay with me, now, this story has plenty of plot—Jerry parachutes to safety, Wings recovers his will at the same time that he recovers consciousness from the blow with the fire extinguisher; he turns on the Japanese and shoots one down just as they encounter the Hell-Diver Squadron. Jerry Austin finds her way safely to the Hell-Divers' base, the Americans win the air battle and defeat the Japanese invasion, and Wings, now back in his accustomed role of Captain Boggs, sneaks back to duty!

Then there was *Calhoun of the Air Cadets,* but he wasn't very interesting, and the feature was quickly discontinued.

Not so the long-running comedy relief feature of *Wings Comics, Greasemonkey Griffin* by "Kip Beales" (who may even have been a real person for all I know).

"G.G.," as he was known, ran along for years and years in *Wings,* despite getting the worst reader response of any feature in the magazine. The Fiction House comics took a leaf from the pages of their companion pulp magazines and ran letter pages, a nearly universal practice in the comics of the 1960s and 1970s, but a rare thing in the so-called Golden Age. In *Wings Comics* the letters page was called, naturally enough, *"Wings'* Air Mail," and readers were encouraged to send their comments on the stories and art to the editors.

The page was divided into two sections, one featuring "long" letters of as much as two paragraphs, the other with capsule remarks a line or two in length. This format hardly permitted the development of lengthy discussions like those in "The Vizigraph," the letter column of *Wings'* Fiction House companion, *Planet Comics.*

But it did allow for comments from as many as 40 or 50 readers each month—and there's nothing to keep a reader coming back for more like finding *his* letter and *his* by-line on the letters page! A common practice among "Air Mail" correspondents was giving a breakdown of the value of the magazine—I never saw this in any comic published by anyone other than the Fiction House group. Here's the way one Earl Nietsttew (hmm—backwards that is Wettstein, a more likely name) of Minneapolis rated *Wings* in the August, 1945, issue:

4 cents for Captain Wings. Best drawings and stories.
3 cents for Jane Martin.
1 cent for Clipper Kirk.
1 cent for Suicide Smith.
Half cent for Air Mail.
Quarter cent for Skull Squad.
One-eighth cent for Greasemonkey. Kick him out.
One-sixteenth cent for the story.
One-sixteenth cent for Wing Tips.
Total 10 cents for one of the best comics on the market.

Earl Nietsttew's opinion of Greasemonkey Griffin was not out of line with those of the majority of the "Air Mail" correspondents. G.G. was exactly what his name suggests—a ground-borne mechanic of the lowest grade, assigned to an air base somewhere in Great Britain. Typically, his adventures involved his getting caught up in the middle of spy-plots or other intrigue, getting carried away in high-powered warplanes and/or experimental craft, and blundering through to triumph only to close out with a final pratfall.

The artwork was superior to the writing in the yarns, but somehow, to me, there was very little empathy with Griffin himself. I did not feel that Greasemonkey Griffin was a *person*— he was just a figure going through plot situations. And in varying degrees this was true of all the folks in *Wings*—they weren't made of flesh, they were just shapes performing acts and, while I could sometimes get behind their adventures on a pure thrills-'n'-excitement level, and while I certainly dug those pictures of airplanes (if I'd been older I might instead have dug the pictures of ladies), they were no substitute, even to an eight-year-old reader, for the feeling of real *companionship* offered by some of the more character-oriented comics.

Well, I suppose that's true to this day, and it applies to novels and motion pictures as much as to comics.

There were a couple of other features in *Wings* that deserve mention. The "story" that reader Nietsttew thought worth one-sixteenth of a penny was of course the standard text short story that comics carried to meet postal regulations. I never read a single one in *Wings,* and seldom any at all; the only ones I found consistently worthwhile were the *Jon Jarl* series by Otto Binder, which ran in *Captain Marvel Adventures;* fully 99 percent of the text stories in comics were throwaways, printed only because the mailing-permit regulations called for text material. They weren't written to be read, they were written to satisfy the postal reg's, and that is what they did, and that is all that they usually did.

Wings ran a few nonfiction features—a series of illustrated biographies of military aviation heroes (Lieutenant Edward H. O'Hare, Wing Commander Douglas Bader, Lieutenant Commander "Butch" O'Hare—and, yep, he was the same Edward H. O'Hare; they really dug him at *Wings*—Sergeant "Shorty" Gordon, Lieutenant Harold "Swede" Larson, Major Marion Carl, Lieutenant Colonel Francis Gabreski, Sergeant Meyer Levin, and so on) was one such feature.

Another was "Wing Tips," a page of tips on flying and aircraft maintenance. I've never been able to figure out for sure whether the people who put out these features—and similar ones ran in a number of aviation-oriented comics—really believed that aviation cadets and actual Air Corps personnel were reading them and learning anything useful, or whether it was all a shuck to make kids think they were reading stuff aimed at real aviators. I've never been able to figure that out, and if you have, I think I'd prefer you not to tell me. Let us preserve at least a *few* bright illusions.

There was a captive fan club run through *Wings Comics,* similar to the Supermen of America, Junior Justice Society, Captain America's Sentinels of Liberty, Captain Marvel Club, and others. This one was called Wings of America, and when you joined you got a neat metallic membership pin to wear on your shirt, but wartime materials problems stopped that. The announcement was terse:

Special Notice: Due to the metal shortage, *Wings Comics* is no longer able to obtain membership pins for *Wings of America.* Club emblems will not be available to our readers until after the war. We suggest that all our readers buy War Savings Stamps every month to speed Victory.

Ironically enough, that announcement appeared in *Wings Comics* for August, 1945—the month the war ended! Still, I have been unable to find any evidence that Wings of America was revived after the war. Too much trouble for too little return, I suppose—or maybe it was just that the sense of involvement was going out of the business.

There were a couple more continuing story features; I should mention *Clipper Kirk* (by "Cliff DuBois") but it was so much like all the others that I hardly know what to say except "more of the same." In this precious 1942 edition of *Wings,* the *Clipper* strip opens with a symbolic splash panel—a Grumman Wildcat fighter decked out in British markings dives at a Messerschmitt 109; the Grumman's machine guns are blazing away, the Messerschmitt is on fire and its pilot is apparently trying to climb out and parachute before he is killed. Ominous black clouds back up the scene, while a red-robed skeleton reaches one sinister, bony hand for Death's due.

The story itself opens with Clipper Kirk sitting in a café in Port Said getting his orders from his CO. (That's a nice way to get your orders, I suppose—when I was in the Army we did things somewhat differently.) A few minutes later Kirk joins his girl friend Tonia at another table. Kirk himself is a typical sandy-haired,

square-jawed, *Wings Comics* hero. Tonia—could you have
guessed this?—is super-shapely, with long, wavy dark hair and a
yellow dress that shows her amazing pectoral development at one
end while it reveals her lovely legs nearly to the thighs.

"Clipper," Tonia says, "I'm worried. That waiter at your table . . . he was eavesdropping."

"You mean Henri!" Kirk replies. "Nonsense, Tonia, he was only waiting for our order."

Of course Tonia was right, as anyone with half an eye could
have told. Henri is swarthy, frowning—no, *scowling* is a better
description—and watching Kirk and his CO out of the corner of
his eyes while walking in the other direction. A dead giveaway for
a spy, if he doesn't trip and half-kill himself with that stunt.

Yes, Tonia is right, Kirk gets ambushed and shot down, is
bombed by his attacker, and barely escapes with his life. How's he
going to get out of this? Well, dig it—

He just strips to his underwear ("I'd best get rid of these R.A.F.
duds!"), flags down another German plane that just happens to fly
overhead after dark, and passes himself off as a German. ("Heil
Hitler, comrade!" Kirk says, "A dog of the R.A.F. shot me down
and left me for dead." The reply: "Heil Hitler . . . come aboard!")

The Nazi aviator flies Kirk to the secret German base and as
they stand around drinking beer, who drives up but Henri the
treacherous waiter with Tonia as his prisoner! "You see, Clipper,"
explains the luscious Tonia, "the waiter noticed that you were talking to me after I returned to Port Said that day."

Clear enough.

Okay, Kirk and Tonia overcome Henri and a Nazi sentinel;
Kirk sends Tonia home with the waiter and sentinel as prisoners,
and "At dawn Kirk is among the Luftwaffe airmen seated in a Stuka, ready for the flight." In midair Clipper shows his true colors by
shooting down three Stukas, tricks two more into colliding with
each other, flies back to the Nazi base and bombs it, then abandons
his plane in the desert when it runs out of fuel.

Just at this point, who drives up on her way back to Port Said
but—Tonia! Lovely, just lovely. Did I mention that coincidence
often played a role in these stories?

The whole thing was really great fun if you could take it on the
right level.

As the years went by the features in *Wings* evolved in several
ways. Captain Wings, for instance, pretty well dropped his identity
as Captain Boggs the ground officer and became just another hero-

aviator. That is, what little interesting characterization there was to him faded away. Instead of flying whatever aerial flivver he could lay hands on while his men were using the modern aircraft assigned to the unit, he got himself a sleek North American P-51 Mustang with a custom paint-job—stark black-and-white, with stylized bird-wings painted on its wings, and eyes and mouth painted on its nose. The latter device was of course borrowed from the practice of Chennault's Flying Tigers, although their standard aircraft was the Curtiss P-40 rather than the Mustang.

At various times in his career Wings moved around the world, fading to a kind of background narrator rather than central character (at this point his adventures were drawn by Lee Elias in a style much reminiscent of that of Milton Caniff), but he stepped back onto center stage to engage in a series of old-style air adventures at the time of the Korean war.

The quality of the writing and drawing varied, of course. In one of the finest *Captain Wings* stories of the "narrator" period we find Captain Wings reading the diary of a dead Flying Tiger pilot. The diary tells how the pilot sold his services to a Chinese warlord only to discover that the warlord is collaborating with the Japanese.

The flier is making plenty of money, but he faces a crisis of conscience (Captain Wings and his sidekick Lieutenant Griper turn up in the story at this point, in secondary roles) and finally crashes his plane, deliberately, to avoid killing Wings and Griper.

Whereupon his *ghost* is summoned by the ghosts of an American buddy and a Chinese girl—the warlord's daughter—and shown scenes of Japanese aggression and atrocities, a Japanese soldier shooting a Caucasian priest and raping an American girl, and so on. "That might be your Martha, Tom—if we don't win," the second ghost says. "He lies. Don't forget that farm. It's yours for the asking. Come, come, we must hurry!" urges the ghost of Loto, the warlord's daughter.

Tom makes his decision: "Get out of my way, Loto. You're right, Jake, there are things more precious than money. Things money could never buy!"

He somehow makes it back into his own body and is revived by Wings and Griper. "Sure, I'll be all right . . ." Tom says. "I've got work to do—got to join you Army guys! I've got to fly again—fly for both Jake and Martha and the kids!" And we fade out on Tom receiving the Medal of Honor, having downed an even dozen Japanese aircraft.

Then there was Jane Martin, at first a flight nurse, then after the war a saleswoman for an airplane company, and later still an airborne reporter. Her adventures weren't substantially different from those of the male heroes, except for the even greater opportunities offered the artists to include cheesecake shots, which they did with alacrity.

Jane got tangled up with the expected array of bright-yellow, fiendish Japanese, gross and brutal Nazis, and (after the war) gangsters and thugs. In her latter years she did some cold-warrioring as well, smuggling anti-Communist refugees out of Eastern Europe and the like.

Wings only ran one costumed adventure hero in its decade and a half of life; he was the Phantom Falcon but, except possibly for the idea of the costume itself attracting readers, I can't think of why he was included. He had no particular superpowers *à la* Superman, nor any of the Batcave-Batmobile-etc. gimmickry of Batman. He was just a standard *Wings Comics* aviator-adventurer, only he wore this tight costume with a hood and a cape . . .

I think the Phantom Falcon was Clipper Kirk in disguise. Or maybe he was really a fellow named Chet Home. It doesn't matter much.

What does matter is the one other major feature of *Wings Comics,* which I've been saving for last: *Ghost Squadron!*

It may be just my personal bias in favor of the fantastic at work, but I must state that of all the features in *Wings,* the one I enjoyed the most was neither the fast-paced adventuring of Captain Wings or Suicide Smith, nor the leggy, spunky Jane Martin, nor the perpetual comedy-of-errors of Greasemonkey Griffin, but the *Ghost Squadron.*

The Squadron had a run of a good many years; I don't know the exact issue number in which it first appeared, or that in which it last appeared either, but it was not in the earliest or the last issues of *Wings.* It was by-lined by our old friend "Capt. Derek West" and among the artists who worked on the feature was Maurice Whitman, who was not technically on a par with such *Wings* artists as Bob Lubbers, George Evans, Lee Elias, and Bob Powell, but managed to instill a spirit of brooding menace into his stories that more than overcame his inadequacies of detail. His characters might be anatomically imperfect, but they had identifiable natures that brought them closer to the vividness required in proper fiction than most of the *Wings* crew ever had.

I think the peak period for the Ghost Squadron was the late 1940s and, in the moldering copies of *Wings* I've managed to dredge up, three tales in particular of the Ghost Squadron stand out. Perhaps not coincidentally they all were published within a relatively short span of time—December, 1947, April and June, '48. Captain West didn't give his individual stories titles, it was just *Ghost Squadron* issue after issue, but I have given these three stories titles just for my own satisfaction. I call them "The Society of the Flying Skulls," "The Adventure of the Polish Bride," and "The Room of a Million Windows."

"The Society of the Flying Skulls" opened with an English flying cadet—well, perhaps Irish—named Charlie Kelly being invited to join a sort of air-cadets' fraternity of just that name. He is told to report for his initiation at midnight, where he will be required to pass a flying exam in an ancient biplane. Of course he's a new cadet and doesn't know how to fly, but everyone knows that it's all a put-up job, the trainer is rigged to remain stationary.

Before going for his initiation Charlie takes his girl Gwen Morrison to a dance, where he proposes to her. She accepts and they plan to be married as soon as the war is over. (Well, the story was published in 1947; World War II went on and on and on in the comics.)

But Charlie's rival Joe, who had been after Gwen's prospective fortune, un-rigs the trainer; Charlie steps into it at midnight, it taxis down the field, rises into the air, dips into a dive—and Charlie is killed!

Flash forward a year. Gwen has recovered from her grief, Joe has now proposed and been accepted, and there's no waiting for him. We see a fancy full-dress wedding with Charlie's ghost (ghosts look greenish and shadowy in *Wings Comics)* hovering around, trying to warn Gwen against Joe. He fails, though; Joe and Gwen are married and Gwen's dad gives them a wedding present of 50,000 pounds—nearly a quarter million dollars in those days!

Joe goes on to combat duty—Spitfires versus Focke-Wulf 190s—and when a buddy needs help, Joe refuses to give it.

"He's ridin' me hard. For the love of heaven, help me, Joe!" crackles the radio.

But Joe thinks: "Not me—I'm goin' to play deaf. Why should I risk my neck for Larry. Maybe I am yellow but I'm goin' to live!"

Back on the ground Joe weeps crocodile tears over his dead pal, making the excuse that his radio was out of order so he never heard the cry for help. But a ground mechanic checks out Joe's radio and finds it in perfect order. "How would you like to read the headlines, 'Millionaire's son-in-law court martialed for cowardice?' And you will read 'em, Joe, unless you make me a little present—of ten thousand pounds," the mechanic threatens.

Joe heads for Morrison Castle to get the money. His father-in-law had converted the place into a convalescent hospital for wounded servicemen, and Gwen is working there as a nurse. Joe finds old Mr. Morrison leaning over a balcony late at night and shoves him off. The old man dies, a coroner rules the death accidental, Gwen inherits a fortune, and Joe pays off his blackmailer.

But—several weeks later, Joe again visits the castle. The little daughter of a hospitalized soldier shows Joe her toy flying model. "Why—it's the same model as that old training ship Charlie died in," Joe thinks.

The toy airplane gets caught in a tree; Joe tells the little girl he'll get it for her and climbs a ladder—and the moment he takes the toy in his hand he's fascinated. "An old PT-13. And it has the same number twelve."

Charlie's ghost hovers. "That's right Joe. It's just like the murder plane."

"Why—that doll pilot—it looks like me!"

"It is you, Joe. *That pilot is you!*"

"I am on a ladder," Joe frantically tells himself. "I'm getting the plane for a little girl. *No! I am in the plane!*"

Now little Julia calls, "Captain, are you sick?"

But Joe is lost: "The plane's taking off. It's taxiing down the runway!"

And now Joe seems to be sitting in the trainer, with Charlie's ghost behind him, and the controls won't work, and "I've gone into a spin! I'm going to crash!"

And Julia calls "Please come, somebody. The captain's going to fall!"

And we see the plane crash with Joe in it—while we also see him falling to the ground, landing on his head, breaking his neck.

And while Charlie's ghost summons that of Joe, saying "You're dead, Joe . . . and I've had my revenge," a passing soldier looks at the corpse and says "What a horrible death for a hero!"

All I can say is, *Phew!* That's heavy stuff for a shoot-'em-up and leg-art book!

Four issues later, while Captain Wings fought the mysterious Mr. Atlantis for the world's mineral resources and Suicide Smith met the Jivaro tribesmen of Vengeance Valley accompanied by some super John Celardo cheesecake, Captain West came back with "The Adventure of the Polish Bride."

This one came to him in the form of a letter from one of its leading actors, Lt. John Howland, whose sweetheart Hulda was being treated in West Germany for amnesia. Howland thinks the treatment is too rough on Hulda—every time she gets back a flash of memory she bursts into terrified screams.

He breaks in and removes Hulda at gunpoint, steals a Bell P-63 King Cobra fighter plane, and heads with Hulda for her home town in Poland. (At least the war was over in this story.) A ghostly voice comes over Howland's radio, and a ghost monoplane appears, both offering to guide Howland to Hulda's home town. They land and see a ghostly vision of Polish cavalry, then in an old and half-wrecked church they come upon—Hulda's mother! An ancient crone, looking a bit like the actress Maria Ouspenskaya, whom you may remember from the *Wolfman* films.

"I know you," says Mama. "I knew you would come back for the wedding. I have waited a long time for you."

Hulda falls to her knees and begs, "Tell me what happened, Mama. I can't remember anything. Please tell me, Mama!"

But Mama only says, "Don't touch me! Do you understand? Don't touch me!"

What's this? Hardly standard comic-book fare.

Howland addresses mama: "Listen—Hulda's been sick—she's got to know who she is—so speak up and tell her what you know!"

Mama points to a stained-glass window, where Howland looks and sees a scene from the past. He sees a Polish cavalry encampment in 1939, sees Hulda and a handsome Polish officer, Leopold, who was her fiancé.

Now Hulda, too, sees the vision of the past. She sees herself climbing a tower the night before her wedding. She sees herself sending military information to the German agent Kurt in return for jewels to wear at her wedding. "Such a little work for such a grand present," the ghostly Hulda whispers as she sends off a carrier pigeon to Kurt.

But in the morning there is no wedding. With Hulda and John Howland we see the German forces smashing into Poland, Leopold leading a futile, courageous cavalry charge against Panzer armor. We see Leopold crushed beneath Nazi tank-treads.

And now, back in the present we hear Hulda scream: "Forgive me, Leopold! I didn't understand they would butcher my people!" Hulda plunges from the church window and dies on the ground.

Her mother, in proper Ouspenskaya fashion, comments, "It is better so, for now she can make her peace with those she betrayed."

Heavy, heavy stuff for comics.

And then there was the story of "The Room of a Million Windows," one of the rare successful multilevel fantasies ever created. If you're wondering what I mean by a multilevel fantasy, you'll see in a minute.

The scene is set in a ghostly looking but luxurious drawing room where beautifully gowned figures of women and impeccable gentlemen in evening dress are gathered around a chess board. The players are two lovely women. One is blonde, and wears a peach-colored gown that demonstrates her attractions in standard *Wings Comics* fashion. Her opponent has black hair, wears harlequin eyeglasses, a low-cut red gown, and long, sophisticated red gloves; in one hand she holds a foot-long cigarette-holder.

Outside a window, amazingly, can be seen an American Navy plane and a Japanese fighter of World War II vintage engaged in a deadly dogfight. (Ah, World War II was back on, we see.)

A narration panel reads: "Nobody knows the whereabouts of the *room of a million windows* . . . and there is no name for *the sisters* who wage their endless duel there . . . nor can you tell when your number will flash across that mystic screen of fate, and a finger will point, and a voice speak . . ."

Yes, as the two strange sisters pursue their game of chess, we realize that they are controlling destiny, that the participants in the aerial battle correspond to the pieces on the board, that the moves in the chess game are reflected in the war outside!

The dark sister takes the lead in the game. The American plane is shot down, its two-man crew find themselves in a Pacific jungle. One man is courageous, he wants to hide in the jungle, continue the war. His companion is weak, cowardly; when Japanese searchers invite their surrender over a loudspeaker he wants to give up. The Japanese now set out through the jungle after the Americans.

And in that celestial gaming room, the sisters discuss their game:

"See, sister, it is all over. You have no chance. Shall we start another game?"

"No! I don't concede. I still have another move on the board. There—that's it!"

Back in the jungle the two Americans quarrel. A Japanese scout overhears them, throws a grenade. Broken bodies are hauled away.

In the room of a million windows: "The game is over, sister. Your move was feeble. Now I have you checkmated."

"Not yet. You overlooked this piece. There's still a chance."

Back on earth, a Japanese surgeon speaks to a military man.

"That one is dead, honorable captain. But there is a chance this one might live."

And now we see the ghosts of the two Americans. The courageous one is eager to get back into his body and back into the war. The coward is a coward still: "It isn't fair," he complains, "I wanted to surrender."

The doctor works furiously, but there is a bright flash in the room as the electricity short-circuits, and in the celestial setting we hear the light sister complain to the dark: "You cheated! You upset a piece! And just as I was recovering, too!"

"Why, sister," her opponent answers, "everything is fair in this game. It's your move."

"But—but you've put the coward's spirit in my strong one's body. You've weakened my strategy. Still, I'll play on."

And on earth the ghost of the brave flier watches dismayed as his body recovers with the weakling's spirit in it! The Japanese get the coward to sell out, to broadcast for them, and finally to lead a flight of Mitsubishi 00s against an American carrier.

Tension builds amazingly as Captain West cuts between the pending battle on earth and the chess game in the room of a million windows, until the light sister (playing white) moves a piece.

"So, you finally moved, eh, sister?" gloats her foe, moving her own, red piece. "It was very stupid indeed. I have you nicely cornered now."

"Ah, sister," replies white, "you fell into my trap! Watch this."

"You . . . you've broken my defense . . . stolen the weak piece and put the strong in its place!"

And outside we see a Zero being hit by something bright. "The lightning ball—my chance to regain my body!" exclaims the brave flier's ghost. "And I did it . . . I'm back in my own body again. Now I'll show those Nips something!"

And so, to the successful conclusion of the battle, while above the light sister gloats, "It's over, sister. I've won again!"

Wow!

Wings Comics struggled on until 1954, its aviators switching from old prop-driven craft to jets, switching as the times changed from the foes of World War II to criminals and spies, to Communist agents and Korean, Chinese, and Soviet enemies, but somehow the fun had gone out of war. There was no more glamour to it, no more excitement. It had become a dirty, ugly, and depressing business, and even the bright colors, the square-jawed heroes, the leggy and busty heroines of *Wings Comics* couldn't make it fun again.

So *Wings* died, the last of the old-fashioned, pure pulp-type air-war comics, in 1954. The last issue carried a brave slogan: *"All NEW! Jet Aces of Warbird Skies!"* But the genre was played out. Other aviation comics came to other fates—and of course, when I opened this chapter I mentioned *Wings, Military,* and *Air Fighters* as the great three, and then talked only about *Wings,* The others are a different story, and I'll tell it in another chapter.

But *Wings* could just never get over its infatuation with war, and when the American people fell out of love with war, *Wings* had nowhere to go, and so it ended, an idea whose time had come . . . and gone.

THE PROPWASH PATROL FLIES AGAIN

SUCH WAS THE NATION'S disenchantment with war at the time of the Korean conflict that it laid *Wings Comics* by the heels; that's a statement I'll stand by pretty stubbornly if anyone feels like debating, but I will concede willingly that there were other factors involved. After all, it wasn't just the war-oriented comics that fell away in the 1950s.

Most of the superheroes disappeared and, while many of them had been involved in World War II and the Korean War, others had concentrated their efforts on combatting criminals, spies, monsters, and other assorted menaces, all of which continued to be available. And the crime comics and horror comics suffered catastrophic cutbacks, chiefly as the result of Dr. Fredric Wertham's pseudoscientific barrages.

Even television, first coming into its own as a major entertainment medium, may well have been a factor in the decline of the comic-book industry, as was the general effect of inflation, which drove the cost of publishing upward at a steady pace. (The final collapse of the 10-cent price barrier on standard-size comics was a blessing in disguise: it permitted the publishers to peg their prices to general economic conditions instead of an arbitrary level established years before by historical accident.)

So much for economics, but why did *Wings* fail aesthetically? The fact is that *Wings Comics* and all the rest of the Fiction House group failed aesthetically because of a gross imbalance in the ingredients of their stories. The category of the story hardly mattered. Fiction House's six major titles over the years were divided into three categories—*Wings, Rangers,* and *Fight Comics* featured war stories, with *Wings* of course further specializing on *air-war* stories; *Jungle* and *Jumbo* concentrated on jungle adventures; *Planet Comics* dealt in science fiction.

And yet all of the magazines utilized the same formula: uninterrupted and generally violent action spiced with ample cheesecake. The backgrounds that provide atmosphere and sense of involvement were minimal—there were nice drawings of airplanes and the other implements of war, jungle beasts, spaceships and bug-eyed monsters—but very little to give the reader a sense of the stories taking place in real locations.

And the characterization of the continuing heroes and hero-ines—characterization, the most important single factor in fiction—was next to nil. Was Captain Wings really anybody? How about Flint Baker or Hunt Bowman or Lyssa of *Planet?* What of Ka'anga or Sheena, Fiction House's entries in the Tarzan derby? Or Rip Carson, Hooks Devlin, Señorita Rio, all leading figures in Fiction House's war books?

Nobodies, blanks, nonentities, Leckishes.

Leckishes?

A little autobiography. When I was a boy we had an imaginary fellow named Leckish, who used to hang around our family. When the telephone rang and my father answered and spoke briefly, and my mother asked who had called, my father would sometimes grunt, "Leckish, it was Leckish."

That meant that it was a wrong number, or a particularly objectionable solicitor, or something of the sort. Junk mail came from Leckish. Door-to-door salesmen were Leckish. Dull and forgettable movies starred Leckish.

Leckish was a *nebbish.*

Almost everybody in the Fiction House comics, and certainly in *Wings Comics,* was Leckish.

But fortunately not all the aviation heroes of those days were Leckishes, not by a long shot. Let's take a look at a few who weren't.

Let's look, first of all, at the Blackhawks.

The Blackhawks (the name applies in plural to a fighting team, in singular to any member of the team but especially to its leader) were the creation of the Quality Comics Group owned by Everett M. Arnold. Quality never attained the massive growth of the huge DC and Fawcett operations, but it was nonetheless one of the real leaders of the industry. The name *Quality* was well chosen; Arnold and his staff assembled a group of characters that included Plastic Man, the Spirit, Dollman, and Kid Eternity, as well as Black-hawk—a lineup that could stand up to any in the field.

Blackhawk first appeared in *Military Comics,* where he was the lead character from the very first issue, August, 1941, through the entire history of that magazine (it changed titles to *Modern Comics* in 1945), which ended in 1950, and beyond in a *Blackhawk* comic for an eventual 235 issues. That last point can take a little clarification: one of the Quality titles was originally titled *Uncle Sam;* as such it lasted only eight issues, but with No. 9 it became *Black-*

hawk. As *Blackhawk* it reached issue No. 107 under the Quality aegis. At that point the Quality group went out of business but *Blackhawk* was taken over by DC and continued to the ripe old age of *243* issues!

What was the secret of *Blackhawk's* success? Why did this feature last so long, and why is *Blackhawk* so well and vividly remembered today when *Captain Wings* is only a vague and dusty recollection?

The answer does not lie in the plotting of the *Blackhawk* stories, which were, admittedly, a bit more complex and subtle than the rough shoot-'em-ups of the *Wings* characters, nor does it lie in the drawing, although as a separate matter the drawing in *Blackhawk* was far superior to the average of the comics industry.

The answer lies in one word: *vividness.*

The characters in *Blackhawk* were individually delineated, about as "subtly" as Doc Savage's assistants Monk, Renny, Long Tom Roberts, Theodore Marley Brooks, and William Harper Littlejohn. Which is to say, they weren't characters so much as one-dimensional *caricatures,* single characteristics stretched to cover whole personalities, but they had their vivid and contrasting characteristics, which the *Wings* crew never did.

And there was a sense of camaraderie and, yes, hominess among the Blackhawks. They flew matching airplanes, followed the same leader, whom they regarded with loyalty and respect approaching worship; they worked together, fought together, and even lived together on Blackhawk Island, a place a little like Wonder Woman's Paradise Island. And this base of operations offered the reader a kind of psychological home-base; if ever you settled back, an invisible third companion to the illustrious pair of Baker Street, relishing the very familiarity of each sound, each implement, each odor in Mrs. Hudson's famous rooming house, you are familiar with the phenomenon.

Well, from Doc Savage to Wonder Woman to Sherlock Holmes, the comparisons are oddly assorted and yet significantly unified in that all who have encountered these varied adventurers bear forever after a recollection of them; the key ingredient lies neither in the construction of plots nor the rendition of the stories, but in the *vividness* of the characters and their headquarters.

What about *Blackhawk,* then?

That first issue of *Military Comics* was a multicharacter but single-theme magazine. That is, the features introduced an assortment of continuing features: *Blackhawk, Death Patrol, Miss Amer-*

ica, The Yankee Eagle—but there was a common theme, action against the wartime enemy. Of course the United States was not yet participating officially, but the Quality folks followed the same approach that the people at Fiction House did—they used stories of foreign aces, and of Americans fighting under foreign flags. Plus, the device of Americans combating foreign operatives who threatened the nation even in "peacetime."

The international makeup of the Blackhawk team is illustrative. The leader, Blackhawk himself, was introduced as a Polish aviator; in later years this version was modified to explain that, no, he was really an American who had volunteered to fly for heroic little Poland in her resistance to the onslaught of 1939.

He never spoke with an accent; his language was always standard English spotted with colorful epigrams and wisecracks that marked almost every comic-book hero.

In that opening story, an outnumbered and outgunned squadron of Polish resistance aviators are methodically slaughtered by the Nazi "Butcher Squadron" commanded by Captain Von Tepp. (Later on a Baron Von Tepp appeared in the series—he was the captain's brother.)

One by one the brave Polish aviators crash in flames until a single freedom-flier escapes—Blackhawk, swearing vengeance against Von Tepp and the Butcher Squadron, against all Nazis, and against the forces of oppression everywhere. (He was called "Jack" in the origin story by Will Eisner; in a different, later origin story he was called "Bart Hawk"—but *all* the rest of the time he was called "Blackhawk.")

As an origin story it wasn't bad, except maybe a little lacking in the bizarre and the exotic that we have learned to expect from comic-book heroes, but it does have a slightly familiar ring to it. In fact, it sounds one hell of a lot like the story of the Lone Ranger; substitute the Polish air force for the Texas (or was it Arizona?— no matter) Rangers, substitute Nazi aviators for western thugs, and substitute for the lone surviving cowboy-lawman a lone surviving aviator-hero. It matches pretty well.

The Blackhawks wore no nation's uniform; being a sort of multinational volunteer force throughout their career, they donned a uniform of their own design in a dark blue shade. Each was equipped with a visored military cap with brass insigne, military tunic closed by a *horizontal* flap and metallic buttons high on the chest, leather belt with brass buckle, broad-topped trousers of the riding-jodhpur variety, and well-polished black leather boots.

Blackhawk himself was further distinguished by wearing his tunic open at the throat, displaying a yellow scarf, and by a stylized hawk's-head symbol blazoned against a yellow circle on the front of his uniform.

The other members of the Blackhawk team were added early in the series, and with one exception fit neatly into the mold of aviators loyally following the lead of their commander. The lineup varied somewhat over the years, but usually it consisted of six members: Andre, Stanislaus, Hendrickson, Olaf, Chuck, and Chop Chop.

Most prominently featured in the series was Andre, a dashing Frenchman with a turned-up pencil moustache and slicked-back hair. True to stereotypes, Andre was an insatiable ladies' man, forever disappearing in pursuit of a skirt, and "vividified" (to coin a term) by his French accent.

Flying over an island outpost, the Blackhawks spot a distress signal. Andre is detailed to land and investigate. On the ground he is met by a sexy brunette who says, "Thank heaven you saw my signal, sir!"

Andre's response: "Mort de ma vie! Had I known zere was so beautiful a ma'm'selle I would have landed sooner! Permettez-moi . . . ze name is Andre . . ."

A confederate of the beautiful lady's steps from hiding. "Good work, Dorna!" he growls, "He came into your trap like a rabbit!"

Andre says "Ze trap? Have a care . . . I am of ze *Blackhawks!*"

Why, a fella could practically learn to speak the French language from a stack of Blackhawk adventures, if he concentrated on Andre's dialog.

Hendrickson was an interesting fellow. There was a sort of standardized young-mature look that most heroes showed, varied usually only for kids. But Hendrickson (or Henderson as it was occasionally rendered) was a fat, jolly old coot with pure white hair and a big, snowy moustache. But he kept himself in good shape despite his corpulence, and kept up with his comrades on earth and in the air.

The nationality of Hendrickson was somewhat dubious—at first he seemed to be Dutch, bearing out the theme of the Blackhawks all being refugees from Nazi-conquered nations in Europe. But that changed, of course, and one of the ways in which it changed was that Hendrickson became an anti-Nazi German.

This might seem to be a minor distinction, but in fact it set Hendrickson in particular and the Blackhawks in general onto a more sophisticated and in a sense more decent level than most other wartime comics. For those comics were widely guilty of rather vicious racism, the caricaturing of blacks as shiftless, cowardly, and unintelligent being only one aspect of the phenomenon.

Another was the characterization of the citizens of enemy nations as subhuman beasts—Japanese were portrayed as bucktoothed, sadistic fanatics; Germans, as brutal monsters.

It's odd that in *Blackhawk,* where national stereotyping was used as the chief characterizing device, an important distinction was made: that between a political system and a people. Hendrickson was graphic evidence that the enemy was not the German people but the Nazi political movement. And throughout the career of the Blackhawks, with only a few regrettable exceptions relatively late in the game, distinctions were drawn between tyrannical governments and the peoples they controlled.

And as for Hendrickson—how was he characterized beyond those physical items? Why, the same way Andre was, by his dialect. As the Blackhawks see an inventor off to his secret laboratory, Blackhawk himself comments, "There goes a great man, gang—vanishing into the unknown with perhaps the greatest secret on earth today!"

"Jawohl!" chips in Hendrickson, "Und if someding should happen to Dr. Vardan, der vorld might never know!"

The other Blackhawks included the Swede Olaf ("By gar! I ban going to—"), the Pole Stanislaus, and the American Chuck.

Plus Chop Chop, the Chinese cook and comic-relief man. Chop Chop must have stood all of four feet high, and had an almost round head to go with his almost round body. His ears were huge and stood straight out from the sides of his head, his hair was pulled straight *up* and tied in a red bow that flopped about, and he had buck teeth that, to scale, must have been easily three inches long and an inch wide—*each!*

He was oddly dressed, too—green shirt and trousers, red shoes, apparently a red sleeveless tunic over his shirt, and a short yellow vest over the tunic.

Chop Chop was usually pretty cowardly, endeavoring to hide behind Blackhawk or anyone else handy when danger threatened, although if sufficiently provoked he could turn on his tormentor with a meat-cleaver that he kept handy for use in his duties as official chef of the Blackhawks. How did he speak? Are you kidding?

"Well, stlange interlude! Tough clooks still aflaid of Chop Chop, even without goldy pencil boom! Is most stlange! Everywhere Chop Chop go, evelybody scleam and lun away in gleat flight!"

Chop Chop was Blackhawk's Woozy Winks, his Doiby Dickles, his Alfred the butler, and his Uncle Marvel all in one. He flew with Blackhawk in his plane many times, accompanied the team on their missions, suffered privation and imprisonment with them with never a word of complaint except for an occasional "O woe!" and he attained his reward in the form of a series of solo adventures in the later years of *Blackhawk Comics*. These adventures generally carried Chop Chop into exotic settings (as the mainstream Blackhawk stories carried the team into many parts of the world) and in August, 1949, we learned that Chop Chop was the identical cousin of His Royal Highness Chop Chin, Emperor of Won Lung, a small Asian kingdom. In the course of the adventure Chop Chin offers Chop Chop his throne, but the loyal chef refuses—he'd rather fight and fly and cook for the Blackhawks. Okay.

The artwork in *Blackhawk* was almost always first-rate; it was produced by a number of artists, but is most often associated with Reed Crandall, a fine craftsman who passed through the comic-book factories in the forties, contributed much to the greatness of the EC group in the fifties, and in the 1960s turned to book illustration with fine results.

Crandall himself is hardly the man you would expect to turn out those crisply rendered, military-looking figures. He is himself a rotund, jolly farm-boy from Iowa; the first time I met him (to discuss some book illustrations) he even wore the archetypical farmer's straw hat. I think it was the only one on Manhattan Island outside of theatrical costumers' shops.

But Crandall had an education in fine arts, and his drawings of human figures above all else were marked with a kind of vigorous grace that fit perfectly the motif of the somewhat stern, serious Blackhawks.

Second only to the humans in the strip were the airplanes the Blackhawks flew. In the early years of the strip they flew Grumman F5F Skyrockets—one of the oddest looking airplanes of the World War II era, and hence one of the most distinctive that could have been chosen for the Blackhawks to use.

The F5F was an experimental naval fighter; I do not believe that any of them ever reached combat outside the pages of *Military Comics* and its successors *Modern* and *Blackhawk.* The standard U.S. Navy fighter at the outbreak of World War II was the stubby little Grumman F4F Wildcat, a single-engine monoplane with the blunt nose typical of radial-engine craft.

Looking for a hotter airplane to replace the Wildcat, the Navy got the gull-wing Corsair from Vought-Sikorsky while Grumman proposed the Skyrocket. This was a twin-engine plane, and the oddity of its appearance arose from the mounting position of the wing: instead of being set somewhere back along the body, the wing of the F5F was in front of the airplane. The nose of the fuselage extended only partway into the trailing edge of the wing. The result was an airplane that looked like none other before or since, and this was the "official" plane of the Blackhawks!

(As things worked out, the Navy passed up the F5F and Grumman came back with the F6F Hellcat, a sort of "stretched" Wildcat with a more powerful engine and heavier armament. It was quite successful. There was also an F7F Tiger Cat, a twin-engine model again, but few if any of these saw combat service either.)

Over the years the adventures of the Blackhawks were generally edited by Harry Stein; later, by Alfred Grenet. Stories were written by a goodly number of people, including several of the top comics scripters of the era: Ed Herron, Bill Finger, Joe Millard, and the sometime pulp-fantasy writer Manly Wade Wellman. There were several artists, too; before Crandall got hold of the feature it had been drawn by Will Eisner and Charles Cuidera.

But Crandall was the classic *Blackhawk* artist.

After the war ended the strip had to find new directions, but the changes were actually less extreme than you might expect. In place of Nazi or Japanese militarists, the villains tended to be the leaders of private armies or other paramilitary organizations bent on world conquest. The Blackhawks traded in their Grummans for modern aircraft, switching first to somewhat modified Republic F-84 Thunderjets, and then to Lockheed F-104 Starfighters.

They continued under the aegis of the Quality group until 1956, and survived the suspension of the Quality comics by shifting over to DC, but DC unfortunately didn't really know what to do with the Blackhawks. Their adventures, which had always stuck fairly close to realism, grew wilder and wilder. The traditional dark-blue Blackhawk uniforms were swapped for some sort of garish red-

and-green concoctions, and the Blackhawks became just another nondescript bunch of adventurers. DC even revamped Chop Chop into a short, slim, tough, jazz-talking judo expert, trading one racial stereotype for another. The final death of the title in 1968 seemed more a release than a deprivation.

But for the classic years of the Blackhawks, with good, tight writing and fine Crandall art, the feature must be remembered as one of the all-time best aviation comics.

~ ~ ~ ~ ~

Air Fighters Comics was started with the issue of November, 1941, just three months after *Military*. The publisher was the Hillman group, a company that delved into a number of publishing areas including (some years later) science fiction. The Hillman comics were few; aside from *Air Fighters* I know only of *Clue Comics,* a general hero comic which featured the Boy King (he was a boy king, right, and his costume was superhero tights plus a crown and an ermine robe), Zippo (whose shtick was roller-skates), and Micro-Face (who, yes, had a small face).

The first *Air* Fighters bore a slight resemblance to *Wings Comics.* There were a group of aviator-heroes who might have been expected to continue in the magazine, but they were all pretty nondescript. Leckishes, if you will.

The Black Commander was featured on the cover, which advertised ten gripping air-action features, but none of them amounted to anything: *Tex Trainor, Test Pilot; Crash Davis, Navy Ace;* and the like.

A month went by. Two months. Three months. Six months. No second issue of *Air Fighters.* A fella might think that the magazine had gone out of business. Well, it hadn't quite, but it had gone back to the drawing board for a reworking, and when it reemerged it had a new lineup of features, two of which interest us today. One of these was *Airboy.* The other was *Sky Wolf.*

Airboy was the joint creation of Ed Cronin, the editor of *Air Fighters,* and Charles Biro. Biro was one of the classic creative geniuses of the so-called Golden Age; his greatest success came with the Lev Gleason group, where, in collaboration with Bob Wood, Biro was responsible for *Crimebuster* (in *Boy Comics),* *Daredevil* (the fellow in the blue-and-red costume with the spiked belt, no relationship to the later Stan Lee character of the same name), and *Crime Does Not Pay,* which was the all-time classic crime comic.

For publisher Alex Hillman and editor Ed Cronin, Biro dreamed up an aviation-oriented hero with a full complement of personality-establishing gimmicks: Airboy was an instant success when he appeared in the second issue of *Air Fighters,* a full year after the first. By the twenty-third issue of the magazine it had been retitled *Airboy,* and as *Airboy* it was published for the remainder of its history, lasting until May, 1953, a total of 111 issues in all.

Other features in the revamped *Air Fighters* were pretty routine fare, not essentially different from the weak lineup of the first issue. The new *Air Fighters* crew included the Bald Eagle (yep, he was bald), the Black Angel (a lady pilot who wore black tights), and Iron Ace (a pilot who wore armor and whose plane also carried retractable armor shielding). A friend of mine accurately described these things as "routine slaughter-the-Japs-and-Huns stories."

But Airboy . . .

In common with Jack Cole's classic Plastic Man, Airboy started his career in a monastery, tended by the friendly and solicitous monks. The lad was named Davy Nelson, apparently an orphan (although we later learned otherwise on this score) left in the care of the monks, particularly kindly old Father Martier. He was also befriended by other friars—Father Alonzo, Father Aloysius, Father Justus, Father Gregory.

But Father Martier was Davy's particular friend and benefactor, Father Martier, who was a lover of nature, whose particular fascination was the bats who flew about the monastery in the California dusk. Father Martier, who studied those bats and their mode of flight, and who struggled to build a model plane that would duplicate the flight of those bats.

Eventually he succeeded, creating a full-scale ornithopter, an airplane that could fly by flapping its wings like a bat or a bird. (In fact, for a while it was called the bat-plane in the story but, perhaps to avoid confusion with Batman's batplane, the term was switched to bird-plane, and Airboy called the ornithopter Birdie for many years.)

The bat-plane or bird-plane sported a sleekly pointed nose, a smooth bubble cockpit, a single pair of wings halfway back on the fuselage, and a vertical rudder. Both the wings and the rudder had curving, swept-back leading edges and ribbed, bat-like trailing edges.

At first the bird-plane flew entirely by flapping its wings, which were covered with a flexible rubberoid material that facilitated their movements. The plane could take off and land vertically, hover in one spot, or fly at great speeds. In later years rocket exhaust tubes were added at the tail to facilitate even higher speeds.

At about the same time that Father Martier was working on his ornithopter, a local gambling figure attempted to take over the monastery and convert it to a gambling casino. There was a crooked mortgage, taken mainly to provide funds for commercial development of the new aircraft, and to make sure that the mortgage would be foreclosed, the gambler sabotaged the ornithopter so that Father Martier crashed and was killed on a test flight.

Young Davy Nelson, a lad of 15, dismantled the wreckage, discovered the sabotage, rebuilt the bird-plane, and donned the costume that he was to wear ever after as Airboy. He wore a red jacket with a huge letter *V* (the wartime motif of "V-for-Victory" of course) slashing its front from shoulders to waist. He wore blue breeches and brown leather aviator's gloves and boots. A pair of aviator's goggles mounted on a brown leather strap circled his California-wavy blond hair, and were pulled down when he flew Birdie with its cockpit open.

During the war Airboy fought the usual run of German and Japanese menaces. His activities were delineated by a number of artists—copies in my possession are variously signed by Bernard Sachs, Fred Kida, "Zolne" (Dan Zolnerowich), John Giunta, Dan Barry—and Carmine Infantino, who went on to become the editorial director of the entire DC comics line a quarter-century later.

Like the characters in *Gasoline Alley,* Airboy aged at a normal rate, an unusual accomplishment for a comic-book hero, most of whom were frozen in at one age for their entire careers. (Even odder has been the experience of Superboy, whose aging takes place at a severely retarded rate, about one-third normal.)

Aside from standard Axis foes, Airboy periodically encountered villains of a distinctly exotic nature. One such was Misery, a weird, cadaverous being whose eternal mission seemed to be the overseeing of the Airtomb, a huge dead-white aircraft to which deceased aviators went. Another, of more equivocal nature, was Valkyrie, a gorgeous sort of *femme fatale* cast in the mold of Milton Caniff's Dragon Lady.

Still another was Keller, "the fantastic Eastern man of mystery." Keller, a famous stunt flier, had disappeared after being blamed for a fatal accident, and turned up years later as the dictator of a lush Pacific island, where he taught the natives to construct airplanes in the form of ancient war galleys, and commanded both natives and aviators abducted from the outer world (for example, Airboy) to take part in fantastic aerial gladiatorial games.

Among the captive gladiators Airboy encounters an old acquaintance, Jimmy Collins, and they plot successfully to escape. As the two aviators wing their way eastward over the Pacific they work out a few more details of the weird incident. Collins says: "That's it, Airboy! Keller was mad . . . but he knew enough to build only short range planes, so nobody could escape . . . and now that he's dead, I'm sure those people will throw out the air battles he sneaked into their life . . ."

"I hope so, Jimmy," says Airboy, "but the U.S.A. will want to *know* . . . there's still a bunch of captive pilots to free!"

Although Airboy was at first an apparent orphan, his father turned up alive and well, like Little Orphan Annie's periodically reappearing Daddy Warbucks, in November, 1946.

"Take a good look at your *Dad!!*" the story was blurbed. "He's pretty okay, eh? Maybe you'd like to have *him* around as your 'partner' if things got *tight* for you as they did for Airboy. But how would *you* stand up?? What if it was a bright sunny morning, the kind of morning that to dreaming fliers opens the door to the 'wide blue yonder'—and also opens a newsboy's mouth . . ."

And thus we were off into an outstanding Airboy adventure, opening with Airboy, "young prince of the skies," judging a model airplane meet at a local airport.

In the midst of the competition a really superior jet-powered model lands. In its cabin is a note addressed to Airboy, telling him to go to a local movie palace. He obeys, sits down in the last row at the Pix, and in a few minutes a well-dressed, middle-aged businessman enters, sits down beside Airboy, and—"Why! It's . . . *you! Dad!*"

Airboy's father, Professor Nelson, explains that he has been at work for all these years, with three associates, on a form of super jet engine that will eventually carry man to the moon! So great is the secret that the four scientists totally isolated themselves from the outer world for the duration of the war.

Professor Nelson explains: ". . . so we vanished from the public eye! That's why someone else had to take care of you . . . but the war is over! And I suspect a Professor Fitzner of our group of wanting our discoveries for evil purposes of his own!"

After the show, however, Professor Nelson is kidnaped back to the secret island where he, Fitzner, and the others had their laboratory. Airboy pursues; his father, misled by his treacherous partners, nearly kills Airboy in a dogfight—but both land safely, and Airboy kills Fitzner. (No qualms about killing in these comics!)

"Fitzner tricked me, told me you were dead," says Professor Nelson. "Then I saw you! He was going to use the results of our experiments to gain power and money. But he didn't get a chance! *You* saw to that, my son!"

Other menaces faced by Airboy were designed to send a shudder through the reader, and as often as not they succeeded at that task. One such tale was a two-parter that ran in the December, 1948, and January, 1949, issues of *Airboy,* a story called "Airboy and the Rats." This mini-epic ran a total of 30 pages, plus two covers, and those who read it two decades ago still speak of it with awe.

The theme, set in a flashback to the Egypt of 3,000 years ago, is that of man's fratricidal self-destructiveness—and the sinister, patient intelligence of the rats, who wait in the shadows to take over the world when man has relinquished his hold. And where once Pharaohs moved in splendor there is only debris. "For today," the narration runs, "the *rats rule!* And this jumble of ruins is but one ancient civilization inherited by the furry terrors! There are the jungle-covered towers of Asia, the great stone temples of the Aztecs, and many more! It's fantastic . . . and yet, true! And in the year 1948 . . . in the City of New York . . ."

Two men stand, discussing the state of the world. "It gives me the shivers!" says one, "Look at the headline in that paper in the gutter there!"

The headline reads: "ANOTHER WAR MAY END CIVILIZATION!"

The second man says: "Atom bombs . . . jet planes! They'll ruin the world yet!"

The paper is swept down a sewer. The artist follows it, revealing a minor headline: "Authorities Amused by Professor's Warning of Rat Menace."

But deeper in the sewer, rats are gathering. They are able to converse with one another, and their leader is addressing them:

"The day so long awaited has arrived and we, the rats of the western world, have been chosen to make the first move!"

The narration proceeds on through a tale of worldwide catastrophe, as rats cut off entire cities, massacre populations, destroy crops and factories. Airboy leads the opposition.

At the end of the first installment New York City is saved by pouring millions of gallons of oil into the Hudson River, soaking and destroying an army of rats swarming to attack the city.

But the following month the rat hordes renew their assault on human civilization. This time they amass a single grand army in the great gorge below the Grand Culvert Dam. Rats—billions of rats! And their headquarters has been found by Airboy through the device of deliberately allowing himself to be captured.

Now, using a secret radio transmitter concealed in his clothing, Airboy calls in an air strike that will destroy the dam and the assembled army of rats. But Airboy as well will be killed unless . . .

He summons his airplane, Birdie, with the same radio transmitter. Operating on remote control the airplane swoops low over the towering wall of water, drops down, picks up its master, and carries him to safety just as the waters of the Grand Culvert Dam crash down, wiping out the army of rats.

But are the rats defeated for once and all? "I know a little about them now," Airboy says. "Enough to know their cunning and strength—and *they* know that *I'm* wise to them—so they'll be scouting *me* as long as I live!"

That response of Birdie to Airboy's desperate summons raises an interesting point in regard to this particular feature. As the essence of valid fiction is human interaction, most comics heroes had to have some continuing foil, whether boy-sidekick, other assistant, running foe, police contact, and so on, with whom to interact.

In Airboy's case, this foil was his ornithopter Birdie. Airboy used to speak to Birdie as you or I would speak to another human. He called the aircraft his "girl," praised it, sympathized with its wounds when it was damaged, thanked it for its aid when it saved him as in the rats story . . .

It was a distinctly odd relationship, but it gave Airboy somebody to talk to, and he needed that. In his last adventures he was employed by one Tex Calhoun, a millionaire oilman interested in scientific experimentation. Calhoun provided a human figure for Airboy to relate to, and also answered any bothersome questions about the source of Airboy's money. And there was Professor Nelson, and there was Valkyrie. But mainly, Airboy talked to his airplane when he was lonesome.

He faced one more chilling foe in the immortal Zzed, whom he encountered twice in 1950, in January and then again in May.

Zzed was a sinister figure—he looked a lot like the motion-picture actor John Carradine, with a gaunt, bony face, long ragged hair, and battered ancient clothes. He lurked in a mysterious and gloomy swamp in Georgia, where he waylaid and murdered passing travelers.

Meanwhile, across the continent in California, Airboy and his employer Tex Calhoun are visiting Calhoun's laboratory, where a staff scientist, Dr. Jenkins, has devised the theory that the great bulk of "brain energy" generated on the earth is not used, but is drained off into space, where it is concentrating at the behest of—something! And this great cluster of "brain energy" is moving through space, back toward the earth.

Back in Georgia Zzed murmurs strange, ancient words, prayers and incantations, until a weird tentacular apparition descends from space. There is a brilliant explosion and Zzed exclaims *"It is done! Now Zzed is master of mankind!"*

Now there are alarming reports of riots and violence in great cities throughout the world—it is, of course, the invader from space, powered by its collected "brain energy" to spread anarchy and hatred throughout the world. Airboy and Tex Calhoun make their way to Georgia and confront Zzed, who gloats: "I have the collected intelligence of all the years—*the star brain!"* Using this power Zzed can control all men, for the star brain exploits evil and hatred, and there is evil and hatred in some amount in all men. The cause of humanity looks entirely hopeless until—Airboy gets a little child, innocent of evil and hatred, to destroy the apparatus with which Zzed controls the star brain.

Zzed is defeated, but escapes, shrieking mad laughter in the finest tradition of his kind.

Zzed reappeared in a two-parter, May and June, 1950, and his swansong was a wild mélange of melodramatic impedimenta—storms wracking the world, Airboy personally summoned by President Truman to save the world, Zzed operating from a new headquarters at the North Pole, an infernal device slowly melting away the polar ice cap, frozen mammoths and dinosaurs emerging into the modern world, etc.

I won't even try to recreate the story, you can do the job in your own imagination. It was a beaut!

And then there was the story of the tiny sea-slug accidentally raised by Airboy in a diving bell—the slug that began to grow—and grow—and *grow*—until . . .

I guess that by 1953 Airboy had just plain grown up. He wasn't Airboy any more, he was a man, and he put aside his melodramatics and probably took a job as a test pilot for an aeronautical engineering firm, or became an airline pilot at $40,000 a year or . . .

Airboy—Davy Nelson—are you still up there somewhere in the wide blue yonder? I'd like to know about it if you are.

~ ~ ~ ~ ~

I said that when the revamped *Air Fighters* appeared in November, 1942, a year after the weak first issue had come out, the two noteworthy features in it were *Airboy* and *Sky Wolf.*

Airboy, okay; *Sky Wolf,* well, the statement was true but, I must confess, somewhat misleading.

Drawn by Mort Leav and written by Harry Stein, *Sky Wolf* was basically just another war-flier strip. There were four Sky Wolves, differentiated roughly as were the Blackhawks (or Doc Savage's helpers), and their gimmick was that they flew in a brace of double-airplanes, craft vaguely resembling the F-82 Twin Mustangs that served in Korea but capable of splitting into mirror-image pairs of asymmetrical single-engined craft for extra maneuverability in dogfights.

Sky Wolf himself was distinguished by a sort of helmet-hood that he wore, which was formed like the head of a wolf. It did give him a fierce and dashing appearance, and his epic struggles against the Nazi Colonel Von Tundra, a sort of half-man, half-machine rebuilt from the human wreckage of an air crash, were fairly exciting.

The Sky Wolf's three companions, the Turtle, "Cocky" Roach, and the Judge, were a pretty adequate crew of fliers, too.

But the turning point in the adventures of Sky Wolf and Colonel Von Tundra came in their second recorded encounter (that is, because of the unsuccessful trial issue of *Air Fighters,* the *third* issue of the magazine). There has been a terrific dogfight. Both Sky Wolf and Von Tundra crash-land, but both emerge safely from the wreckage of their respective fighter planes. And this is what they met:

It walked in the woods.

It was never born. It existed. Under the pine needles the fires bum, deep and smokeless in the mold. In heat and in darkness and decay there is growth. There is life and there is growth. It grew, but it was not alive. It walked unbreathing through the woods, and thought and saw and was hideous and strong, and it was not born and it did not live. It grew and moved about without living.

It crawled out of the darkness and hot damp mold into the cool of a morning. It was huge. It was lumped and crusted with its own hateful substances, and pieces of it dropped off as it went its way, dropped off and lay writhing, and stilled, and sank putrescent into the forest loam.

Standing there was . . . a massive caricature of a man: a huge thing like an irregular mud doll, clumsily made. It quivered and parts of it glistened and parts of it were dried and crumbly. Half of the lower part of its face was gone, giving it a lopsided look. It had no perceptible mouth or nose, and its eyes were crooked, one higher than the other, both a dingy brown with no whites at all. It stood quite still . . . its only movement a steady unalive quivering.

Pretty unappetizing apparition, and of course if you ever had the creepy pleasure as a kid to read of the adventures of the Heap in *Air Fighters/Airboy Comics,* you know exactly who that is.

The—thing was probably the most bizarre creation in the entire history of the comic medium. Odd heroes and odder villains thronged the four-color page. There was Fawcett's Hunchback, DCs metallic Robotman, and surely a high (or low) of some sort in the person of a hero called the Bouncer. Yep, his power was that— he bounced.

On the villain side there was Dr. Weerd, there was the Snail, there was the Rat, there were endless others. There was Solomon Grundy, a foe of Green Lantern's, and of a somewhat more equivocal nature there was of course the Frankenstein monster himself in the long Dick Briefer series and in many other shorter-lived incarnations.

But there was never a match for the Heap.

His origin story—well, his origin story was told and retold and retold with amazing frequency over the years, frequently with little fillips added or variations in detail that were not always consistent with earlier versions. But in skeletal form, the origin of the Heap went something like this:

Back in the latter days of World War I—sometimes the narration said 1917, sometimes 1918—there was a savage dogfight over a Polish swamp. The German squadron involved was no less than the famous Flying Circus of Baron Manfred von Richtofen. One of the greatest of Richtofen's fliers was another young German nobleman, the Baron Emmelmann (sometimes rendered as von Emmelman). Emmelmann had left behind in Germany a beautiful young wife and a darling infant.

In the great sky battle the baron is shot down. Parachutes were not used in World War I; if you were shot down, you rode your plane down, hoping to survive a crash landing. Few did.

But Emmelmann was possessed of a fanatical will to live. His love for his wife, his need to see his child were such that he would not let go the spark of life that remained in his mangled body after the smoke of his crash had cleared.

Over the years he lay there in Poland, not dead nor alive either. The life of the swamp grew together with the broken flesh of his body. A mindless, unconscious *thing* lay there for a quarter of a century, until, in the early days of World War II, there was reenacted a scene above the swamp similar to that tragic incident of October 12, 1918. (Or '17.)

The Heap rises from the swamp. It feeds on a stray sheep. In time it becomes master of its domain.

And now, in the little Polish town of Rodz, the Nazi Colonel Von Tundra, accompanied by the beautiful double-agent Frisco, holds tyrannical sway over the hopeless Poles.

That dogfight takes place. The Heap comes upon Sky Wolf and the Nazi half-man, and seizes the Nazi. Half-unconscious, the Heap carries its prey into the town where it sees a Wehrmacht soldier. It takes one look, this great, shaggy mass, and—hearts fly through the panel as the Heap falls in love!

Yes, in those early days the Heap was portrayed as a partly humorous feature, and as the years went by, while the character and the strip itself evolved (after a while the Heap was separated from Sky Wolf, and later Sky Wolf was dropped from the magazine), the Heap was never treated wholly as a horror feature.

At the end of the first installment of his adventures, the Heap is apparently blown up in an aerial bombing. But he returned again and again, his repeated "deaths" about as convincing as those of the filmed versions of the Frankenstein monster. You remember how *he* was variously burned, exploded, drowned, frozen, or whatnot, always to return when his services were needed again. So it was with the Heap, and after a while they stopped even pretending to kill him off. We all knew he'd be back soon anyhow . . .

When the Heap returned after that Polish episode his origin was retold with variations. Now the dogfight had taken place in the air over Siberia (!), his first food after regaining his mobility was a dog rather than a sheep, and the soldiers into whose encampment he blundered were Japanese troops garrisoned in wartime China rather than Germans in Poland.

Further, who turns up but the Baroness von Emmelman, working as a nurse! The Heap has a predictable run-in with the Japanese soldiers, a soldier turns his gun upon the Heap, but at the last moment he shoots not the Heap but Baroness von Emmelman instead!

Thus the Heap, "that formless thing of the swamps," "this hulk of the living death," goes from tragedy to tragedy. He is "killed" but the remains are imported to the United States by one Professor Herman Kringle, a henpecked little man who uses the revived Heap to murder his wife. The Heap is shown as immensely strong—he picks up a twin-engine plane in one scene and throws it through the air!

In still later appearances the Heap is charmed by a small boy playing with a model of a World War I fighter plane—somewhere in the murky mind of this thing there stirs a memory of its past.

By 1946 the Heap had his own series in *Airboy Comics;* he adventured for a while with the boy Rickie Wood, but then wandered on again, appearing here and there throughout the world, with ever and again a return to that Polish (or Siberian) swamp in 1918 (or 1917) and a new retelling of the origin story. After a while there began to be Olympian overtones. The comic showed us quarrels among the Greek gods and goddesses, Ceres in particular, the Earth goddess, crying out against the cruelty and violence of the war god Ares.

Now it was by personal intervention of Ceres that the plant life of the swamp united with the spark in von Emmelman to create the Heap, and the Heap is hence a creature of peace and justice, hulking about the world fighting against oppression and violence. (Can you fight against violence? Well, people claim today to "fight for peace" and in an era when we "save" Asian cities by totally obliterating them, why not fight violence?)

In later years the Heap travels to France, to South Africa, back to Poland (now the swamp was near Wasau), and to America again. Almost every story had eerie overtones to it, and almost always the Heap was portrayed as a melancholy figure, an outcast from all life, a creature of pathos as much as of terror, if not more of pathos than terror.

Whether the creators of the Heap were conscious of this characteristic, or if things just worked out that way, I do not know; but consciously or otherwise they hit upon the great secret of monster story-telling. For if the monster is just a bogeyman waved to frighten children, he never will amount to much.

But if the monster is *pathetic,* then he is Quasimodo, then he is Karloff's Frankenstein monster, then he is truly touching and memorable.

And so was the Heap, that great, shaggy, half-man, half-plant, that child of the goddess Ceres, that tragic ace of the Flying Circus.

We see the Heap carrying the broken body of a child to its swampy home, there to tend her with the gentle tenderness of the huge and the mighty.

The Heap could bring tears of pity to our eyes as well as gasps of terror to our lips.

That was his greatness, and that was the strange appeal that brings back his image to this day, the appeal of a very powerful image that stirs something deep within the subconscious memories of us all. Perhaps deeply buried recollections of those days when we were ourselves tiny babies, carried about and handled by our parents, huge creatures of inconceivable power . . .

One might wonder why the adventures of the Heap have never been chronicled in straight prose, but the fact is that they have. There is a story by the fantastic-fiction writer Theodore Sturgeon, called simply "It," which first described a thing remarkably like the Heap.

"It" was published in the famous science-fantasy magazine *Unknown,* with several illustrations by Edd Cartier. "It" appeared in the issue of *Unknown* for August, 1940, over two years before the Heap made his first appearance in the *Sky Wolf* strip. And in case you're wondering how closely It resembled the Heap, turn back to that description that I quoted. You know, the one beginning "It walked in the woods . . ." and ending ". . . a steady unalive quivering."

That description was not lifted from any blurb or narration panel of a *Heap* story. Nope. That's Sturgeon's own description of his nameless monster "It."

Hi there, Heap!

One thing we can note concerning comic books: the publishers admire success, and they make known their admiration in the proverbial "sincerest form" of admiration: imitation. Over the years following the discontinuance of *Airboy* with its feature *The Heap,* the image of that huge, hulking, powerful, half-human creature recurred again and again in the comics. Probably the most significant example was the Thing, a member of Marvel Comics' Fantastic Four hero team.

But by the 1970s several publishers seemed to decide, almost simultaneously, that it was time to bring back the shambling monster in more nearly his original form. Thus in quick succession the Skywald Publishing Company actually revived the "original" Heap in *Psycho,* an oversized black-and-white comic of the type pioneered by the EC Picto-Fiction series in the 1950s and developed to success by Jim Warren's *Eerie* and *Creepy* in the sixties . . . Marvel brought out its carbon-copy Man-Thing . . . DC joined the party with the Swamp-Thing.

But the crowning vindication of Sturgeon's original vision came when Marvel introduced a new comic called *Supernatural Thrillers* in December, 1972. The entire first issue was devoted to a faithful adaptation of "It," using much of Sturgeon's original text as running narration and dialog! It had taken 32 years for "It" to come full-circle, from the pulp pages of *Unknown* magazine to the full-color panels of *Supernatural Thrillers,* but the story that had started off the entire fantastic sequence had finally been recognized and received the attention of a comic-book audience that had seen only imitations for those three decades.

IT'S MAGIC

Dick O'Donnell
(Don Thompson & Richard A. Lupoff)

WHEN YOUR EDITORS first approached me with the request to write a chapter for them dealing with magicians in the comics, I agreed at once. Although I must confess that I long ago stopped reading the strips in the *Honolulu Advertiser* except for one or two favorites, and although I had not picked up a comic magazine for 20 years or longer, I held a strong, lingering affection for those wild and colorful tales of adventure, and for those, in particular, dealing with the exploits of magicians.

For there were magicians galore in the newspaper comic sections and in the early comic magazines of the 1930s and 1940s. I set out to dredge what information I could from my memory, supplemented this with some treasures culled from a few bundles of flaking newspapers that have lain in my attic for untold years, and was aided immeasurably, on a recent visit to the mainland, by Mr. Bill Blackbeard of the National Newspaper Archive and Academy of Comic Art.

One of the first things I learned in my researches was that the first great comic-strip magician was not my old friend Mandrake, but a secondary character in a little-known daily feature by Mel Graff, called *The Adventures of Patsy.* Appearing in the early 1930s, Patsy was a little girl who got herself into endless hot water, much of it in mythical kingdoms of the Graustark or Zenda variety, where she would embroil herself in palace intrigue at the drop of a hat.

For several such adventures, which Mr. Blackbeard kindly showed me in tinted reprints in the *Famous Funnies* magazine, Patsy enlisted the aid of a mysterious *Phantom Magician,,* who was clad in the outfit of tights, cape, and domino mask favored by so many later adventure heroes including the Phantom (no relation despite the similar name) and Superman and Batman and their compatriots without number.

But while the Phantom Magician was an interesting precursor, the first truly important comic-strip magician, and by far the greatest of all time, was Mandrake, the creation of Lee Falk and Phil

Davis, the same Falk and Davis who later created the non-magical Phantom.

Telling the youth of today that Mandrake was a great feature, I have found, is an exercise in futility. They know of that master of mystical adventure only through the modern newspaper strip—drawn since Davis's death by Fred Fredericks—or through latter-day comic-book revivals. Both are weak, puerile things, with tame and simplified plots, no pace, crude and characterless drawing. Certainly a reading of this *Mandrake* leaves one with no impression of anything very worthwhile.

But, ah, when I think of the thrill of reading the *Mandrake* feature as it existed 35 years ago, when Falk and Davis were at the peak of their energies, I can come to only one of two conclusions. Either Mandrake was a truly great strip which has been laid low by the passage of time—or else my memory of it has acquired a luster with the years that utterly distorts and deceives me in my recollections of those pages.

In those days of the 1930s that seem so long ago, I used to go down to Diamond Head to watch for the Matson Liners headed in from the mainland with all manner of goods and supplies, including usually some three-week-old copies of the *San Francisco Examiner,* a Hearst paper that carried *Mandrake* in both its daily and its Saturday editions, for in those days Hearst used to put out two color sections each weekend, the full-sized Sunday section that carried *Prince Valiant* and *Blondie* and the other heavyweight strips in head-on competition with other Sunday papers . . . and a tabloid-sized Saturday color section.

Because no one else carried a color section on Saturday, Hearst could run secondary features in this section and still gain a competitive advantage over rival Saturday editions. *Mandrake* was included in the Saturday lineup, shining there all the brighter because of the relatively lackluster strips that accompanied it.

The Matson Liner would steam into Pearl Harbor and I would know that within hours my father would reach into his pocket and pull out a whole dollar, and send me to the big newsstand on Kamehameha Boulevard, where I would buy a run of *Examiners* and hurry home with them, and while Father read the political news and the sports sections, I would devour the comic strips from the daily papers and the color comic sections from the weekend editions.

One of the earliest *Mandrake* adventures that I read was "The Kingdom of Murderers." I believe that this was the first *Mandrake* color adventure—the daily strip had begun in 1934, and a few months later the weekend series commenced with this tale.

Already Mandrake's appearance was fairly well settled—he was a tall, well-built man with dark, neatly combed hair and a sharply trimmed moustache. He was dressed in full tails with a silk top hat and a crimson-lined black cape.

In short, he appeared as a stage-magician, a prestidigitator, a fast-finger man if you choose to take apart that word, but he was, in the comics, far more than that. He was an actual magician, possessed of supernatural capabilities. This is only one of the many ways in which the strip grew pallid in later years, for by the 1950s Mandrake typically would "gesture hypnotically," following which a mild trick, such as a disappearance or the substitution of a bunch of flowers for a tommy-gun, would be seen, leaving the reader uncertain as to whether this was mere illusion—or more.

In his early years Mandrake had unquestioned magical powers, and exercised them quite freely in the course of his adventures. Mandrake's servant and aide, Lothar, was present from the outset, at first portrayed with deep, blue-black skin and red lips, but within less than a year he had attained the rich brown pigmentation that he was shown with thereafter.

The omnipresent (and insipid) girl friends, Trina and Narda, did not join Mandrake for many years. In his earlier adventures he enjoyed the company of a series of female friends. In "The Kingdom of Murderers," early in 1935, Mandrake's female companion was one Rheeta, a lovely although taciturn blonde whom he had transformed to human form from a tawny-coated pantheress. No illusions here, no hypnotic gestures. He outright turned the pantheress into a human woman.

In that tale, Mandrake agrees to assist two agents of the International Police in penetrating the "secret and hidden kingdom of murderers," and after one of the police agents is himself assassinated, Mandrake, Lothar, Rheeta, and the second police agent, Pierce, get under way.

Mandrake has captured the assassin of Pierce's partner and, when the killer refuses to guide them to the hidden kingdom, Mandrake calls up the murderer's *shadow* and commands it to lead them. En route to the kingdom they are harassed by "ghosts," but make their way into the kingdom anyway, and discover that the "ghosts" are projections of an infernal machine operated by members of the kingdom of murderers.

Mandrake turns these killers into beasts—an ape, a seal, an ostrich, and a horse.

He encounters the king of this hidden retreat, the killer Bull Ganton, who plans to execute Rheeta (no women allowed) and enslave the others. Instead, a wrestling match is arranged between Lothar and the champion of the murderers, to take place on a trestle over a pit of flames.

While Mandrake and Bull Ganton look on, Lothar hurls his foe off the trestle—Mandrake rises, gestures, and raises the victim from the pit, safely back to the trestle. "A simple trick I learned in India," Mandrake explains.

There follow complex reversals of fortune as Ganton imprisons Mandrake and has him strapped into the "dynamite chair," an explosive device of execution; Pierce sets loose a flock of carrier pigeons summoning all of the murderers in the world to the hidden kingdom, Mandrake breaks free, and so on. In the end the kingdom of murderers is destroyed and Mandrake and his companions return to the outer world.

By the next year Mandrake's adventures were making the hidden kingdom of murderers look mundane. Take, for instance, "Mandrake in the X Dimension." A scientist has discovered that beings from the X dimension are kidnaping Earth people for unspecified purposes. His own daughter disappears into the X dimension, so he sends Mandrake and Lothar in a machine of his own devising to rescue the girl.

Here Mandrake and Lothar find a world worthy of Alex Raymond's Mongo—"wheelmen of living metal instead of flesh" use captive humans to work their mines for coal and metals and to curry to the needs of these heartless living robots.

For them, oil is food and rust is the only disease! Humans toil as miners, oilers, and polishers. Rebellion is met with instant repression. All metal things in this world live—when a miner sits down to rest for a moment, a scrap-metal band curls about his throat and chokes him until he yields or dies!

Mandrake and Lothar rescue the girl and the other prisoners of the X dimension, of course, and after their return to our own world, the master magician and his giant servant entered one of the finest of all Falk and Davis's fantasies, "The Land of Dementor."

Dementor is apparently more a Graustark than a truly alien land, but its ruler, the monstrously fat Prince Paulo, is himself a fascinating creation, alternately comical and horrifying in his manias. Mandrake encounters him first with the prince riding a horse facing backward; Mandrake remarks on this silly practice, and to Prince Paulo's demand he says that he was merely talking to himself.

"Well!" responds the Prince, "You're a man after my own heart! I always talk to myself because I like to converse with intelligent people!"

Paulo shows Mandrake his castle (which is built upside down) in which he keeps a young man imprisoned in an electrified cage, jolting him with current whenever he wishes him to sing. Paulo also keeps the beautiful Sybil, "loveliest flower in Dementor," imprisoned in a giant fishbowl.

When Mandrake tries to straighten things out, Paulo has him seized and thrown into a dungeon. Suddenly huge pointed metal girders begin to transfix the room, like a magician's swords in a sword-box; Mandrake dodges one after another, but he exclaims: "Whew! This *is* a tight spot! Magic's no help against machinery!"

But Mandrake does use magic to send an astral projection to summon Lothar, who pulls Paulo away from the machinery and frees Mandrake.

Now a great duel ensues:

Paulo calls out his army against Mandrake.

Mandrake transforms himself into a 100-foot tall giant towering over the troops!

Paulo calls out a huge cannon and fires it at Mandrake!

Mandrake shrinks to normal size and multiplies into a regiment of swordsmen!

And so it goes, until Mandrake triumphs over Paulo and the mad ruler is replaced on the throne by Marlock, a noble who also proves to be the mourning father of Sybil, who is reunited not only with her father but also with Dormus, her sweetheart, the singer.

I think that in this adventure Phil Davis's art was at its finest. The human figures are without exception beautifully rendered and gracefully appealing, even that of the gross Paulo. Sybil is lovely, Mandrake is noble, Lothar is powerful. The castle is beautifully rendered, the drafting of the "spike room" looks like a creation of imaginative artist M. C. Escher, and the scenes of the duel between Mandrake and Paulo are works of art, each panel.

But if Davis's greatest work was in the Dementor sequence, Lee Falk's writing may have been at its peak in the 1938 adventure, "Mandrake on the Moon." (Not that Davis's art is poor either—it is very fine, up to the strip's level.)

In this tale, Mandrake, Lothar, the scientist Professor Thursby, and his beautiful daughter, Laura, travel to the moon in Thursby's rocket ship, *Stardust.* The story is a combination of pure fantasy—for, after all, that is what magical stories are about—with science fiction and elements of myth.

The notion of traveling to the moon in a rocket ship, of course, was science-fictional; otherwise the travelers might have gone by flying carpet, astral projection, or other mystical means. Having reached the moon, they don breathing helmets (science fiction) but no vacuum-suits (fantasy). Laura and Lothar fall into a crater but, even though the fall is some 60 feet, they land unhurt and are able to jump back out (science fiction).

The surface of the moon proves to be uninhabited and essentially rather dull, so the four travelers climb back aboard their craft and fly to the far side of the moon. The near surface *had* shown an ancient wall of clearly artificial construction; perhaps the far side will reveal its makers' identities.

On the far side is revealed, "hanging between barren peaks . . . a great shining dome." The travelers land the *Stardust,* find an entranceway into the dome, pass through a series of air-locks, and confront a gorgeous, coral-tinted bird as tall as a man! Shades of Stanley Weinbaum's "A Martian Odyssey"!

But no, the bird is revealed the next week to be a pet. Its master—a handsome man, identical in form to Earthmen, dressed in a flowing toga. Without a word he leads Mandrake and his party on a tour of a lovely city, Lunatopia, magnificently delineated in Grecian architecture with flowing fountains, music, luscious food and drink, no apparent labor. At bedtime the Earth-folk are shown how to use lunar "air-mattresses" which actually do float in the air.

Once spoken communication is established between Earthmen and Lunarian, the lunar being explains the history of his people. There had once been a magnificent civilization on the moon when that world was young and lush and Earth was still younger and uninhabited. As the moon grew old and lost its air and the waters of its seas, its people had migrated *en masse* to the ancient earthly continent of Atlantis, where they had reconstructed their great civilization.

A golden age passed and then Atlantis began to experience the cataclysms that led to its eventual disappearance. What to do? The Atlanteans returned to their spaceships and sped back to the moon, leaving behind only a few stragglers and diehards on Earth. Back on the moon they constructed a series of domed double-cities on the side of that world facing away from their lost Earth. Each city contained a surface community of beauty, culture, and comfort, and an underground city filled with automatic machinery which performed all the work.

The few Lunarians who remained on Earth became the ancestors of modern mankind—and the originators of the legend of Atlantis!

Now the visiting party's host takes them on a tour of the underground machine-city. "The machines generate their own power and lubrication," he explains. "For centuries they've worked without being touched by human hands! They're perfect!"

Mandrake says: "Amazing! But why do we have to see them from behind these bars? It looks like you keep your machines in jail!"

"We do! It sounds silly—but they were built so long ago, we know nothing about them! Some believe the master-machines *think* just like we do! Yes—we're a little *afraid* of them!"

Shades of E. M. Forster's "The Machine Stops"! The theme of decadence and domination by machinery is pursued to its logical revolt-of-the-robots conclusion, but rather than closing the lunar sequence for Mandrake, this leads to still another adventure—for the moon's flaming and molten core is inhabited by *fire people.*

Mandrake and his companions proceed to an encounter with these fantastic beings, and so the strip proceeded, and none except a few researchers and collectors have seen its like in a generation and a half.

The difficulty here is that *Mandrake the Magician* and other classic newspaper adventure strips, including the great *Flash Gordon, Prince Valiant, Tarzan,* and Falk and Davis's own *Phantom,* were designed, created, and published in a certain manner, intended to be read in a certain manner, and those who approach them in a different manner, albeit through no fault of their own, simply fail to comprehend the art form.

The problem is two-fold, one of graphic presentation and one of structure of continuity.

Mandrake and other newspaper comics were drawn in rather large size, intended to be presented on either full-size newspaper pages or (as with *Mandrake)* at least tabloid size. Each panel was fairly large, and the artists—Phil Davis, Alex Raymond, Hal Foster, Burne Hogarth—were able to lay out a scene and put into it a number of figures and an amount of graphic detail and technique appropriate to its size.

Even today I can look at a *Mandrake* page from a 1935 Saturday *Examiner* and see that each panel is a work of art.

When the Mandrake strips were collected by the King Features Syndicate and republished in *King Comics, Magic Comics,* and the David McKay Feature Books from 1936 onward, they were reduced in size by approximately 65 percent. The reader can follow the story-line well enough, but the beauty of the drawings is almost totally lost. There remains, perhaps, enough of a suggestion of Phil Davis's delicate brushwork and line to permit one to imagine what the page should look like, if one has seen full-size pages, but for the reader who knows *Mandrake* only through reductions such as these, there is simply no way of understanding the art and detail that went into the strip.

As for story structure, comic-book readers are accustomed to tales constructed in conventional short-story pattern: a problem is presented, it is further developed and complicated, and it is finally resolved. This is, of course, the classic beginning-middle-end structure.

Newspaper strips are simply not made this way. They are, in one sense, totally open-ended serials, but in fact they run in cycles, generally of 13 weeks' duration (a quarter of a year).

Within those 13 weeks it is necessary (in a weekly strip) to have 13 episodes, *each* with a beginning, middle, and ending. (Cliff-hanger technique merely displaces the end of each week's episode to the opening of the following episode.)

Each episode is a semi-independent unit, yet over a period of 13 such episodes a full adventure develops.

A batch of half-a-dozen Saturday *Mandrake* pages in an issue of *King Comics* is simply not the way the strip should be read. And, in fact, the complete adventures collected in the McKay *Mandrake* Feature Books, while better than the King format, were still not ideal by any means.

I can only suggest that the reader find some way of getting access to a series of the old Hearst Saturday color sections, then turn to the *Mandrake* page in each and prepare himself for a remarkable treat. Of course, doing this may take magic.

~ ~ ~ ~ ~

Once the comic book began to come into its own and specially created material began to displace reprinted newspaper strips as the dominating content of these magazines, it was not surprising that a number of magicians appeared, some of them rather closely based on Mandrake, others not nearly so much like him. Just for amusement I have made a list of some 30-odd of these sorcerers, the magazines in which they appeared, and the publishers of the magazines.

Perhaps some will ring a bell for you; if not, just speculate upon the endless variations on this theme represented herein. I follow the list with comments on just a few of the most interesting specimens as they seem to me.

There were: Balbo the Boy Magician (*Master, America's Greatest,* Fawcett); Blackstone (at least four different series published by Vital, Marvel, EC, and Street & Smith); Hale (*Dynamic, Punch,* Harry "A" Chesler); Houdini (*The Great Houdini);* Ibis the Invincible (*Whiz, Ibis,* Fawcett); Jupiter, Master Magician (*Prize Comics,* Prize); Kardak, the Mystic Magician (*Top Notch,* MLJ).

There were a great many magicians whose names began with *M*—alliteration as a device was favored long before Spiro Agnew came along—and left. These included: Magar the Mystic *(Red Raven,* Timely); Mantor the Magician *(Human Torch,* Timely); Marvo the Magician *(Lightning,* Ace); Marvelo, Monarch of Magicians (*Big Shot,* Columbia); the Master Mystic *(Green Giant,* Pelican Publications); Monako, Prince of Magic *(Daring Mystery,* Timely); Merlin (*National Comics,* Quality); Merzak the Mystic (*Mystic Comics,* Timely); Dr. Mystic, the Occult Doctor (*The Comics,* Dell); Mystic Moot and His Magic Snoot (*Ibis,* Fawcett); and Mystico, the Wonder Man (*Startling,* Better Publications).

After that they're scattered again: Nadir, Master of Magic (*Adventure,* DC); Norgil the Magician (*The Shadow, Doc Savage,* Street & Smith); Dr. Occult (*New Fun,* DC); Colonel Porterhouse (*Whiz,* Fawcett); Red Reeves, Boy Magician *{Silver Streak,* Comic House); Sargon the Sorcerer (*All-American, Comic Cavalcade, Green Lantern, Sensation,* DC); Solar, Master of Magic (*Captain Aero,* Holyoke); Stardust the Super Wizard (*Fantastic,* Fox); Tao-Anwar, Boy Magician (*Super-Magician Comics,* Street & Smith); the Wizard with Roy the Super Boy (*Shield-Wizard, Pep,* MLJ); Yarko the Great Master Magician (*Blue Beetle, Wonder World,* Fox).

And then in the *Z's* there's another cluster: The Great Zarro (*Great Comics,* Great Publications); Zatara the Master Magician (*Action, World's Fair, World's Finest,* DC); Zatanna (*Adventure, Justice League of America, Supergirl,* DC); Za-Za the Mystic (*Za-*

Za, Charlton); Zambini the Miracle Man (*Zip,* MLJ); Zoro the Mystery Man (*Slam-Bang,* Fawcett).

The list is assuredly incomplete, but I think it captures the bulk of the magical fraternity among comics heroes of the past nearly 40 years. A few of those mentioned deserve some comment.

Blackstone and Houdini, of course, were both magicians in real life, of the prestidigitational sort. Houdini specialized in amazing escapes and was thus in a sense the prototype of Jack Kirby's modern Mister Miracle. Blackstone went in more for the white-tie-and-tails illusionist approach; in his various comic-book incarnations he turned his powers to the entrapment of criminals, and gave a few magic pointers to his readers.

Mystic Moot was a somewhat remote parody of Ibis the Invincible, alongside whose adventures Moot's appeared. Moot was the creation of Basil Wolverton, one of the all-time masters of the grotesque and the comical; as Ibis derived his power from the magical Ibistick, Moot got his from his nose. His adventures were very funny, and usually confined to half a page.

Colonel Porterhouse was a comic-relief feature that appeared in Fawcett's *Whiz Comics,* and would be of little concern here except for a series of adventures early in the 1940s in which the Colonel was depicted, in each *Whiz Comics,* reading that same issue of *Whiz* to his little niece and nephew. In each issue, Porterhouse concentrated on a different story, and his pages were turned into a parody of that story—in one issue, Captain Marvel; in others, Spy Smasher, Lance O'Casey, Golden Arrow, and, of course, Ibis.

The Porterhouse parodies were very funny, possibly superior even to the Harvey Kurtzman-*Mad* parodies of a decade later. Perhaps with the thawing of the long-standing DC-Fawcett impasse, they could be revived and reprinted in collected form, or at least run as a reprint series in one of DCs magazines.

Dr. Occult and Dr. Mystic were very similar characters created by Jerry Siegel and Joe Shuster in the years before Superman finally emerged. Students of the history of comics heroes must regard the Occult-Mystic figure as a definite prototype of Superman, performing many of the feats Superman later performed, but doing so by supernatural rather than superscientific means.

Of all these magicians, by far the most significant two were Zatara the Master Magician and Ibis the Invincible.

Zatara appeared from the first issue of *Action Comics,* thereby setting the pattern of a magical feature in support of major superheroes. He was closely patterned on Mandrake, with traditional formal dress (he wore morning clothes and silk hat rather than tails), slicked-down hair, and crisp moustache.

For the giant Lothar, Zatara substituted an Asian giant, Tong. (Both Lothar and Tong also resemble Milton Caniff's Big Stoop and even Little Orphan Annie's companion Punjab, but that is of only passing concern.)

The early Zatara strips were drawn by Fred Guardineer, whose style was well suited to comic-book pages—he drew with a heavy, vigorous line and used large areas of solid color. The master of this principle, of course, was Clarence Beck, who drew Captain Marvel.

Zatara's power, according to the narration panels, lay in his eyes, and he was on occasion rendered *hors de combat* by being blindfolded. But when performing feats of magic, he spoke magic words—at first mere jumbled phrases, later the words of command with the sequence of their letters reversed. As—"SGUHT, PEEW YENOM!" Slow-witted readers, after a few issues, were advised by narration panels to read Zatara's words backwards for a surprise.

A few of Zatara's earlier adventures had some of the high-soaring imagination of Mandrake's. One example was "The Terror from Saturn" in *Action* No. 14, in which a flaming triangle appears on Earth bearing word of a possible interplanetary war with Saturn. Zatara, aided by the scientist Djersinsky, travels to the ringed planet where he encounters a race of bald, green-skinned humans whose Prince Porra might have served as the prototype for DCs later John Jones—J'onn J'onzz, Manhunter from Mars.

Zatara undergoes a few Mandrake-like adventures among the Saturnians, convinces them that they can solve their own problems on Saturn and need not invade Earth, and returns home.

A more typical adventure, however, was that of Zatara at the New York World's Fair, in *World's Fair Comics* for 1940, the predecessor of DCs *World's Finest Comics,* which exists to this day. In this adventure (not signed, and clearly not by Guardineer) a group of thugs invade the fairgrounds and Zatara hunts them down and rounds them up with bits of magic.

Many artists worked on Zatara; Joseph Sulman was one of the most prolific, and was rather good; even Joe Kubert got his artistic hands on the master magician at least once. The main obstacle in the strip was not the art, which was no worse than the comic-book norm, but the writing, which was unfortunately no better than the comic-book norm.

In common with many DC heroes of the 1940s, Zatara used a basically exotic identity-gimmick and power in very mundane situations. He would, in one story, go after bank robbers and turn their guns to flowers; in another he used a city-wide television hookup to command thugs to give themselves up to the police.

In a fairly amusing yarn in *Action* No. 31 he turned the leaders of two warring nations into manikins and forced them to a successful peace conference, having first used his powers to minimize casualties and aid escaping refugees; in another he used his magical powers to trick a potential rival into giving up a magic lantern, which Zatara then destroyed to preserve his own uniqueness.

In brief, where the greatest achievement of Falk and Davis in using Mandrake was not the conception of the character himself but the imagination with which he was carried into exotic adventures, the failure of Zatara lay in the lack of imagination applied to the plotting of *his* adventures.

Zatara disappeared along with so many others during the great character washout of the late 1950s and was presumed totally lost until his daughter (!) turned up in the late 1960s looking for her dad! The Zatara-Zatanna theme has been used several times in that series (of which more later) and, while Zatara has never been revived as an independent feature, it remains a possibility.

~ ~ ~ ~ ~

The second of the two significant *comic-book* magicians was Ibis the Invincible, who originated in the first issue of Fawcett's *Whiz Comics* in 1940 and was to Captain Marvel thereafter as Zatara was to Superman.

Ibis was not closely based on Mandrake or Zatara—the similarity was limited to the theme of utilizing magical powers as the basic characteristic of an adventure hero. The writing and drawing were the product of the usual anonymous Fawcett crew, generally farmed out to the Binder or Beck-Costanza studios; very likely the best single drawing of Ibis was the one by Mac Raboy for the first issue of the single-character *Ibis* comic launched in 1942. The cover, which is reproduced in *All in Color for a Dime,* shows Ibis using his magic wand, the Ibistick, to raise a figure of a woman or goddess clad in ancient dress from a cloud of green smoke that billows above a huge sorcerer's urn.

Ibis had a full-fledged origin story, a short version of which appeared in *Whiz,* a more complete version in that first issue of *Ibis.* In this tale Ibis, properly known as Amentep, had been a prince of Egypt some 4,000 years ago. An evil Pharaoh, misled by the false priest Mesu, abandoned Osiris and the benevolent gods of Egypt and made league with Set, the Master of Inferno, and a legion of demons.

The evil Pharaoh lusted for power, glory—and the resplendent one, the Princess Taia, betrothed of Amentep.

As the people were ground under Pharaoh's heel, Amentep spoke out, leading protests against tyranny. He was thrown in jail, and there received from his uncle the fabled wand of mystical power, the Ibistick. In rebellion against the tyrant, Taia fell, an arrow in her breast. Enraged, Ibis beheaded the tyrant and, in grief, commanded the stick to slay himself. It refused—it would do no harm to its rightful master.

So Ibis instead commanded it to make him sleep some 4,000 years. Revived in modern times, dressed in a dark business suit with only a red turban to distinguish him, Ibis found the mummy of Taia, used the Ibistick to revive her—she had been in suspended animation, not dead—and proceeded to a series of modern adventures.

These adventures ran for some 15 years. Many of them dealt with mystical topics—Ibis in combat with demons and dark gods of various sorts; when this was the case, the stories, however limited their logic might be, generally offered something interesting to the reader. When, as occasionally happened, Ibis fought ordinary criminals or spies, the strip tended to descend to the poor level of the weaker Zatara yarns.

If there is a lesson to be drawn from all this, it would seem to be that an exotic hero must have an exotic challenge to hold him up; plunged into a mundane setting and plot, as was so often done, the exotic hero merely looks silly.

All of the magicians I have mentioned so far were essentially mortal men gifted with certain supernormal powers. There was yet another class of magicians in the comics, heroes whose might so far exceeded that of a mere Mandrake, Zatara, or Ibis, that they truly transcended the category of "mere" magicians and became— something more. These were the mind-bogglers, the farthest-fetched heroes in all the history of the comics: Doctor Fate and the Spectre.

~ ~ ~ ~ ~

There are many comic-book heroes whom I remember more for their potential—alas, all too often never really tapped—than for the actual stories. Chief among these were Doctor Fate and the Spectre. Both had concepts that stretched the mind, but both had too many adventures that were, despite the supernatural elements shoveled into them, prosaic.

The Spectre could grow larger than the solar system or shrink smaller than an atom. He could fight a duel with comets as weapons (against a foe who could do the same!). He could ski on stars, raise the dead (with one exception), stop time, and talk with God.

The Spectre really was omnipotent. He could, quite literally, do *anything.*

It sounds like a good deal, I hear you cry. How does one qualify for this sort of superheroship?

Well, first you have to die. The Spectre really was a spectre—a ghost.

The Spectre was a creation of the fertile mind of Jerry Siegel—who had, with fellow Cleveland high schooler Joe Shuster, created Superman. Siegel's by-line appeared on every story in the Spectre's entire run in *More Fun Comics,* where he appeared in issues No. 53 through No. 101 (February, 1940, through January-February, 1945). Artist Bernard Baily drew the strip; he did Siegel one better by signing it both at the beginning and at the end of each story. Baily also drew the early adventures of Hourman.

Siegel may have felt that if Superman did so well with his powers, Spectre would do even better with more. It's sort of like, if a little bit of salt is good, a cupful will be great; the result is about the same.

For a while, it is fun to follow the adventures of a hero who can do anything, but after that it gets kind of boring. Spectre could do anything except create suspense, it seemed. Besides, he was pretty frightening in appearance and attitude.

The Spectre was the ghost of Jim Corrigan, a "hard-fisted" police detective who was beaten by crooks who had kidnaped his fiancée, Clarice Winston. The crooks dumped him into a barrel and encased his still living form in concrete, then chucked the whole thing into the river. You can't get much deader than that and it is not a pleasant route to take to get to be a superhero, no matter how powerful.

Jim Corrigan's spirit rose from the barrel and headed for Heaven, with only a momentary pang at leaving Earth and his fiancée. He was looking forward to eternal rest but a voice—obviously God's, although never explicitly stated to be His—told him that he could not have his eternal rest until he had wiped out all crime on Earth. *All* crime, mind you. A tall order, but he was promised special abilities.

He returned to the river where his body lay and discovered that he did not need to breathe, that he could walk on water, levitate, or disappear at will, grow or shrink to whatever size he wished, and walk through walls. Armed with these powers and many more he didn't yet know he had, he went to rescue Clarice from the hoods who had killed him.

This turned out to be a two-part origin story *(More Fun* No. 52 and No. 53) and that was where the first part ended. Although the Spectre appeared in full costume on the cover of No. 52, Corrigan never got to wear a costume until part two.

With a mere 52-word synopsis, the second part began exactly one panel later. The last panel of the first installment showed Corrigan walking into the wall of a warehouse; the first panel of the second showed him emerging, halfway through the wall, in the room where "Gat" Benson's gangsters were menacing Clarice.

The hoods never had a chance. Their bullets either bounced off Corrigan or passed through him harmlessly, depending on his whim. One by one, he called the thugs to him and had them look into his eyes, where they saw either Death incarnate or the very pits of Hell. They died or went mad at once. One wild shot had struck Clarice and he touched the wound; it closed and healed and vanished. She remembered none of this.

Corrigan figured that life as the wife of a ghost was no life for the woman he loved, so he broke his engagement with no explanation to her. Clarice refused to accept that and the series continued with the stock comic-book situation of the heroine chasing the reluctant hero with marriage as her object. But there were some differences from other strips using this device. For one thing, Corrigan was more than willing to marry her but felt that his lack of mortality (not necessarily immortality; with his powers, it is conceivable that he *could* have wiped out crime and got what was always referred to as his "eternal rest") prevented this; I'm not sure why. Also, Clarice was in love with Jim Corrigan, not with his alter ego—nobody but the most ardent necrophile could have loved the Grim Ghost, as he was called with the traditional comic-book love of alliteration.

For some reason, Corrigan made a costume for Spectre the hard way, sewing it laboriously by hand (a strange talent for a hard-fisted police detective) when he could have created it from moonbeams, spider webs, or cool night air with a perfunctory thought.

His lack of skill as a tailor may have accounted for the bagginess of his green shorts, which he wore over a skin so deathly white that it looked almost as if he were wearing snowy tights. Green gloves, cloak, and a floppy hood completed the costume. The face of the Spectre was the same deathly white, with dark, shadowed eyes (close-ups often showed the pupils to be tiny skulls) and a grim, tight-lipped mouth. He was quite imposing, more than a little frightening.

To assume his identity as the Spectre, Corrigan needed no convenient phone booth—though just how convenient *is* it to change clothes in a phone booth?—or facile alibi to explain his absence while the Spectre was in action. He could go about his business, talking, eating, fighting crime, while the Spectre, like a supernatural amoeba, split invisibly off from his body and took on a corporeal form of his own. The two halves of Corrigan's personality could exist simultaneously and independently, so no secret-identity problems ever arose. Eventually, when Corrigan's concrete-encrusted corpse was about to be discovered on the river bottom, Corrigan was restored to life absolutely independent of the Spectre, who kept right on fighting crime and the supernatural entities that began appearing right after he made the scene. I said earlier that there was one exception to Spectre's dead-raising abilities: I meant Jim Corrigan. God (the Voice) did that at the Spectre's request.

In a more or less typical story *(More Fun* No. 61), newspaper headlines praising the Spectre enrage the police chief, who orders Corrigan to arrest the Spectre. One of Center City's biggest promoters is just then threatened by the Spectre—actually a bogus Spectre—and is turned to gold in front of the chief and Corrigan. A witness who is about to name the culprit also is turned to gold. Corrigan is given a free sample of chewing gum by a feeble social outcast and, seeing a car following him, plays a hunch and turns himself to gold. Two men jump from the car, pick him up with astonishing ease, considering how much a gold six-footer would weigh, and toss him in the river. The Spectre emerges from the water and follows them, foiling another assassination attempt by turning the gum to worms.

When one of the hoods calls the boss to report the incident, the Spectre shrinks, enters the phone, and races through the wires—a trick revived in the sixties and given to the new version of the Atom—only to be frustrated when the boss breaks the connection.

Corrigan visits Clarice and meets Gustave Gilroy, who knows a scientist who is trying to change the atomic structure of objects. Spectre bombards the scientist with L-rays, which cleanse his mind of evil. The L-rays were a bunch of letter L's which came out of the Spectre's eyes. He then finds Clarice in the grip of the bogus Spectre, who has kidnaped her father. Just then, he is caught in the grip of an "occult occurrence" this happened in several stories, with no explanation and with varying results—which flings him an hour back in time as Jim Corrigan. Using the extra time, Corrigan arrests the real Spectre, turns him over to the police chief, escapes, and then goes back as Spectre to nail Gustave (now, oddly, called Gustaf) Gilroy, the man masquerading as the Spectre. Gilroy confesses and commits suicide by turning himself to gold.

Whew. All that and more in just one short story.

God was presented as somewhat sneaky. In one instance, just as Clarice is about to be killed, the Spectre is called away by God.

Clarice has a bullet heading toward her skull and God has chosen that time to decide that the Spectre is getting a raw deal and to offer him a choice of taking his eternal rest *right then* or of going back to wipe out all crime. Of course, should he decide to take up the harp, that will be the end of Clarice. (Presumably, Clarice has not led a blameless life, else he would be assured that she would join him in Heaven.) He chooses to return to earth to finish off crime and save Clarice.

The strip was weakened later by the introduction of Percival Popp the Super Cop, a supposedly funny, big-nosed, buck-toothed bumbler who rose from supporting character to star, with Spectre taking second billing. It was one heck of a long fall from what the Spectre could have been.

~ ~ ~ ~ ~

Doctor Fate also appeared in *More Fun Comics* (No. 55 through No. 98; May, 1940, through January, 1944). For the first dozen issues, he had no secret identity and his origin was unknown. This was most effective. Doctor Fate was always in costume and dwelled in a doorless and windowless tower in "witch-haunted Salem," surrounded by musty tomes, weapons, and devices both of advanced science and advanced necromancy. He exited his tower by walking through the walls or by using some arcane machine. He was a wizard of incredibly ancient origin and virtually unlimited powers; he certainly was not a stage magician who happened to possess some real magic. He had been a wizard back when the Druids were altar boys.

Dr. Fate wore blue tights with yellow boots, shorts, gloves, and cape. On his chest was a large golden medallion of unspecified purpose, strung on a cord about his neck. His head and face were covered by a completely smooth bullet-shaped golden helmet with only two eye-holes.

A girl named Inza, whose presence in his life was not explained, wandered at will about the world and called on Dr. Fate whenever she was in difficulty. She got in trouble often, usually as a result of some slumbering wizard's awakening or some bush-league Merlin stumbling across the Book of Thoth and becoming a major-league Merlin. Things like that happened all the time.

Dr. Fate had achieved complete control of energy, and blows or bullets directed at him were turned into power for him. He could emit rays of energy which were capable of knocking over buildings or thoroughly disposing of unsavory characters. He had a crystal ball and spells for all occasions at his command. He could fly, too.

Gardner Fox, who wrote the earliest stories, had obviously read a great deal of H. P. Lovecraft, although the strip was not directly derivative. The hints of elder gods and vanished civilizations, of wizardry that was actually a form of science far beyond what we have attained, and "witch-haunted Salem," which smacks unmistakably of Lovecraft's Arkham, all point to a familiarity with Lovecraft's writings. Most of the stories were illustrated by Howard Sherman. The unknown letterer made his mark on the strip, too; he made his E's with the center bar longer than the other two, making the dialog look as if it were filled with hyphens. It was different—hard to read, but different.

Dr. Fate whips Wotan (apparently unrelated to Norse mythology, Wotan had a green skin, a Mephistophelean face, and wore red tights with a high, stiff, flaring collar and a green floor-length cape) in his first appearance, in No. 55. In the next issue, he goes to the land of the dead to make sure Wotan is really there. He is not, so Dr. Fate returns to Earth and whips him again, leaving him in a magical trance, encased in an air bubble and hidden beneath the Earth. In a later story Wotan is freed, and this time Dr. Fate kills him.

Doctor Fate took the cover and lead spot in *More Fun* away from the Spectre and he deserved to. His stories had much more of an air of mystery, helped largely by the fact that no one really knew much about Dr. Fate.

Then, in issue No. 67, they went and spoiled it by giving him an origin story which threw out the ancient wizard bit entirely. In the origin, he is young Kent Nelson, exploring in the Valley of Ur "in the year 1920 or thereabouts" with his father, Egyptologist Sven Nelson. Sven thinks the pyramids had been built by people from another planet; he doesn't think the Egyptians knew enough to do the job. Kent finds a man standing in an open casket and, following telepathic directions, turns a lever and frees him from suspended animation. The man is Nabu the Wise, who is close to half a million years old and from the planet Cilia. His people built the pyramids; unfortunately, Sven never learns his theory was right because he dies of poison gas prepared by Nabu's people to prevent intrusions. Nabu attempts to make up for this by teaching Kent the secrets of the universe. He then gives young Kent the costume and name of Doctor Fate and disappears without a word of explanation. Since these stories appeared in the early 1940s, Doctor Fate had suddenly gone from being millennia old to being barely 20. The Lovecraftian aura was shed with the years.

The beautifully mysterious face-covering was sawed off just below the eyes, revealing the Doctor's nose and mouth and concealing only his hair, forehead, and the area around his eyes. His powers were sawed off, too; starting with the idea that he was only invulnerable from outside harm and that his lungs were vulnerable to lack of air, they developed the idea from simply making him susceptible to gassing or drowning to the point where he could be rendered unconscious by strangling him or by hitting him in the solar plexus to knock the air out of him.

Then they decided to make him a real doctor, an M.D.—he got through medical school and became an intern in just half a page—and he spent the bulk of the rest of his career chasing petty crooks.

Both the Spectre and Doctor Fate have been revived from time to time by DC. The Spectre had his own book briefly in the sixties and Doctor Fate has made several guest appearances in *Justice League of America* and *World's Finest Comics.* The revivals stick to the original powers and costumes but really don't offer much else.

Some magicians also made an appearance in the superhero revival of the 1960s. The best of these was Doctor Strange, who began in Marvel Comics' *Strange Tales* and has appeared in his own book and as a frequent guest in other Marvel comics. Originally drawn by Steve Ditko and written by Stan Lee, he has undergone many changes of writer and artist without losing any of his extravagant speech patterns or much of his flamboyant costume. Strange (who actually is a physician-type doctor, according to yet another of those belated origin stories that come along by afterthought) lives in Greenwich Village and has an Oriental servant named Wong and an Oriental teacher known as the Ancient One.

Strange has black hair, white at the temples, and the moustache that few who weren't magicians could wear in the comic books without being either a villain or the girl friend's father. He wears a loose blue suit and a voluminous cape with a stiff, flaring collar of red and yellow; he wears a magic yellow amulet on his chest, an amulet that occasionally opens as an eye (the all-seeing Eye of Agamoto) and blasts Dr. Strange's opponents. For a while, he wore an all-over skintight black suit which covered even his face, but that was dropped. He tended to be colorful, but it was hard to follow his stories and even harder to worry about him, since the magic was of such an anything-can-happen variety: Dr. Strange could be thoroughly beaten at the end of one book and remember another, winning, spell at the beginning of the next. The stories were good, though, and the artwork was often excellent, even after the enormously talented Ditko left Marvel.

The now-defunct American Comics Group (ACG) created a horrendous flop in the magician category with Magicman. He was a soldier in Vietnam who turned out to be a descendant of Cagliostro and had magical abilities. He outfitted himself out of a costume trunk and looked as if he was on the way to the Artists and Models Ball. He wore a vaguely Arabian Nights costume with a fruity little string mask and made his magical gestures with limp wrists. Worse, he had a dumb and sadistic sergeant for comic relief and they hung around together even after they got out of the service. Fortunately, the strip did not last long. He appeared in *Forbidden Worlds* No. 125 to No. 141.

As noted, DC revived the Spectre in the 1960s. He had some tryout appearances in *Showcase,* a comic book where new comics were tested, then ran briefly in his own book. He had a few good stories, but he didn't seem to have his old verve; maybe the fact that his stories were censored by the Comics Code Authority contributed to his early demise.

DC also brought back Sargon the Sorcerer, a minor magician who had the power of controlling anything he had ever touched— as with most superhero limitations, this was badly abused by lazy writers who decided that, since he had touched the air, he could make the air do anything he wanted and he could beat up crooks with hardened air. When DC brought him back, it was as a villain in *Flash Comics.* Eventually, however, he reformed and helped the Justice League of America and became a good guy again.

The best and longest-lasting of DCs new versions of old magicians was Zatanna, a hitherto-unmentioned daughter of Zatara. Zatara had last appeared in *World's Finest* in 1951; in 1964, his daughter appeared on the scene, looking for her widower father. As far as we comic-book readers knew, Zatara was wifeless and childless in 1951, but Zatanna was obviously mature, certainly more than 12 or 13 years old.

She sought her father through a series of comic books, seeking the help of different DC heroes. She first appeared in *Hawkman* No. 4 (October-November, 1964) as "The Girl Who Split in Two!" The story was written, as were the rest of the stories in the series, by Gardner F. Fox, who had created Doctor Fate. Editor of all the books in which Zatanna appeared was Julius Schwartz. While searching for the source of certain art objects that had mysteriously appeared in the museum, Hawkman found in China a gibberish-speaking statue of a girl. Hawkgirl found another statue of the same girl, also speaking gibberish, in Ireland. When the two statues were brought together and merged, the result was the living Zatanna and the gibberish was revealed as two halves of the same words. She had split herself in two to try to simultaneously look for her father in two different places, but the result was immobility and incoherence. She had magically placed the art objects in the museum with what remained of her powers in order to attract Hawkman and Hawkgirl. Freed now, she said the words "ANNA-TAZ RAEPPASID"—using the same magical method as her father—and continued her quest.

Her costume was reminiscent of her father's but with considerable difference. Both wore top hats and morning coats but, where Dad wore gray trousers, Zatanna wore gray hotpants and mesh stockings. She also wore high heels and had a definitely feminine appearance. She sought her father in *The Atom* No. 19 (June-July, 1965), where "the world's smallest super-hero" helped her track down a wizard called the Druid in an atom world; in *Green Lantern* No. 42 (January, 1966), where "the emerald gladiator" helped her battle the Warlock in another dimension; and in *Detective* No. 355 (September, 1966), where she bypassed Batman ("the caped crusader") to seek Elongated Man's help and "the stretchable sleuth" helped her recover a copy of the magic book of *I Ching*—don't ask me why she didn't just pick up one of the many paperback reprints of the book. Each time, she got a little closer to finding Zatara.

The series concluded in *Justice League of America* No. 51 (February, 1967), where all those heroes plus Batman helped Zatanna rescue her father from a magical world.

Zatara was kind of forgotten after that, but Zatanna has appeared frequently in *Justice League of America* and in her own series in *Adventure* and *Supergirl.*

She appears to be more popular than her father and it really isn't surprising; he may be a more powerful magician, but she has really great looks and attracts adolescent males of all ages—with the most powerful magic of all.

THE BIG RED CHEESE

ONE BALMY WINTER'S day nearly 30 years ago, in the sunbaked village of Venice, Florida, two small boys dressed in tee shirts, short pants, and sneakers wandered into the town drug store. In addition to being Venice's sole pharmacy, the store was the town's main source of beach goods, the local ice cream parlor and short order lunch counter, and the only newsstand this side of distant, metropolitan Sarasota.

The taller of the two children looked to be seven or eight years of age: chubby, jolly, extroverted. The smaller boy was his brother, younger by three years. In general he resembled the older boy, but evidenced a more contemplative and introspective nature. Despite being the younger of the pair, he would more likely remember such a day.

The treasury of the two boys comprised exactly twenty cents, entrusted to the more experienced judgment of the older child. It was entrusted wisely. The boy used the coins to purchase a chocolate ice cream cone for himself, a strawberry cone for his brother, and, to be shared by the two children, a copy of the first fat issue of *Whiz Comics.*

The littler boy quickly and sloppily dispatched his strawberry ice cream, gave away the dry biscuity cone, and turned his attention to the colorful world of *Whiz Comics,* where that day he made the acquaintance of a friend and adventuring companion for years to come, whose eventual disappearance from the colored pages of comics was a real loss to many besides that one child. I refer, of course, to the greatest of all comic book heroes, Captain Marvel.

As for remembering that day, the younger boy does—vividly: the sights and odors of that bright day near the Gulf of Mexico, the palmettoes and the scrubby grass that eked uncertain existence from the rocky, sandy Florida soil, the texture and taste of that pink ice cream with its red embedded bits of berry. That ten-cent book of wonders starting with the original story of Captain Marvel. Mostly, I remember Captain Marvel.

His career started with Billy Batson, a poverty-stricken orphan newsboy, hawking his papers on a night-dark street outside a subway kiosk. A dark and mysterious figure beckons to Billy, then disappears into the underground. Billy follows, only to find himself ominously alone in an apparently abandoned subway tunnel.

The tunnel opens eventually into a huge vault; lining the wall of the chamber Billy saw seven gigantic, evil-looking statues representing the traditional seven deadly sins. Passing beyond the shadowy effigies Billy came to an even larger chamber in which stood a great throne carved from a monolithic block of stone. Above it, suspended by the merest thread, hung a huge square-cut block of the same material. Beneath the murderous weight, seated on the throne, was a tall, thin man clad in a simple, floor-length robe. His hair and his long beard were of purest white.

Billy stood awed before the ancient one. The seated figure spoke, and, although the comics were a printed medium, I could hear his voice, cracking and aged but yet carrying the authority of the mighty and the righteous. (For how many years was that printed visage my personal vision of God?) "Billy Batson! I am Shazam, an ancient Egyptian wizard. I have fought evil, but my time is up! You shall succeed me!"

"Mine, sir?" was all that Billy could stammer.

"Yes. You are pure of heart. You have been chosen. Speak my name!"

The boy shouted "Shazam!" A mighty bolt of lightning and a deafening bass peal of thunder filled the chamber. The frightened child was gone. In his place stool a veritable giant of a man. Clad in a tight-fitting red costume and white cape, the symbol of the lightning that heralded him blazoned upon his chest, the world's mightiest mortal, Captain Marvel, had been born.

He was a huge, massively built figure, covered with bulging muscles. He had thick black hair, heavy eyebrows, a powerful mouth above a broad, cleft chin. A golden sash encircled his waist and his boots were of the same hue. Sleeve trimmings reminiscent of those worn by naval officers decorated his cuffs, and gold workings like those of a naval officer's cape rimmed his own.

No sooner had the heroic figure appeared than a final strand supporting the stone gave way. It crashed to the throne, filling the space between the graven arms. Of Shazam there was nothing left. In a moment a cloud arose, assuming the shape of the dead ancient, risen from his own dust.

"Shazam!" shouted Captain Marvel. Instead of Billy Batson's boyish falsetto it was an heroic voice that pronounced the name of the wizard. Again the thunder and lightning, and in an instant Captain Marvel had disappeared to the limbo from which he had been called, replaced once more by the child, Billy Batson.

"Go now," solemnly intoned the shade of the wizard. "Fight the forces of evil. When you have need of the powers at my command, you need only speak my name, and you shall be transformed into Captain Marvel, possessor of all the powers of the six gods whose initials form my name: the wisdom of Solomon, the strength of Hercules, the stamina of Atlas, the power of Zeus, the courage of Achilles, the speed of Mercury."

With this speech even the shade of the wizard faded from mortal view. Old Shazam's bland mixing of gods, heroes, and a biblical king did not bother a small reader on the Gulf Coast of Florida. Nor did Billy Batson note the anomaly as he slowly retraced his path to the street.

Back on the sidewalk Billy himself thought that he might have been having a dream, so strange and thrilling had been his experiences of the night. The stranger who had gestured mysteriously, the hall of the seven statues, the wizard and his words of power . . . .

But the first time he was faced with the need of Captain Marvel (it involved mere mundane crime, with little to hint at the odd and exotic cases to follow), Billy tested the promise of Shazam and found it a truthful one.

Shortly Billy won employment as boy newscaster for radio station WHIZ. His association there with Sterling Morris continued throughout the published career of Captain Marvel, even into the early days of commercial television in the 1950s. Also for that entire period Billy wore a yellow-collared red shirt and blue slacks. Billy lived in a comfortable apartment, alone save for his Negro valet, Steamboat Willie.

Steamboat Willie was the exemplification of the racial stereotype of the era, as popularized in innumerable pulp magazine stories, radio dramas, motion pictures (perhaps there most of all), and other popular media. He had huge fat lips and gigantic popping eyes, dressed flashily, spoke a peculiar illiterate jargon, served faithfully and humbly except when terrified (which he usually was) of menace human or supernatural, and of course he was thoroughly drenched in superstition. Although obviously a grown man in the employ of a half-grown boy. Willies always addressed his employer as "Mist' Billy."

Trying to evaluate the stereotypes of that era, the modern critic is left near to speechless puzzlement. The comic black of the popular arts is of course only the most obvious and extreme case, but few, if any, identifiable groups escaped the establishment of a demeaning "type." There were the standardized caricatured Jew, Irishman, Italian, Indian, Russian, Chinese, Spaniard, Mexican, Swede, and so on through every conceivable national, racial, and religious grouping.

The strange aspect of the matter is that the writers (and artists and actors) who created and perpetuated such types were seldom, if ever, vicious in their intentions. The portrayal of Steamboat Willie was essentially a friendly and sympathetic one! It was simply assumed, as a pre-condition to the writing and the drawing of the character, that this was the way black people looked and spoke and behaved: As if there were a Platonic ideal Negro, of whom all Negroes were more or less faithful reflections.

There were of course other characters who appeared early in the saga of Captain Marvel, and who won enduring roles in the series. Among the most vivid were the villains, two of whom stand above all the rest: Dr. Sivana and Mr. Mind. And, once the popularity of Captain Marvel had been established, Fawcett Publications saw to it that the popular feature spun off a number of variants of itself, designed to exploit a market of almost unbelievable size.

That first Captain Marvel story in *Whiz Comics* started a series of well over 1,000 stories featuring either Captain Marvel himself or other members of the Marvel Family. *Whiz Comics* itself was a kind of variety book, featuring a cast of running heroes who appeared in one adventure apiece in each issue. In addition to Captain Marvel the lineup included Spy Smasher, a costumed adventurer whose exploits concerned—right—smashing spies; Lance O'Casey, a freelance sailor who plied the South Seas in search of danger and romance; Golden Arrow ("the Robin Hood of the West"); and Ibis the Invincible, an Egyptian prince revived in modern times to do battle with the aid of occult powers.

There was also *Colonel Porterhouse,* an amusing feature about an elderly windbag who amused a pair of children by reading them *Whiz Comics* each month and projecting himself into the role of a selected hero for a lampoon of that hero's current adventure. The Colonel Porterhouse technique was revived with fantastic success by Harvey Kurtzman in *Mad* over a decade later, and in recent years has been revived again in such comics as *Not Brand Echh* and *Inferior Five.*

With *Whiz* selling briskly, Fawcett added a companion devoted entirely to the exploits of their big hero: *Captain Marvel Adven-*

tures. Later there was a *Marvel Family Comics* featuring Captain
Marvel, Captain Marvel, Jr., and Mary Marvel. There were various
lesser Fawcett periodicals featuring the red-suited hero, and two
attempts to promote him in text form. One was the *Captain Marvel
Story Book,* a shotgun marriage of the comic book and pulp magazine featuring alternate pages of text and illustration.

The other (which appeared in 1941—*very* early in the Marvel
cycle), was *Captain Marvel and the Return of the Scorpion.* As for
where the Scorpion was returning from, that's another matter, as
we shall see later. But this publication was a Dime Action Book,
one of four issued by Fawcett as their own entry in the Big Little
Book sweepstakes.

Resembling the more famous Whitman series, the Dime Action
Hooks were approximately four by five inches in dimension, containing 192 pages of alternating picture and text.

There were only four—devoted to Captain Marvel, Spy Smasher, and two other Fawcett heroes, Bulletman and Minute Man. Despite their crude artwork and not very polished writing, these four
little books are among the scarcest of collectors' treasures today.
An example from *Captain Marvel and the Return of the Scorpion*
by Otto O. Binder:

> "Oh, a wise guy!" rasped one bruiser, built like a gorilla. Not
> quite realizing just whom he was facing, he leaped forward and
> swung at the crimson figure a haymaker that might have broken
> the neck of an ordinary man. The blow landed solidly on Cap-
> tain Marvel's chin. Its only effect was to make the thug yell in
> pain as his knucklebones were crushed.
>
> "Tit for tat," murmured Captain Marvel and, smiling pleas-
> antly, he shot his fist out at the thug's chin like a steam-driven
> piston. The thug sailed backwards through the air, landed
> among his henchmen, and piled them all upon the pavement.

The *Captain Marvel Story Book* came later by some years, and
was not restricted to such simple writing. Its format, providing
full-page presentation of Beck's drawings (occasionally even a
two-page spread), gave Beck an opportunity to shine, and many of
the illustrations are among the most memorable of the whole Captain Marvel art canon. A sample of the text from a 1949 *Story
Book* titled *Captain Marvel and the Gargoyle Men:*

Captain Marvel was left to his thoughts. But his thoughts refused to mesh. Intruding upon them was the image of a beautiful woman, a woman such as he had never seen before. Captain Marvel shook his head. He tried to think of his friends, but the image of the woman persisted in superimposing itself upon his thoughts. He even thought of Sivana, but even the unforgettable face of that old villain faded into the beauty of this strange new woman. Abruptly Captain Marvel leaped to his feet.

"I'm going back to see what the gargoyle men are doing," he told Dr. Cuchin. "You'll be safe here until I get back."

With that he sprang into the air and vanished into the distance.

In the publishing industry, ever since the early 1960s, there has been a boom in the publication of heroic adventures. Many of the older heroes have been revived and new ones have been added. A glance at the paperback section of a large bookstore reveals a whole lineup of flamboyant adventurers in and out of fancy dress: Captain Future, Starwolf, Tarzan and many other of Edgar Rice Burroughs' heroes, Conan, the Phantom Detective, Secret Agent X, Dusty Ayres, the Avengers (I refer to the comic characters, but the British television stars are there too), Captain America, Brak the Barbarian, Doc Savage, the Shadow, and so on.

A paperback edition of one or several of the *Captain Marvel Story Books* would not be out of place. Certainly the writing is at least equal to the pulp level of many of the reprints and the newly written books, and the appeal of the character is great. But it has not happened and is not likely to, for reasons we shall shortly see.

Another feature familiar to the readers of *Captain Marvel Adventures* was *Lieutenant Jon Jarl of the Space Patrol.* Almost all comics in the 1940s and early 1950s ran two-page short stories in solid text format. Not that the publishers particularly wanted to, and most of the readers generally skipped over them in reading the pictorial stories, but concern over postal and copyright regulations caused the inclusion of these pieces. (More recently they have been abandoned in favor of letter columns and "news" pages—actually promotional material for the publishers' own products.)

In *Captain Marvel Adventures* a series of these two-page stories was devoted to Binder's creation, Lieutenant Jarl. They were frequently charming little pieces, usually with a clever twist to them, and I suspect that the copyright to them might be cleared, and that they would make a most unusual paperback original.

There were about 84 of them. Here's one small quotation from *The World Stealers* (1947):

> It was a giant space ship, over a mile long! And from its stern came out a long beam of some amazing radiation that seemed to be *towing* Earth along, like a barge behind a tug.
> Jon radioed Headquarters. "Attention! Huge space tug pulling Earth out of its orbit."
> The answer came back in a bellow. "Don't you think we know it? Good lord, the whole universe is changing around us as we leave Earth's orbit around the Sun. Stop that ship, Lieutenant! We can't get a cruiser there for hours. Stop that ship!"
> "And this," groaned Jon, "is my vacation!"

For little *little* children there was even a funny animal version of Captain Marvel, *Hoppy the Marvel Bunny*, complete with the magical word of Shazam, lightning transformation, red suit, and super powers. Hoppy appeared in Fawcett's *Funny Animals* and in a periodical of his own.

As I have stated elsewhere, it is unfortunate that comic books seldom carried complete and accurate credits in that golden era. Certainly it would be fascinating to know exactly *who* did *what* in the founding days of the Fawcett comics dynasty, but only a tentative picture can be sketched from fragmentary records and memories of events nearly 30 years old.

It does seem fairly certain that Captain Marvel was the brain child of Bill Parker (writer) and C. C. Beck (artist). Parker was a Fawcett wheel horse who had been drafted from the company's magazine department to help launch the comic line. He found the illustrated adventure strip an uncongenial art form and succeeded, once the Fawcett line of comics was successfully launched, in having himself returned to his former area of work. He devoted himself to such periodicals as *Mechanix Illustrated* until his death some 20 years later.

Beck, on the other hand, found the comics very much to his liking, and remained the chief artist of the Fawcett comics line from the founding days in 1940 until the end of the line in 1953, when he moved to Florida and went into commercial art.

Parker and Beck devised their hero as Captain Thunder and planned to feature him in the projected *Thunder Comics*. Except for the names, "Thunder" was very much "Marvel" and *Thunder*

Comics was equally *Whiz Comics.* A first issue of *Thunder Comics* featuring Captain Thunder was prepared as a kind of trial run, but never went beyond the Fawcett offices. (A collector who could produce a copy of *Thunder Comics* today would have a treasure beyond compare. A copy was offered in 1963, but after its purchase had been arranged and payment made, the sale was cancelled on the grounds that the magazine had been ruined by water damage. Whether the item ever existed at all, outside the seller's imagination, is unknown.)

Between that practice run on *Thunder Comics* and the issuance of the first *published* issue, the transformation of titles took place. As a result, the *first* issue of *Whiz Comics* was called Number Two. One more woe for collectors and bibliographers.

In addition to Bill Parker and C. C. Beck, quite a few other men played a part in the early days of Fawcett's comics venture. Ralph Daigh was editorial director for the entire Fawcett operation, and Al Allard was art director. Ed Herron served as comics editor until he was drafted in 1943, and later contributed many fine scripts. His successor was Rod Reed. But for most of Fawcett's greatest years, their top comics carried the names of Will Lieberson as executive editor and Wendell Crowley as editor.

The team of Joe Simon and Jack Kirby was called in to launch *Captain Marvel Adventures.* The ground was prepared by a one-shot called *Captain Marvel Thrill Book,* an oversize comic printed in black-and-white (but with full color covers). Then came *Special Edition Comics,* a standard sized comic in full color, devoted entirely to Captain Marvel and his exploits. Finally, *Captain Marvel Adventures* was launched.

Simon and Kirby didn't stay around the Fawcett establishment very long, however, but went on to a seemingly endless stream of comics done separately and in collaboration. Both are still active in the comics industry, sporting a credits list that staggers the imagination. Most enthusiasts would agree, I am sure, that their greatest success was scored with Captain America.

After Bill Parker went back to the model airplanes and the hotrod how-to-do-it set, Otto O. Binder entered the picture as the lead writer for Captain Marvel. Binder was one of three brothers who had already made their mark on the pulp magazine industry. Jack Binder (it's pronounced with a short *i,* by the way) was a pulp illustrator who later did considerable drawing for the comics, including Fawcett's comics.

Earl and Otto Binder were writers, beginning their career under the joint pseudonym of Eando (E-and-O) Binder in 1932. Earl shortly left the team, but Otto kept the established by-line as his own, and turned out well over 100 pulp adventures, ranging from short stories to novels, in the years that followed. Some of Binder's most popular stories were series: the Adam Link stories about a sentient robot, the Anton York series about an immortal scientist, and the "via etherline" series tracing the exploration of the solar system.

Binder appeared in *Amazing Stories, Astounding Stories, Wonder Stories, Fantastic Adventures, Weird Tales, Comet, Dynamic Stories,* and so on. Before coming to Fawcett he worked on a number of smaller features for lesser comics publishers. He was brought to Fawcett by the original comics editor, Ed Herron. Binder broke in on some of the secondary Fawcett heroes, then took Captain Marvel in hand and shepherded him for all of the Captain's remaining days.

The popularity of Captain Marvel skyrocketed so spectacularly that Fawcett soon advanced *Captain Marvel Adventures* to a schedule of one issue every three weeks. It fell back to monthly but after World War II it advanced to publication every two weeks, at the peak of the magazine's success.

Peak circulation was well over 2,000,000 copies per issue—a figure never reached by any other comic before or since. In those years before postal regulations required circulation disclosures, publishers were skittish about revealing their sales, but Captain Marvel's chief rival, Superman, is believed to have peaked at 1,600,000 copies. An enviable figure itself, but no match for Fawcett's champion.

Fawcett remained in the superhero business until 1953, although during the last few years the road became increasingly rocky. After some early experiments in which page size went as large as a tabloid newspaper or as small as a Dime Action Book, and prices ranged from five cents for standard-size comics of 32 pages plus covers up through fifteen cents for the jumbo-sized comics, the Fawcett line, like the rest of the industry, settled on a standard 64-page saddle-stapled product selling for a dime.

A combination of paper shortages—and later, a profit squeeze—forced the reduction of the standard comic, first to 48 pages, then to 32. Costs were rising but the standard price seemed immovable. Simultaneously, the popularity of the costumed adventure hero was waning. By the 1950s Fawcett was flailing about trying to find a new winning formula in the western, sports, horror, adolescent humor, and other fields, but none recaptured the great appeal of the once mighty flying men and women.

There was, of course, one other factor in Fawcett's eventual abandonment of its comics line, which has led to endless discussion and a great deal of misunderstanding. This was the famous lawsuit between National Periodical Publications and Fawcett Publications. It might also be known as Superman versus Captain Marvel.

There is a great deal of argument about who was really the first great adventure hero, or superhero, or costumed hero—who set the style for the hundreds and thousands who have followed. A case can be made for such pulp magazine adventurers as Doc Savage or the Shadow, or for Baroness Orczy's Scarlet Pimpernel, or Cooper's Deerslayer. Those who would stick to panel art cite the Phantom, or even Popeye the Sailor. Classicists may cite Ulysses or Jason, Samson, David, or Gilgamesh.

But there is no denying that Siegel and Shuster's Superman set the style for comic book heroes by combining the vividly colored tights and dual identity of the Phantom with the super powers possessed by heroes of earlier media.

And once Superman's success had been established, the presence of so powerful a rival as Captain Marvel proved intolerable to the holders of the Superman copyright. National instituted a lawsuit against Fawcett charging that Captain Marvel infringed upon the copyright of Superman, and seeking to obtain an order that Fawcett discontinue Captain Marvel and pay damages to National.

On the face of it, National had considerable merit in their case. The similarities of Captain Marvel to Superman were substantial. The powers of the two heroes were similar: great strength, invulnerability lo most forms of peril, incredible speed, an ability to leap great distances that quickly turned into the power of outright flight. Certainly the physical appearances of the two were much alike: tall, muscular men with dark hair wearing tight-fitting brightly colored costumes, blazoned with emblems upon the chest, and with a cape and boots. Captain Marvel's costume was red while Superman's was blue, and the golden lightning upon the chest replaced Superman's large monogram; these were small differences.

In both cases the hero possessed a mufti-clad alter ego employed in the news media. Superman's Clark Kent worked as a
reporter under editor Perry White of the *Daily Planet*. Captain
Marvel's Billy Batson advanced in his first adventure from newsboy to boy radio newscaster working for Sterling Morris of station
WHIZ.

Even the arch-villains of the two strips were very much alike.
Superman dealt with Ultro, a bullet-headed, mad scientist. (Ultro
later gave way to the not-very-different evil genius, Luthor.) Captain Marvel tangled with Thaddeus Bodog Sivana who was billed
as the world's maddest scientist (in contrast to the world's mightiest mortal), but who preferred the self-bestowed title of Rightful
Ruler of the Universe. And of course Sivana sported a scalp just as
bald as Ultro's.

The talents behind both strips emerged from the world of science fiction. Otto Binder's background I have already sketched.
Jerry Siegel and Joe Shuster were teenage science fiction fans
when Eando Binder was first a familiar by-line in the pages of
Amazing Stories and other pulps. From their homes in Cleveland,
Siegel and Shuster began publishing a mimeographed science-
fiction fan magazine called simply *Science Fiction,* in 1932. By
the third issue (January 1933) they featured a story called "The
Reign of the Superman" by the pseudonymous Herbert S. Fine—
Siegel—and drawn by Shuster. Here is a brief excerpt:

A grin of superiority crossed the Superman's face.

"I can do four things that no one else of the planet can emu-
late. They are: intercept interplanetary messages, read the mind
of anyone I desire, by sheer mental concentration force ideas
into people's heads, and throw my vision to any spot in the
universe.

"Furthermore," he added, "during the night my mind has as-
similated all the knowledge that exists in the universe . . . I am
a veritable God!"

Aside from this early stirring of Superman, the issue contains at
least two other portents of things to come. One is a letter from Julius Schwartz, then a science fiction fan, later a highly successful
comic book writer and editor in the National stable. The other is a
mention of *Interplanetary Police,* a projected newspaper strip by
Siegel and Shuster. Somehow the project failed, but very shortly

they were on their way with transitional heroes called Dr. Occult and Dr. Mystic, and finally, Superman.

But whatever the background of the two great heroes, and whatever derivation of the one might be traced to the other, there was little or no imitation as the years passed—at least, on the part of the Fawcett crew. Many men contributed scripts to the Marvel saga, including Bill Finger (who pioneered the Green Lantern series for National), Carl Formes (who did many stories for Fawcett), and Bill Woolfolk (better known today for his bestselling novels). Still, Otto Binder was the top Fawcett scripter, turning out some 529 Captain Marvel stories alone—more than all other writers combined.

And Binder points out that he and the other Fawcett regulars, at management direction, studiously *avoided* even looking at National's comics for fear of even unconscious plagiarism!

What final disposition would have been made of the National-Fawcett lawsuit had it reached a final judgment will never be known. As it was the suit dragged on for years, with legendary proceedings in which National's lawyer, Louis Nizer, presented Superman-Captain Marvel scrapbooks as evidence. In response to which Fawcett's lawyers presented similar scrapbooks to show that whatever Superman had done before Captain Marvel, Popeye had done before Superman.

Certainly one by-product of the suit was a reluctance on the part of merchandisers to take on Captain Marvel novelties for fear of being caught in the maelstrom. As a result, Fawcett found itself in the novelty business, merchandising Captain Marvel statuettes, stationery, tie-clips, hats, and other products.

What prevented the suits ever reaching a definitive judgment was Fawcett's decision in 1953 to abandon its foundering comic book line and concentrate its resources on the far more lucrative areas of its business—areas such as paperback book publishing, how-to-do-it books that had spun off from the successful *Mechanix Illustrated* magazine, and other periodicals such as *True* magazine.

Fawcett settled out of court with National, agreeing to suppress and never revive Captain Marvel and the rest of the Marvel Family, and selling off or abandoning the rest of their features. *Ibis the Invincible* and a few others were taken over by Charlton Publications, but in time they disappeared entirely. At least one Fawcett title, *Hopalong Cassidy,* was taken over by National, but it too disappeared eventually.

And so what was unquestionably the greatest battle ever to take place in the comic books ended not in a landmark decision, but in a quiet, out-of-court settlement!

But to get back to the 1940s, it became unpleasantly clear that the *Superman* feature, after a brilliant initiation and immense commercial success, quickly lost the imaginative spark that had at first been present. Siegel and Shuster discovered to their dismay that they had lost legal title to their creation to the publisher, and the writing and artwork were taken over by a series of hired men doing the bidding of a commercial publisher. A rereading of those Superman stories reveals a kind of literal-minded, almost mechanically grim outlook. The stories might have been written by a machine.

But *Captain Marvel* seldom ceased to be interesting and imaginative, with real suspense, clever gimmicks, legitimate plots, and a delightful air of almost whimsical fantasy to the stories. Perhaps the reason behind this is something that Crowley, Lieberson, and Binder realized, something about supermen (with a lower-case *s)* that too few writers ever grasp.

Whether the writer is a pulp novelist like E. E. Smith chronicling the adventures of a Richard Seaton or a Kimball Kinnison, or "Kenneth Robeson" creating a Doc Savage, or a comic book scripter pitting some tights-clad super-adventurer against an arch-criminal or mad scientist, there can be no real suspense in the story of a superhero combatting a merely ordinary villain.

One way out of this dilemma is to face the superhero with a supervillain, thus restoring a balance of opposing forces in the story. The temptation then is to make the hero maybe a little bit *more* super than the villain, shortly requiring the ante to be upped again, and again, until a totally incredible battle of the gods results. (For samples of this phenomenon, see some of the adventures of a comics hero called the Spectre.)

An alternate maneuver is somehow to un-super the superhero. I can recall, for example, one incident from those bygone days, when Superman developed amnesia, thereby losing knowledge (and effective use) of his super powers. That incident took place in the radio series. And along the way Superman, of course, acquired an immense slew of super-companions, both villainous and heroic. And, of course, the theme of Kryptonite, that mysterious mineral which, in its varied forms, has such strange and powerful influences upon Superman, has been developed *ad absurdum.*

But I'm writing about Captain Marvel, am I not?

Captain Marvel faced an impressive collection of foes, the two most prominent being Dr. Sivana, whom I mentioned earlier, and Mr. Mind, a mystery villain whose true identity was not revealed until well into the lengthy serial adventure which covered his entire career.

Sivana's origins were somewhat obscure. He seemingly held royal status among the residents of the planet Venus, who were portrayed in the traditional pulp-magazine form of frog-like amphibians. Sivana, however, was wholly human, albeit scrawny, bald, snaggle-toothed, and myopic. In the early days of the series he was portrayed as having two offspring, although a Mrs. Sivana was nowhere in evidence.

In the original Sivana family constellation the son was a tall, muscular, god-like, blond young man named Magnificus. He appeared only briefly, and only in the Venusian sequences of the feature.

Beautia Sivana ("byoo-tee-a," not "byoo-shuh," according to Otto Binder) played a large and quite intriguing role. She accompanied her father to Earth and appeared in many of the Marvel stories of the 1940s. She too was tall, extremely well formed, and blessed with lush, wavy blond hair. Unlike her villainous father, who was the sworn enemy of Captain Marvel, and who provided Marvel with his most popular epithet, "that big red cheese," Beautia had distinctly ambivalent feelings.

She was a loyal daughter, and as dutiful as she could be. Further, at least at the outset, she shared her father's ambitions for universal empire. Unfortunately for her peace of mind, however, once she had seen the mighty figure of Captain Marvel she became hopelessly infatuated with him. In one very early story, before the full dimensions of Captain Marvel's invulnerability had been established, Sivana invented a gas gun which would have killed any ordinary man, and which succeeded, at least, in rendering Captain Marvel unconscious. Torn between daughterly loyalty and romantic attachment, Beautia deserted her father and nursed Captain Marvel through his recovery—then returned to Sivana's side.

As for the other side of the relationship, things were even odder. Remember that in one aspect of his existence Billy/Marvel was just a boy. In the early days he was, in fact, rather a *little* boy, although of indeterminate age. To Billy Batson, Beautia Sivana was a grown-up woman of incomparable glamour and charm. Billy was definitely smitten, but with the kind of touching "crush" that a child often has on an adult of either sex.

Metaphysical theses have been written on the exact nature of the transformation that took place when Billy shouted the word *Shazam* and disappeared in favor of Captain Marvel. To be quite fair about it, Billy himself often spoke of "calling on" rather than "changing to" Captain Marvel. And, in at least one story, Billy was seen to cheat on a written examination by *whispering* his word and obtaining a wraith-like presence of the Captain, who provided correct answers to the exam.

But all of this notwithstanding, most aficionados are in agreement that Captain Marvel was Billy Batson's alter ego (and vice versa); that in a metaphysical sense they were the same person in two different embodiments; and that in truth Billy did not so much give way to Captain Marvel as become magically transformed *into* Captain Marvel, retaining even as Captain Marvel, the basic personality and identity of Billy Batson.

If all of this seems a digression, take a moment to consider yourself a small, uninitiated boy, with a crush on a gorgeous mature woman. Now—you are miraculously and instantaneously transformed into a man. Bodily. That gorgeous woman all but flings herself upon you. How do you react? Be honest now—you are flustered, confused, embarrassed, even frightened. And that, raised to the nth power, is how Captain Marvel reacted to the advances of women in general and Beautia Sivana in particular.

Oh, it was a strange and wonderful relationship.

In the later years of the series Beautia disappeared, presumably returning to the planet Venus to rejoin her brother Magnificus. The two Sivana offspring were replaced by another pair who had apparently been held in reserve all those years on the cloudy planet. The two new Sivanas were Sivana, Jr., and Georgia Sivana.

Junior was a younger edition of his dad, distinguishable chiefly by his non-baldness and his highly visible argyle socks. Georgia was a female counterpart of her brother: scrawny, angular, ugly, bespectacled, brilliant, and evil; her mental acuity was distinctly an inheritance from daddy.

Dr. Sivana and the later little Sivanas were all scientific wizards, forever dreaming up inventions that would permit them to commit outrageous crimes ranging from astounding thefts to walking through prison walls, from traveling through time and altering history to wrecking the entire world. Captain Marvel for his part was supposedly endowed with the wisdom of Solomon, but he did not always use it. The evil schemes of the Sivanas were constantly being thwarted, of course, but their perpetrators always returned with newer and more novel plots.

~ ~ ~ ~ ~

The proliferation of superheroes is one of the more interesting aspects of the whole superhero phenomenon. I don't mean only that scores of publishers entered the lists, with literally thousands of would-be champions, but that successful superheroes often fissioned into variations of themselves. Captain Marvel very early gave a kind of odd parthenogenetic birth to three Lieutenants Marvel when it was learned that in addition to the original Shazam-blessed Billy Batson there were three *other* Billy Batsons in the land.

By the magic of superheroic proliferation, these other Batsons—Tall Billy, Fat Billy, and Hill Billy—were also able to turn into red-suited super-beings by pronouncing the magical name simultaneously with the *original,* "Real" Billy. While holding lesser rank than their senior counterpart, they occasionally banded together as the Squadron of Justice.

The artwork that went into the Fawcett comics, most particularly the Captain Marvel feature, was remarkable for its charm. Charles Clarence Beck brought to the comics page a style that combined simplicity with a high level of humor, a sense of color and design that matched perfectly the tongue-in-cheek attitude that pervaded the Marvel feature. Although over the years many artists worked on Captain Marvel and its related strips, Beck's influence never ceased to be felt, and at least occasional glimmerings of the original sprightly conception appeared up to the very end.

The first really important proliferation of the Marvel strip was the introduction of Captain Marvel Jr. Junior was conceived by Ed Herron and usually drawn by Mac Raboy, who later took over the *Flash Gordon* Sunday feature originated by the late Alex Raymond, and drew it until the time of Raboy's own death.

Captain Marvel Jr. originated in the Captain Marvel lead story in an early issue of *Whiz Comics.* A poor newsboy named Freddy Freeman, apparently mortally injured in an encounter with a supervillain named Captain Nazi, was found by Captain Marvel and carried to the cavern of the wizard Shazam. Marvel summoned the wizard by lighting a brazier, as he had been instructed, and plead-

ed with him to save the youth by means of supernatural interces-
sion. The wizard decreed instead that the World's Mightiest Mortal share his own powers with the boy.

For what seemed to be his final moments of rallying strength,
the boy's eyes flickered open. Standing above him Freddy saw the
mighty form of his hero and whispered: "Captain Marvel!" In the
now familiar burst of thunder and lightning the broken form of the
boy disappeared and was replaced by a tights-clad, colorful figure
of strength: Captain Marvel Jr. His costume was identical to that
of the senior Captain, except for the substitution of blue for red. In
form, however, he retained the size and appearance of a boy—and
went off into a series of adventures of his own in *Master Comics*
(where he displaced *Minute Man* as the leading feature), and in a
later series devoted entirely to himself, as well as the *Marvel Family* series. I should mention, in passing, that the powers of Captain
Marvel, although "shared" with Freddy in the form of Junior, simultaneously continued *undiminished* in the Captain's own exploits.
Another example of the comics miracle.

Twenty years later Will Lieberson told why Junior's magic ex-
pletive was "Captain Marvel" rather than "Shazam." "All those
kids were going to read Captain Marvel Jr," he said, "and every
time they read a story about Junior we wanted to remind them
there was a Captain Marvel *Senior* too, so they wouldn't neglect to
buy more Fawcett comics."

The use of "Captain Marvel" as Captain Marvel Jr.'s change-
word had certain problems with it, that were sometimes either forgotten or simply ignored by scripters. However, they provided
amusing possibilities when remembered. For instance, in any
Marvel Family adventure, Junior could not speak Captain Marvel's name in direct address without changing instantly to Freddy.
Freddy, when out hawking papers, could not shout a headline including either Captain's name (Senior or Junior) without changing. And Captain Marvel Jr., could not even speak his own name
without changing back to Freddy!

Mary Batson turned out to be the long-lost twin sister of Billy,
and once *she* was found it turned out that the Shazam powers were
in her genes too! Instead of the attributes of Solomon, Hercules,
and so on, Mary was provided with a purely feminine pantheon:
Selena (grace), Hippolyta (strength), Ariadne (skill), Zephyrus
(fleetness), Aurora (beauty), and Minerva (wisdom).

As Mary Marvel she wore a short-skirted feminine adaptation of the lightning suit, but like Freddy Freeman she retained her childish size and form despite her supernatural powers. Once launched from the pad of *Captain Marvel Adventures* Mary was transferred to *Wow Comics* where she superseded Mr. Scarlet (a non-powered costume hero) as top feature. And, in time, there was the customary single-character comic for Mary, and the expected role in the activities of the Marvel Family,

This roll call of Captain Marvel spinoffs seems to go on and on, but there are just a few more, I promise.

Uncle Marvel—in mufti, Uncle Dudley Batson—was a fat old fraud who simply appointed himself a member of the Marvel Family. He made for himself a standard set of lightning-blazoned red tights plus cape and boots, introduced himself to Mary Batson as a long-lost uncle, and joined in the adventures of the family. He was such a good-hearted bumbling fake that although Billy, Mary, and Freddy promptly saw through him, they tolerated and even abetted his frauds, all the while pretending to be fooled.

He devised the technique of shouting "Shazam" simultaneously with the others, and in the din and glare of their magical transformations, slipping quickly out of his street clothing to appear in the Marvel uniform he wore beneath. Of course, he could not fly or perform other marvelous acts, but he was frequently taken along by the other Marvels, who studiously failed to notice when he hitched a tow on a trailing cape and who "coincidentally" happened to intercept bullets and other missiles directed at him.

When presented with a direct challenge to his Shazam powers, Dudley pleaded a case of "Shazambago," a debility of advancing years, and played upon the sympathy of some authentic Marvel—usually Mary—for help. He survived financially by running a benevolent agency called Shazam Incorporated, and eked out his living by serving as host of a Marvel Family television show.

On at least one occasion, however, Uncle Dudley truly saved the day. In the very first adventure chronicled in the first issue of *Marvel Family Comics,* issued in 1945, the world was being ravaged by a terrible and mysterious being who looked like a member of the Marvel Family, and who exhibited all their marvelous powers, but whose self-assigned mission was universal conquest or destruction.

Summoning the shade of the wizard, the Marvels were told this story: 5000 years ago in Egypt, Shazam had sought to create a hero who would combine human virtue and superhuman power for the good of mankind. Selecting an Egyptian named Teth-Adam, Shazam had put him through the initiation ceremony by now so familiar to Marvel buffs. The product of the thunder and lightning in ancient Egypt was then dubbed Mighty Adam and commanded to struggle for the right.

Abandoning the role of Teth-Adam, the superhuman Mighty Adam turned his powers to personal benefit instead of charity, and seized the throne of empire. Enraged, the wizard Shazam confronted him, re-dubbed him Black Adam, and banished him to the most distant star in the universe.

Black Adam had spent the centuries speeding back from his interstellar exile, had finally reached the Earth, and had resumed his march of tyranny. And now, in the chamber of the wizard, he stood in confrontation with the modern Marvels. Black Adam presented an imposing figure: tall, wiry, muscular, with an evil leer on his thin face. His costume was a proto-Marvel suit, the background color black, the trim in the customary pattern of golden lightning bolt, sash, cuff decorations, and boots. (For some reason Black Adam dispensed with the usual Marvel cape.)

At once a mighty struggle commenced, but despite their numerical superiority the Marvels were unable to overcome Black Adam—for, Atlas, and so on. In steps Uncle Marvel, seemingly attempted to achieve rapprochement with the ancient supervillain: "He's so strong," Dudley told his friends, the Marvels, "let's make him a member of the Marvel Family! After all, he got his powers from old Mazham. I mean . . . Hamshaz. No, I mean Shamhaz . . . er, uh . . . ."

"You sputtering old fool," Black Adam interrupted, "You mean *Shazam!*" Thunder! Lightning! In place of the muscular Black Adam stood Teth-Adam, an incredible 5000 years of age.

Before the Egyptian could undo the change by again shouting the word he was silenced by a single blow. Then, the weight of his 50 centuries descending in a moment, he collapsed—into a small heap of dust.

Did I say that was the end of the roll? I lied. There was a Freckles Marvel—a young girl who tried Dudley Batson's trick and appointed herself Mary's chum. And Baby Marvel, a foundling adopted by the Marvel Family and decked out in red-and-gold diapers. But within a single adventure Baby was reclaimed by his mother and left the series.

And there was Levram—that's Marvel spelled backwards. Product of a mad scientist's scheming, he was a sort of reverse-polarity evil reflection of the Captain. And Ibac. Ibac was originally Stinky Printwhistle, a small-time crook who received from Lucifer himself a set of Shazam-like powers.

The letters in Ibac stood for Ivan (the terrible), Borgia (the poisoner), Attila (the Hun), and Caligula (the emperor). Stinky/Ibac changed in a flash of green fire, and even as Ibac he was not too impressive, generally looking like a pro wrestler whose costume comprised only a pair of black leotard bottoms.

Several of Captain Marvel's greatest challenges were spun out for the readers of Fawcett comics in serial form. One very early serial took its theme from the then current World War II—as did many Marvel stories. The war and the war effort were brought up repeatedly, perhaps running second only to the endless recidivisms of the Sivana family, and Hitler, Mussolini, and Hirohito appeared personally, and derogatorily, in many of the comics, as did also such surrogate villains as Captain Nazi, Corporal Hitler Jr. and Nippo.

I mentioned Spy Smasher earlier. Let me say just a bit more about him. He was a non-powered costume hero, sporting a modified version of an aviator's suit, helmet, goggles and cape. He zoomed around the world in the gyro-sub, a unique combination of airplane and submarine, protecting America's interests and fighting her enemies at home and abroad.

For a number of issues of *Whiz Comics* in the early forties the Spy Smasher and Captain Marvel features were combined, and the double-length stories were used to follow the furious struggle between the two. Axis scientists had developed a brain-warping machine and captured Spy Smasher. Using the fiendish device, they had twisted his mental processes so that he became sympathetic to their cause and the mortal enemy of Captain Marvel.

For months he fought the world's mightiest mortal to a standstill, generally using his brainpower to overcome Captain Marvel's obvious physical advantage, and several times he nearly annihilated the big red cheese whom he caught in his vulnerable identity as Billy. (Ah, that vulnerable alter ego of the super-being: what a blessing to script writers it was!)

In the end, of course, Captain Marvel succeeded in subduing Spy Smasher, capturing the brain-warping apparatus, and restoring Spy Smasher to his usual attitudes.

Unquestionably the greatest comic book serial of all time was "Captain Marvel and the Monster Society of Evil," a cooperative product of the efforts of Lieberson, Crowley, Binder, and Beck. This started in the February 1943 issue of *Captain Marvel Adventures* and ran for 26 consecutive installments, ending in the May 1945 edition.

The Monster Society of Evil was a conglomeration of villainous characters, some lifted from Marvel stock and others concocted especially for the occasion. They included Captain Nazi, Nippo, Ibac, the Japanese scientist Dr. Smashi, Herkimer the crocodile man, a giant orange octopus, and assorted others.

Behind them all, operating from the dark and mysterious Planetoid Punkus, lurked the enigmatic Mr. Mind, shadowy master of the Monster Society of Evil. Chapter after chapter passed with Billy Batson about to freeze to death at the North Pole, or be cooked by cannibals (while bound and gagged, of course), or forced to watch helplessly as an interplanetary Big Bertha is fired that will—well, let's catch the flavor of the message that appears at the end of the chapter:

> But how can even the *world's mightiest mortal* stop a shell a thousand times his size?? One shell already heads for *Russia,* to blast that land to shreds! Another is aimed for *America!* Will Captain Marvel save the two great allies—*Russia* and *America*—from utter destruction???
>
> See chapter 12, *"Gsv Ylnyziwnvmg Lu Vzigs!"* Next Month! (Use your code-finder to work this out.)

Eventually Mr. Mind was revealed to be—not some fearsome and gigantic foe of humanity, but—a tiny green worm! A typical bit of Hinder-Beck Marvelizing. And after the tide had turned in the serial, a series of reverse cliff-hangers were used, in which Mr. Mind was about to be crushed under a careless heel . . . or devoured along with a juicy steak by Herman Goering . . . or otherwise eliminated.

At last, though, Mr. Mind is captured in the station WHIZ building, brought to trial for 186,744 murders, prosecuted personally by Captain Marvel, convicted, and executed. Strange that in that day of slaughter of millions, the imagination could conceive of an arch-fiend murdering fewer than 200,000 victims. Truth is not only stranger than fiction. It is infinitely more horrifying.

Another serial opponent of Captain Marvel was Oggar, the world's mightiest immortal. This character, got up in a Roman toga, spent his time promoting the Cult of the Curse, a movement designed to make him the object of universal adoration.

His origin was that of an ancient Olympian. The original version of Shazam's name was Shazamo, but when Oggar proved too nasty to take, the wizard had dropped him from the acronym. Oggar had been banished from Olympus, and now he was back to work fresh mischief.

This kind of rewriting of "history" in the comics leaves me with a sense of disquiet. Each time the Superman origin story is republished with new twists and fillips to convenience modern revisionists, I yearn for the purity of the original version . . . and every time the Captain Marvel origin sequence was embellished it left me equally annoyed.

Besides, wasn't Shazam in Egypt 5,000 years ago, busy with Teth-Adam?

The serial did have one nice twist, though. Captain Marvel knew that Oggar had *one* fatal weakness but he didn't know what it was, so he kept a little notebook and kept checking off possibilities. And Oggar could perform endlessly varied feats of magic, but each one only once. So *he* kept a notebook.

Time after time, there would stand the two opponents, each flipping pages frantically, searching for a device he hadn't already tried on the other. Simultaneously they would cry: "Ah! I have it!" and go to work on each other.

"Magic force! Take Marvel and—*owwwwww!*"

"Here's what I want to try—biting his finger! That didn't do it! Now I'll try yanking out some of his hair!"

"Owwwwww!"

"Still no good! I'll try twisting his nose!"

"Owwwwww!"

"Nothing worked! And the rest of the pages are blank! I need more items on my list!"

"You had your fun! Now it's my turn! Magic force—create an unbreakable plastic ball around Marvel!"

Ping!

"Holy Moley! Holy Moley! I can't break out!"

"Of course not, stupid! That's a magic *unbreakable* ball! You won't break out in a million years! *Haaaa!*"

There was one other major series within the Captain Marvel saga: the adventures of Tawky Tawny, the talking tiger. In this age

of the Esso tiger, tiger-paw tires, tiger grooming aids for tigers—
or men—Mr. Tawny might fit very well. He was intelligent, artic-
ulate, well (if somewhat flashily) dressed, and provided an amusing element in the latter days of the Marvel feature.

But somehow, I never warmed to Mr. Tawny. It may sound
strange, but I think it was because he seemed unrealistic. I mean,
the whole Marvel sequence was about this little boy who could
summon magic lightning to transform him into an invulnerable
flying man. *That* I could believe. But a talking tiger? It just didn't
fit.

At the very end, with the comics industry faltering and their
own reliance on superheroes paying fewer and smaller dividends,
the Fawcetts tried various devices to perk up interest. One was the
introduction of horror elements: King Kull, and the Red Crusher (a
Korean War villain). They even had Mary Marvel leave behind
her little-girl looks for a rather nubile appearance. One might,
through the power of hindsight, criticize the Fawcett management
for not holding on longer—superheroes *did* make a major come-
back some years later. But in 1953 it looked like the end of the
line, so they entered into that wretched consent agreement, and
went out of the hero business.

But Captain Marvel refuses to rest easily. Ever since the demise
of the Marvel Family, those Shazam wraiths have reappeared and
reappeared, in one form or another. There is a whole generation of
men and women who remember the big red cheese and the world's
maddest scientist and the rest of the Marvel crew.

There were those fortunate enough to see the Republic movie
serial of Captain Marvel, with the magnificent Tom Tyler in the
title role and Nigel DeBrulier as the wizard. And—remember "The
Return of the Scorpion"? I promised I'd explain that reference.
The Scorpion was the masked mystery villain of that film serial,
and that's where he returned *from* in the Fawcett Dime Action
Book.

When Batman came to television in the person of Adam West
and became (briefly) a national craze a few years ago, there was a
period of several weeks when you could walk into a theater in
Times Square and see the entire Captain Marvel serial—12 chapters in sparkling black and white—in one afternoon or evening.

I could say quite a lot about that serial—about Frank Coghlan
Jr's delightful portrayal of a slightly older and much stupider Billy, about the supporting portrayals by Reed Hadley, John Da-

vidson, William Benedict and others. Benedict had only a small role as Billy's pal Whitey, but he was so striking that the character was adopted into the drawn version of the feature and ran until Whitey was drafted into the army.

And the serial just won't stay dead. Just recently I went to the Carnegie Hall Cinema to see *You Are What You Eat* with Tiny Tim, Frank Zappa, Malcolm Boyd, and an all-psychedelic cast. And playing with that film, a curtain-raiser perhaps, was Chapter 1 of the old Captain Marvel serial. Camp? Of course—no one in the audience took it seriously with its corny lines and hammy acting. But they loved it anyway. Groans, hisses, cheers . . . a delight.

And some of us still have our ancient Captain Marvel paraphernalia: Comix Cards or stationery or statuettes, or our official Captain Marvel Club membership documents. It cost a dime to join and, in addition to other benefits, members received a personal letter from Captain Marvel himself. And . . . look, you remember that cryptic message in the Monster Society serial? *Gsv Ylmyz-iwnvmg* and so on? If you were a member of the Captain Marvel Club you could *decode* that message.

I wonder if the wizard Shazam will banish me to the farthest star in the universe if I reveal the Captain Marvel Club code. What the heck, I'll risk Olympian-Egyptian disfavor. Just reverse the alphabet: for *a* read *z*, for *b* read *y* and so on. Now that I've shown you how it's done, you can decode that clue yourself. But you'll have to do it yourself; I won't decode it for you.

There were so *many* enjoyable things about the old Captain Marvel stories, and the other features associated with them, that I'm sure that sometime well into the next century there will still be old codgers around who, reminiscing about their childhood scores of years before, will find random recollections unleashing whole floods of bittersweet nostalgia . . .

A particular series, such as the stories featuring Mr. Atom, a gigantic robot who embodied the awesome power of atomic energy. The first story in the series was a beauty. Credit Bill Woolfolk for that, and forget about *The Beautiful Couple*.

Or *Captain Marvel Battles the Giant Earth Dreamer*. A nutty professor tells Billy Batson that he has discovered the universe is nothing but the figment of a dreaming giant's subconscious—*and the giant is about to wake up!* Take it from there.

Or even a single, beautiful, C. C. Beck panel: Billy Batson visiting a crazy surrealistic world in which things work by a different "logic" than they do in our world. Billy looks into a mirror to comb his hair and sees the back of his own head. Or: Sivana captures Billy and tosses him, bound and gagged (natch!) to a giant carnivorous plant.

Or the fantastic leering menacing *funny* face of Mr. Mind. I was always sorry that he was executed at the end of that serial. Couldn't he have reformed and gone on to . . . .

Did you know that Holy Moley and Shazam are struggling to live on as part of the American language? Not three miles from my home is the Sha-Zam boutique! TV's Gomer Pyle often exclaims *Shazam!* And Captain Marvel turns up in the Beatles' song, "Bungalow Bill."

In 1966 a fly-by-night publisher brought out a new Captain Marvel comic book. Credit lines went to Carl Burgos, the man behind the original Human Torch, and to Roger Elwood, a journeyman literary agent and anthologist. It looked hopeful but it was dreadful. The basic conception was unappealing—Captain Marvel's magic word was *Split,* and upon saying it, he would fly to pieces and zoom off in all directions, here a hand to accomplish one task, there a leg to do another . . . . The writing was bad, the artwork worse, and the feature quickly disappeared.

In 1967 there was a delightful development that unfortunately did not last long either. An independent publisher set up a new comic book line and hired Will Lieberson to edit, Otto Binder to write, and C. C. Beck to draw! They worked out two features together.

One was Fatman:

A sensational new fighting hero of *pachyderm* proportions, whose adventures are *overweighted* with thrills as he strikes like a *ton* of bricks. Crooks have *slim* chances as he *tips the scales* against crime at every turn!

But that's not all! Fatman's exploits reach *soaring* heights in *high-speed* action full of *horsepower* punch with *the sky the limit!*

He's Boris Van Bradford, gentle fancier of rare tropical exotics.

He's a Fatman—dreaded nemesis of evil-doers everywhere! He's a human flying saucer, with powers from other worlds!

And his costume, except for the substitution of a stylized flying saucer for the familiar lightning bolt, was a perfect replica of the old Marvel Family standard—this time in a primary shade of green! There were three fat issues of *Fatman.* A decade and a half of writing science non-fiction and spacing it out with straight-faced comic scripts for Superman, Doctor Solar, and Mighty Samson had not dulled the charm and wit of Binder's writing.

Those same years spent editing *Monsieur* and other esoteric periodicals had not dulled Lieberson's editorial skill.

And Beck's years in commercial art must only have honed his talents, for the drawing in *Fatman* glowed with all the charm and wit and general *joie de vivre* of Beck's mid-forties best.

The other Lieberson-Binder-Beck project was to be called *Captain Shazam,* and that name alone should push your thrill button by now, or you're reading the wrong chapter of this book.

But distribution of the new comics was spotty, financing was not reliable, and just at the worst possible moment the neo-superhero boom in the industry experienced a moderate depression. The whole new series disappeared before Captain Shazam had seen a single issue.

It was to weep.

Still, only a few months later yet *another* Captain Marvel appeared, this time from the Timely Comics group that had laid a claim to the word *Marvel* from the first publication of *Marvel Comics* featuring Human Torch and Sub-Mariner back in 1939! Their new Captain Marvel, originally written by editor Stan Lee and drawn by Gene Colan, is an alien spaceman marooned on earth. His real name is Captain Mar-Vell, and while the stories are really rather good, I frankly find it painful to see the blaspheming of the old beloved name.

I suppose that consent agreement between Fawcett and National will keep the *real* Marvel Family in the deep freeze forever. But a whole generation who grew up with those marvelous adventures will never, never forget Billy Batson, Shazam, Freddy and Mary, Sterling Morris, radio station WHIZ, the mad leering Sivanas, or . . .

. . . the Big Red Cheese!

Sporting Memories

FROZEN FINGERS

IF YOU HAD a time machine and could travel back to the late 1940s to attend a football game, you'd barely recognize the game. Leather helmets, blobby-looking pigskins, single-wing and T formations. But the biggest difference was the limited-substitution rule, restricting each team to one new player on each down. No offensive units, defensive units or special teams.

The all-powerful NCAA and the struggling NFL kept changing their minds about limited versus unlimited substitutions. My alma mater, a military prep school in New Jersey, and others in its unofficial league were still using the limited-substitution system. Players were expected to put in 60 minutes on the field. Water boys carrying sloshing buckets of water and ladles would run onto the field and rehydrate athletes between plays.

My brother, Jerry, was the family athlete, while I was the designated intellectual, complete with thick eyeglasses, protruding ears and braces. Jerry was an all-state center.

Prep school football was pretty tough. Metro newspapers couldn't send reporters to all the games, so they created a system of stringers coordinated by a helpful faculty member at each school. These coordinators recruited the most nearly literate kids they could find to do the actual reporting. There I was, something like 14 years old, on the pages of the *New York Times*, *New York Herald-Tribune*, *Newark Star-Ledger*, *Trenton Times*, *Philadelphia Inquirer*, *Philadelphia Bulletin* and our own little weekly *Bordentown Register*.

At each of our team's games, home or away, I would sit with a football scorebook and track the play. I used a double-ended pencil, blue at one end (for our team) and red at the other (for our opponents). Our press box consisted of an elevated section of bleachers. I think I've still got some splinters in my derriere to show for the experience. I'd track the progress of the ball, left and right, solid line for runs, wavy line for passes, dotted lines for kicks, players' numbers marked for each play.

By the end of the game I'd have my whole story laid out in blue and red on a simulated gridiron. If I was lucky I'd get a ride back to our office with my boss, a wonderful teacher named Paul Hartpence, and start writing my stories. Different venues demanded different lengths: 50 words for one paper, 120 for another. No

two could be alike. Typical deadline was 6 o'clock, and I don't
remember ever missing one.

We delivered our copy via a memorable gadget called a teleprinter, an ancient ancestor of today's computer terminal. At the
end I could stretch out and write my story for the weekly *Bordentown Register* and wait for Monday afternoon, after my last class.
I'd walk over to the *Register* office, smell the printer's ink and
deliver my copy, fresh out of my Smith-Corona portable.

The big game each year, Bradley Military Academy vs. Nimitz
Naval Institute, was played the Saturday before Thanksgiving. It
got considerable newspaper coverage as "the Little Army-Navy
Game."

In 1949, the last year that Jerry and I both attended Bradley, a
series of Atlantic storms were dumping rain and sleet on the area.
Not too severe to cancel the game, though. I remember sitting on
our elevated bleacher, totally exposed to freezing temperatures,
keeping track of the plays. My hands were freezing. I could hardly
feel my fingers. I was able to hold my blue-and-red pencil, but to
make my lines for run or pass or kick, I had to shove the point
around. Snow kept accumulating on my glasses, and I had to keep
brushing it off. If I'd had a cup of hot cocoa, it would have made a
world of difference. But I could only tough it out.

On what turned out to be the last play of the game, Nimitz had
the ball on their own 1-yard line, nursing a narrow lead. Their center snapped the ball. My brother—did I tell you he was first-string
all-state as well as my personal hero?—barreled over his opposite
number, slammed into the NNI quarterback, knocked the ball
loose and fell on it for the winning touchdown.

He also came out of the play with a knee injury that put him in
a hospital bed and kept him from playing college football.

I wrote my stories and hit the sports pages with such greats as
Stanley Woodward and Red Smith. I went on from there to a lot of
other kinds of writing, from speeches for corporate big-shots to
Hollywood screenplays, with a stack of novels and other books in
between. Sitting in front of a computer in my home office with a
cup of coffee at my elbow is very comfortable. But somehow, I
must confess, I miss those long-ago days, sitting on a splintery
bleacher bench while the wind wailed and the snowflakes stung,
clutching a red-and-blue pencil in my frozen fingers!

I COULDA HAD A THREE-POINTER

MY OLDER BROTHER, Jerry, was the family athlete. All-State in football, captain of the riflery team (yes, our school had a riflery team), and a power-hitting left-handed first baseman in baseball season. So naturally I suffered from Little Brother Syndrome and tried desperately either to replicate Jerry's achievements or to excel in some other realm.

I opted for the latter. Tried amateur boxing for a while. The good news: I was strong and what was sometimes called "plucky." I could hit hard and I could take a punch. Was never knocked out or even knocked down. The bad news: I had slow hands, and with no amount of striving could I achieve those super-quick reflexes that any successful boxer needs. Plus, when it came to foot-work . . . let's put it this way. Get out your *Illustrated Guide to Sports Terminology* and look up *stumblebum,* and you'll find my portrait.

Next I tried out for the basketball team. The coach believed in giving kids a chance to play, and we wound up with fifteen boys on the squad. I was a third-string guard. Halfway through the season a couple of players were fired for the proverbial "violations of team standards." I think they skipped practice once too often. A couple of days later their two best friends quit in protest.

That left eleven players. Five on the first string, five on the second string, and me. As the last game of the season approached my stats read:

Field Goals	— 0
Foul Shots	— 0
Total Points	— 0
Minutes Played	— 0

Came the season finale and we were locked in a tight contest with another local high school. With just seconds remaining we were down by one point, something like 33 to 32. Basketball was a slower and lower-scoring game in those days.

One of our guards started up the court with the ball and tripped over a defender's foot. Twisted his ankle and went down. Time called. Our guy had to leave the game.

225

For some reason, Coach didn't put in a second-stringer. He sent me in.

Me!

The other guard passed the ball to me. I looked down the court. Our two forwards were jumping up and down on either side of the key. Our center was closer to me, ready to take a short pass. But time was running out and there was only time for one desperation play.

I was at mid-court. I reached back and threw an overhand pass like a soldier hurling a hand grenade. I was aiming at the taller of our two forwards. My aim was lousy. My pass was a couple of feet off-line and three feet high.

Swish! Nothing but net! The buzzer sounded. The score was 34 to 33. We had won. A gasp went up from a gymnasium full of fans, followed by a cheer.

I'll let you in on a secret. Everybody in that gym thought I had made an amazing shot from mid-court. It would have been a three-pointer if three-pointers had been invented back then, but two points were enough to win the game.

To this day, not a soul on the hardwood, not my teammates, not our opponents, not the officials or coaches or fans in the audience knew that I only made that shot because my aim was lousy. But now you know it.

If three-pointers had been invented back then, my crazy winning shot would have been one. Yes, in another era, I coulda had a three-pointer.

Reviews

THE BLACK HOOD

The Pulp Adventures of the Black Hood
by G. T. Fleming-Roberts
Altus Press, 2008, 228pp., $19.95
ISBN 9781440438296.

IF PUBLISHING PARTNERS Martin Goodman and Louis Silberkleit had not had a falling out in the late 1930s, American popular culture might have taken a different path over the rest of the Twentieth Century—and beyond.

Goodman and Silberkleit were limping along with a line of low-end pulp magazines, competing with fast-talking Rumanian-born Harry Donnenfeld's Spicy line, Delacorte, Fawcett, Harry Steeger's Popular Publications, and aging giant Street & Smith.

Then along came something new: the superhero. Mystery men like the Shadow and wild adventurers like Doc Savage got their start in the pulps, but Donnenfeld bought a superhero comic strip for stamp money from a couple of teenagers straight out of Cleveland, Ohio. Donnenfeld ran the feature in a new monthly, *Action Comics,* Superman took the nation by storm, and the race was on to create an army of powerful crimefighters garbed in colorful tights and flowing capes.

Soon there were scores of muscular heroes with amazing powers competing for the dimes of twelve-year-old customers.

Former partners Goodman and Silberkleit went their separate ways, competing in the mini-budget pulp field, and dipping their toes into the new superhero-dominated world of comic books.

Silberkleit brought out a brigade of the tights-and-cape-wearing adventurers: the Wizard, the Comet, the Hangman, the Black Hood, the Shield. That last named, per pop-culture maven Will Murray, was the first patriotic-themed superhero. His outfit looked as if it had been stitched together by a mad tailor trapped in a flag factory. Red, white, and blue stars and stripes, of course, plus a similarly-themed, triangular shield that the hero wore like an umpire's chest protector.

Goodman's heroes were as colorful and as bizarre as Silberkleit's. The Human Torch was an android who could turn himself into a one-man flying conflagration; the Sub-Mariner was a hybrid born of a human and a mer-creature; and Captain America was a

muscular patriot whose outfit looked like something stitched together by a mad tailor locked in a flag factory. Red, white, and
blue stars and stripes, of course, plus a similarly-themed triangular
shield.

Gosh, do you think Louis Silberkleit was peeved? Do you think
the two ex-pals exchanged lawyer letters and threats of lawsuits?
Do you think Goodman backed off? Well, he did, to the extent of
having Captain America's shield redesigned, dropping the triangular format for the familiar bull's-eye shape that's still around after
all these years.

I'm not sure why the Black Hood was as popular as he was, but
for some reason he caught on and had a fairly lengthy career in a
variety of Silberkleit's comic books. There was also a Black Hood
radio show. I've never heard it, and if anybody could provide me
with a copy I'd be very grateful.

And what's chiefly to the point, Silberkleit added a *Black Hood
Detective* pulp to his line. Ten cents a pop, kiddies! After just one
issue the title morphed into *Hooded Detective*. Will Murray suggests that legal problems, possibly involving the better-established
Black Mask pulp, were involved, and he makes a very plausible
case.

The Black Hood's pulp adventures lasted only three issues, dated September, 1941, November, 1941, and January, 1942. The
demise of the magazine may have resulted from paper rationing
imposed by the government, the United States having entered
World War Two on December 7, 1941.

Well, who was this guy? Will Murray recounts his rather tangled origin story in Silberkleit's comic books. An honest cop
named Kip Burland is framed by the mob. Falsely convicted, he
escapes but—a common pulp device—is mousetrapped between
the police and the gang. Mobsters catch up with him and riddle
him with bullets. They dump Burland's apparently dead body in
the countryside but in fact there remains a spark of life.

Along comes a bearded hermit (shades of Mary Shelley's
Frankenstein) who nurses Burland back to health. The hermit happens to be a scientific genius who puts Burland through a series of
treatments that render him a sort-of semi-superhero. He can't quite
fly, and bullets won't bounce off his super-tough torso, but he's
abnormally strong, can jump like a grasshopper, and has amazing
powers of recuperation. (Shades of Steve Rogers, aka Captain
America.)

I would think, under the circumstances, that I'd change my name, move to a distant undisclosed location, maybe grow a moustache or dye my hair, and start a new life, keeping well under the radar. But not so, Kip Burland. He gets himself a lovely, attractive outfit at the local Superhero Haberdashery.

Bright yellow tights, black gloves and shorts, and a black headgear that covers the upper half of his face. At this point I must take a slight detour and mention my young grandson, Ethan. He has asked me repeatedly why Superman wears his underpants "on the outside." Well, Supie is not the only one!

Kip Burland also resumes his life as a plainclothes society playboy. I don't know what he does for money. I also don't know why the mob and the cops have forgot that they both have him—or had him—in their sights. He has a girlfriend, society dame Barbara Sutton, and a potential sidekick-wannabe/rival, former professional athlete Joe Strong.

Lissome Miss Sutton is of course carrying a torch for the Black Hood while dismissing Kip Burland as a useless fop. (Shades of Lois Lane, Superman, and Clark Kent . . . Vicki Vale, Batman, Bruce Wayne . . . Beautia Sivana, Captain Marvel, Billy Batson . . . and so on.)

For the pulp adventures of the Black Hood, Silberkleit obtained the literary services of George Roberts, a solidly competent pulp scrivener who used the by-line G. T. Fleming-Roberts. For the three book-length adventures of the Black Hood, Roberts grappled with some serious problems involved in converting a comic book hero to a pulp adventurer. Roberts was accustomed to writing detective stories for the pulps, and once he tackled the Black Hood, the results resembled pulp detective stories more than they did superhero adventures.

Roberts' favorite device called for a criminal mastermind blackmailing a millionaire—or group of millionaires—with the threat of murder should they fail to comply. (Shades of uncounted Saturday afternoon movie serials!) Kip Burland in both his civilian identity and as the Black Hood becomes involved, as do Barbara and Joe Strong

Kip wears his Black Hood costume under his street clothes, and in at least one instance we see him strip to his tights, hide his civvies in the bushes outside a mansion, and set off to chase the crooks. He seems to have forgot to come back for them. Or maybe I missed that in all the excitement.

In another novel he's involved in a chase through midtown Manhattan and stops to make a telephone call, ducking into a public phone booth while he's at it. He does worry that he'll be recognized in his bright yellow and black superhero suit, but fortunately nobody notices. Next he hails a cab, and that works out nicely, too.

Which reminds me of the day I sat with pals Lenny Kaye and Gary Lovisi in a café on upper Broadway. Just outside, a muscular male individual garbed in a perfect Wonder Woman costume stood at the curb, trying without success to flag down a taxi.

Hmmm.

Roberts modified the Black Hood's costume by adding a flowing black cloak, permitting him to disappear into the shadows when it suited him. (Shades of Walter Gibson's crimefighter, the Shadow.)

These three stories are of course part of their time. Of particular interest, in one of them, precision machine tools are being smuggled out of the country disguised as lead ash trays. And where are they destined? Russia!

Russia?

Clearly, the story was written during the months of the infamous Hitler-Stalin Pact.

Fascinating.

In all honesty, I can't say that these three novels make great reading. Even by pulp standards, they are pretty mediocre. Certainly readable (I've struggled through far worse!) but far from great. I think Roberts was writing at breakneck speed, not uncommon for high-volume pulp creators. Further, trying to fit a comic book semi-superhero into the procrustean bed of a fairly conventional detective story was a difficult exercise at best.

Still, *The Pulp Adventures of the Hooded Detective* is a fascinating artifact of a lost era. Publisher Matthew Moring earns major kudos for putting together a most attractive package, while Will Murray demonstrates outstanding scholarship and, in my opinion, critical perceptions in both an introduction and an afterword to the collection.

We're living in an era when several publishers are vying to make classic pulp fiction available to contemporary readers. For gray-haired oldsters, they represent a trip down memory lane; to younger readers, they offer a literary glimpse into the world of their grand- and great-grandparents.

I was lucky to receive a paper copy of *The Pulp Adventures of the Hooded Detective* from Matthew Moring. If you try, you may succeed in finding one for yourself. But failing that, I'm pretty sure that the collection is available from Altus Press as an e-book.

As for Martin Goodman and Louis Silberkleit—remember them?—both pioneers have of course long since gone to that great comic book factory in the sky. But their heirs and descendants are still at it, and the penny-poor companies they created have grown into a billion-dollar industry.

Goodman's heroes, joined by latter-day comrades like Spider-Man, the Hulk, and the Fantastic Four, are the subjects of one blockbuster movie after another. And as for Silberkleit's successors, while they clearly lost the battle of the superheroes, they found another rich mother lode to mine. Archie Andrews, Betty and Veronica, Jughead, Mr. Weatherbee, Miss Grundy . . . yes, after the better part of a century, they're still plying their wares at Riverdale High.

CAPTAIN FUTURE, VOLUME THREE

The Collected Captain Future Volume Three
by Edmond Hamilton
Edited by Stephen Haffner
Introduction by Chuck Juzek
Haffner Press, 2013, 661 pages, $40.00.
ISBN 9781893887749.

STEPHEN HAFFNER'S PULP-reprint-oriented press keeps turning out these lovingly crafted volumes, to the delight of old-timers (like me) who remember the pulps when they were fresh and new and exciting, and to the illumination of younger readers (like most people) who are discovering them as relics recovered from a lost world of colorful, explosively crafted adventure.

In fact, I find myself wondering how many millions of television viewers have noticed the poster-size blowup beside the front door of Sheldon Lee Cooper and Leonard Hofstadters's apartment in the immensely popular sitcom, *The Big Bang Theory*. In fact, for the sake of any reader who is unfamiliar with this television series, it centers around a group of four academic physicists, all of them male, and their respective girlfriends (or in one case, wife).

The males are all geeks and all science fiction fans. They spend endless hours debating the technology behind their favorite comic book super heroes, they are all hopelessly addicted to *Star Wars* and *Star Trek* and *The Lord of the Rings* and will argue incessantly about Asimov's Three Laws of Robotics.

And there beside their doorway is a blow-up reproduction of the first issue of *Captain Future, Wizard of Science*. I doubt that any of the characters in the sitcom have ever laid eyes on a pulp magazine no less read one, but there it is. And publisher Stephen Haffner, to close the circle, has now published three omnibus volumes out of the eventual five in his intended reissue of the entire Captain Future series.

By the time he had written the ninth through twelfth novels in the Captain Future series, I have a feeling that Edmond Hamilton was growing a little tired of Curt Newton, Grag the giant robot, Otho the rubbery android, and Simon Wright the genius brain-in-a-box. I suspect that Curt would have happily taken a leave of absence from his space-faring adventures, and rocketed off to a happy tryst with the adorable Joan Randall. But such was not to be the case—at least, not yet.

In the four adventures gathered in the present volume, good ol' Cap fights villains as close to home as the lost radium mines on the moon and as distant as alien dimensions and hidden worlds at the center of the galaxy. At least, that's the impression I have. These adventures do tend to run together.

If Captain Future was starting to wish for a respite from his chores, it's obvious that author Edmond Hamilton was definitely starting to wilt. He was not only turning out four Captain Future novels a year, he was also supplying the other science fiction pulps with a steady flow of stories, and even venturing into the world of weird horror fiction with dark fantasy stories for *Weird Tales*.

As a result, the Captain Future stories that he produced did tend to sag after a while. Eventually Hamilton was placed on temporary leave of absence from his task of chronicling the exploits of the Futuremen, and relief writers were called in from the Standard Publications bullpen.

None of these writers have appeared in the first dozen Captain Future novels, but appear they did in the pages of the magazine, and their contributions to the series will be included, I am certain, in later Haffner volumes.

I should add that the Haffner books are lovingly designed and beautifully produced. They include the illustrations from the 1940s magazines, editorials and letter columns, and knowledgeable introductions. In the present volume, Chuck Duzek reminisces about his boyhood reading matter, which ranged from *Planet Comics* to *Captain Future* and other pulps.

Great fun for the nostalgic oldster and a glimpse into the wondrous escape reading of three quarters of a century ago, for younger generations. In fact, one might well lay out a matrix of characters from the Captain Future novels and place the principles of such TV series as *Star Trek* in the compartments. They would fit remarkably well.

CAPTAIN FUTURE'S BACK!

THIS IS THE age of relaunches. Blink your eyes and there's a new installment of your favorite movie franchise, TV show, comic book hero, or pulp character lumbering out of the 1970s or '50s or '30s or whenever. In the pulp world alone there have been modern-day versions of the Green Lama, Doc Savage, the Avenger, the Shadow, the Spider, and I'm sure many others. I've even picked up a rumor that Zorro is galloping back.

But Captain Future? Publisher Stephen Haffner has been reissuing the complete original saga in a series of lovingly crafted omnibus volumes, and I've been reading—rereading—the twenty original novels for the first time in many decades. Okay, they're creaky and clunky and the "science" in them, which was highly dubious even in the 1940s, is now totally absurd.

Even so, I find myself drawn into the stories, loving the characters: Curtis Newton, Otho the android, Grag the robot, Simon Wright the living brain, lovely Joan Randall and irascible old Ezra Gurney, Ook and Eek the interplanetary pets, and marvelous villains like Victor Corvo and Ul Quorn.

Every time I watch an instalment of *The Big Bang Theory* I wait for a glimpse of that poster-size reproduction of the first Captain Future magazine on the wall of Sheldon and Leonard's apartment. Clearly, Chuck Lorre and Bill Prady know their science fiction.

Now Allen Steele has penned a *new* Captain Future novel, editor David Hartwell has guided the book through the editorial process, and TOR Books has published it. *Avengers of the Moon.* Author Steele says he has modernized the solar system so lovingly described by Edmond Hamilton in 1941. Ed and his wife, the wondrous Leigh Brackett, befriended me in 1967 when I was a wet-behind-the-ears new-fledged science fiction writer. I wish I'd got to know Ed and Leigh better, but I will always treasure the precious time I got to spend with them.

I'll confess that I still dive back into those old novels on occasion, and I've just finished reading Allen Steele's new one. Maybe Captain Future is a guilty pleasure for me. Maybe I should be reading Thomas Pynchon or William Gaddis or Dexter Palmer: challenging, brilliant, rewarding novelists one and all. But they don't stop me from loving the works of Leigh Brackett and Edmond Hamilton—and now, Allen Steele.

Allen revises and updates the fondly-remembered origin story of Captain Future and the Futuremen. He reintroduces us to those wonderful characters and their world. He shows us the Moon and Mars, pretty much as we believe them to be in this, the Twenty-First Century. He even provides an ingenious and at least slightly plausible explanation for the many interplanetary humanoids that Ed Hamilton described.

Listen, friend, if you're already a devotee of the Captain Future saga—as I am—rest assured that Curtis Newton and Company are in good hands, in Allen Steele's hands. And if you've never read a Captain Future novel before, you're in for a treat when you read *Avengers of the Moon*. But you would also be well advised to pick up on the Haffner reprints of the original stories. Come on, share with me a great guilty pleasure.

TWO TO KEEP

SUDDENLY I WAS getting emails congratulating me on appearing in *The New Yorker.* No, I hadn't cracked that high-paying and prestigious market with a short story or an essay or a cartoon. Rather, a writer named Louis Menand, a so-called "Critic at Large," had contributed an essay titled "Pulp's Big Moment: How Emily Bronte met Mickey Spillane." In this article he had mentioned me.

Not being a man of undue modesty, I snagged a copy of the magazine (dated January 5, 2015) and found that Mr. Menand's essay was based largely on a book titled *American Pulp.* I tracked down a copy of *American Pulp,* only to discover that, despite its misleading title, this book is not about those grand colorful fiction magazines of past generations, but was almost entirely about mass-market paperback books. I also discovered that my own book on this subject, *The Great American Paperback,* was cited repeatedly in *American Pulp.* Well, flattering, to be sure. But what about the rest of that book?

Having read all its 405 pages, I sat down to put my thoughts on paper (well, actually, on a hard drive) and was about to send it off to Gary Lovisi for the estimable *Paperback Parade* when I came across another book on the subject. Thus, the double review below.

American Pulp: How Paperbacks Brought Modernism to Main Street
by Paula Rabinowitz
Princeton University Press
390+xv pp. Hardcover $29.95, 2015.
ISBN 978-0691-15060-4

When Books Went To War: The Stories that Helped us Win World War II
by Molly Guptill Manning
Houghton Mifflin Harcourt
288+v pp. Hardcover, $25, 2014.
ISBN 978-0544-53502

Paula Rabinowitz, a Professor of English at the University of Minnesota, is clearly a woman on a mission. Her book, very handsomely produced by a prestigious university press, is dedicated to the thesis that the humble twenty-five cent paperback book was the vehicle for spreading great literature among the previously uncultured and unsophisticated American masses, and, to a lesser extent, much of the rest of the world.

Prior to the import of Penguin Books from England and the creation of an American imitator, Pocket Books, high culture and great literature were the province of the moneyed classes who could afford the relatively expensive hardcover editions in which all worthwhile books were published. This, at least, is part of Rabinowitz's thesis. It is not an easy case to prove. Surely public schools and public libraries had a vital role in the enlightenment of the masses, as did advancing technology that brought the world into movie theaters in every town and radio that brought the world into every home.

To ease into the challenge, Rabinowitz describes her own childhood discovery of inexpensive Signet and Mentor books. Her taste was always of a high-tone nature, primarily in non-fiction, but also including novels that addressed controversial social issues. Rabinowitz states that her plan in the present volume involves "investigations of the effects of the paperback revolution on constructions of American racial, class, sexual, and gender relations."

Vital to this effort is the meaning of the word *pulp* itself. Within the traditional communities of readers and collectors of popular (and populist) fiction—primarily genre fiction—*pulp* is a type of magazine printed on cheap wood-pulp paper, bound in glossy, colorful covers, and containing hundreds of pages of exciting fiction: mysteries, science fiction, westerns, war stories (from ancient to modern), swashbucklers, horror tales, jungle adventures and love stories.

A secondary use of the word, common in the publishing industry, involves the process of recycling unsold or discarded publications into reusable paper.

Rabinowitz also uses the word *pulp* in two senses. One is inexpensive media, most particularly the mass-market paperback book, inexpensive, widely available, easily portable. The author focuses mainly on those small books that could literally fit into a purse or pocket, but at times she broadens her purview to include radio shows, motion picture, and other media.

The second use to which she puts the word *pulp* refers to the process of making a work readily available in an inexpensive, popular edition. Thus, a sociological work like *Coming of Age in Samoa* by Margaret Mead or a serious "literary" novel like *Daisy Miller* by Henry James, was considered "pulped" when reissued as an inexpensive paperback by Penguin or Mentor. At least, this is Rabinowitz's use of the word.

It is obvious that Rabinowitz's feelings about "pulping" (in her sense) are mixed. Bringing good reading to the millions, to borrow a phrase used in the 1940s, was certainly an admirable goal, but the colorful, often lurid, packaging and blurbing of these books was not.

Depending on which definition of *pulp* applies, Rabinowitz makes a statement that is either quite reasonable—or one of the greatest howlers since Richard Nixon's famous, "I am not a crook." Rabinowitz says: "Pulps were essentially products of the Second World War. Allen Lane had launched Penguin in 1935 and then, in 1939, Ian Ballantine brought Penguin to the United States for its American branch. But it was also 'stolen,' as E. L. Doctorow recounted, by Robert de Graff and turned into an American product, reviving the paper-bound book in the United States with Pocket Books and its kangaroo logo."

A reader who accepts Rabinowitz's rather unusual definition of *pulp* will find this statement unremarkable. Any reader familiar with the concept of pulp *magazines* will jump out of his or her chair emitting a yowl of astonishment and protest. *These* pulps— covering the alphabet from *Air Aces* to *Zeppelin Stories*—were created in the 1890s and were published well into the 1950s or early '60s. Allen Lane, Ian Ballantine, and Robert de Graff had nothing to do with it.

Having devoted a chapter to the establishment of mass-market paperback publishing in the US, Rabinowitz digs deeply into her subject matter. She establishes the role of mass paperback publishing as "interface," a connecting tissue between culture and society. She introduces each chapter in the book with one or more epigraphs, in this case, the famous Marshall McLuhan line, "The medium is the massage."

A clever play on words, McLuhan's statement has become a touchstone for media theorists. Unfortunately, it is pure hooey. The medium is *not* the message (or "the massage"—*chortle, chortle*). The *message* is the message. If the Yellow Sox and the Earthworms play a baseball game and the final score is Sox 5, Worms 3, that's the message: *Sox 5, Worms 3.* Doesn't matter whether you're at the game and that's what it says on the scoreboard, or you hear it on your car radio on the way home from work, or you see it on the evening TV news or read it on the sports page of the next morning's paper. It's still, *Sox 5, Worms 3.*

Rabinowitz states that, "Paperbacks linked objects and ideas to bodies, brought intimate longing and fear into public view, and circulated social experiences into the privacy of one's home and one's head. Pulps were precursors, imagining their own demise; they were also, paradoxically bulwarks against it."

She goes on, advancing the notion that the availability of socially critical works in mass market form brought not only culture but political awareness to millions of readers. A favored example is *12 Million Black Voices.* If one is to believe Rabinowitz it was the publication of this and Richard Wright's *Native Son,* as well as *If He Hollers Let Him Go* and other works of Chester Himes, equally angry and eloquent, that somehow served to bring about the civil rights movement of the Twentieth Century.

This is very much a *post hoc, ergo propter hoc* argument. It is also what the late James Blish referred to as a "piety." That is, a notion that we would like to believe, a sort of dubious candidate for the status of truism.

Rabinowitz wanders from her major thesis to offer lengthy paeans in honor of African American novelist Ann Petry and Argentine fantasist Jorge Luis Borges.

Petry was the author of three adult novels, one of which, *The Street,* achieved sales in excess of 1,000,000 copies. At present, she is remembered to a degree among feminist historians but has little influence, if any, beyond academic circles. Borges, in contrast, remains one of the most respected and influential sources of science fiction and surrealist literature.

Borges was first translated into English by Anthony Boucher, a major figure in Twentieth Century genre literature, with strong credentials in both detective and science fiction. Borges's first English-language publisher was *Ellery Queen's Mystery Magazine*—a pulp in neither the pulp magazine tradition (e.g., *Black Mask, Amazing Stories,* etc.) nor in Rabinowitz's favored usage, that of inexpensive pocket-sized paperback books. It was and remains a literate and relatively upscale, digest-size magazine.

The question then arises, *What is Señor Borges doing in Rabinowitz's book?* The answer is, obviously, Rabinowitz is a fan of Borges's and she wants to write about him. Not that there's anything wrong with that, but it's rather stretching the boundaries of

American Pulp: How Paperbacks Brought Modernism to Main Street. Speaking of which, it would surely have been helpful if Rabinowitz had offered a definition of modernism. This reader, for one, could not discover such in her book. *American Pulp* is replete with references to modernism (and even to post-modernism, heaven help us!) without ever making clear what either of these terms means.

Well, not to damn with faint praise (or praise with faint damns), Rabinowitz does get back on track from time to time. She has a splendid chapter on the Books in Wartime program that existed during the Second World War. A combine of publishers, with sponsorship and encouragement from the United States government, produced many millions of paperback books which were distributed free to American service personnel and to troops of allied nations. Some editions were translated into other languages.

This chapter is titled, oddly, "Isak Dinesen Gets Drafted: Pulp, the Armed Services Editions, and GI Reading." The "ASE" program was a huge success (undeniable) and Rabinowitz attributes to it the development of a permanent, massive, new reading populace (dubious). The late Frank M. Robinson, a best-selling author of novels including *The Power* and *The Glass Inferno,* served in the United States Navy during both the Second World War and the Korean conflict. Among his other duties, Robinson was a ship's librarian. He reported that enlisted sailors generally read comic books while better-educated officers preferred paperback books.

Did they seek out Dostoevsky or Margaret Mead? Rabinowitz might be disappointed to learn that, per Robinson's report, the two authors most in demand were Edgar Rice Burroughs and Mickey Spillane.

There is also an excellent chapter in *American Pulp* on lesbian fiction in mass market ("pulp") paperbacks. According to Rabinowitz, great numbers of young lesbians learned from these books. And what did they learn? Mainly, it would seem, how to dress (black slacks, white shirts), how to wear their hair (short), and where to meet other lesbians (department stores or artists' studios).

The present writer pleads ignorance of such matters, but it does seem peculiar to regard the very fine novels of Ann Bannon, Mary McCarthy, March Hastings, Vin Packer and other talented writers, as compendia of fashion tips and how-to manuals for apprentice lesbians.

Throughout her book, Rabinowitz appears to be obsessed with finding symbols where the more innocent reader might find only literal meanings. An example is Rabinowitz's interminable battering of a single word, "slip," to which she devotes page after page of analysis. One might think of it as a feminine undergarment more widely worn in past decades than at the present time. Or perhaps as a verb, describing an unfortunate event that might occur on an icy sidewalk in midwinter. But the treatment that Rabinowitz offers this modest four-letter word might well be categorized as semiotics run wild.

Another—and this is a real winner—is this riveting line: " 'All right, draw,' the declaration of the gunman in classic Westerns—those complicated scenes of repressed male homosociality—is now redirected into a command between two urban women artists not quite willing for their 'lips to speak together' of mutual desire."

Huh?

Still, one can always learn. The author Paula Rabinowitz reports that the name *Paula* is common code usage or signal in lesbian literature, indicating a lesbian character. The usage extends beyond paperback novels into another pulp medium, the comic book. Here, in the early Wonder Woman stories, which were drenched with lesbian imagery, sado-masochism, bondage and domination, and bestiality, the evil plotting scientist and Wonder Woman's arch foe is named Paula.

What a surprise.

As it was in the beginning, so it is at the end. Rabinowitz's highly personal and notably slippery definition of *pulp* remains a central flaw in her argument. Is the differentiation between pulp and non-pulp literature closely linked to the difference between genre and non-genre literature?

Let's see:

The story of Abel and Cain in *Genesis*, Shakespeare's *Hamlet*, Edgar Allan Poe's *Murders in the Rue Morgue*, Mark Twain's *Tom Sawyer, Detective*, Anna Katherine Green's *The House of the Whispering Pines*, Agatha Christie's *Murder on the Orient Express*, S. S. Van Dine's *The Dragon Murder Case*, F. Scott Fitzgerald's *The Great Gatsby*, Dashiell Hammett's *The Maltese Falcon*, and Sue Grafton's *"A" is for Alibi* are all murder mysteries. All are by definition genre fiction.

Which are pulp? Which are non-pulp? Upon what basis is this distinction drawn?

The so-called *True History* of Lucian, *From the Earth to the Moon* by Jules Verne, *The First Men in the Moon* by H. G. Wells, *The Moon Maid* by Edgar Rice Burroughs, *Fahrenheit 451* by Ray Bradbury, *Shadow on the Hearth* by Judith Merril, *The Dispossessed* by Ursula K. Le Guin, and *Camp Concentration* by Thomas M. Disch are all science fiction novels. All are by definition genre fiction.

What about Larry McMurtry's *Lonesome Dove,* Owen Wister's *The Virginian,* Ambrose Bierce's "An Occurrence at Owl Creek Bridge"—all are clearly Westerns.

Which are pulp? Which are non-pulp? Upon what basis is this distinction drawn?

If not a matter of genre versus non-genre, how else are we to distinguish between pulp and non-pulp books? Perhaps sheer antiquity or longevity should be our touchstone. But where, then, to draw the line? Perhaps at 1835, with Poe's "Manuscript Found in a Bottle." Or at 1896 when Frank A. Munsey converted *The Golden Argosy,* a children's paper, into *The Argosy,* the first pulp fiction magazine. Or 1935 when Allen Lane created Penguin Books, paperbacks to be sold "as cheaply as a pack of cigarettes." Or 1939 when Robert de Graff founded Pocket Books.

Sorry about that. No answer is provided.

Were Jane Austen's *Pride and* Prejudice and the Bronte sisters' *Jane Eyre* and *Wuthering Heights* non-pulp for a century and more, until they were "pulped," whereupon they became pulp fiction?

Pardon me. This makes no sense.

May we consider the author's intent? If he or she was trying to make a sociological statement the work is "real" literature. If the author was just there to entertain an audience and earn a living, the work is pulp? Alas, that doesn't work either. For one thing, we can't know what Dostoevsky was thinking when he wrote *Crime and Punishment* or what P. L. Travers was thinking when she created Mary Poppins. Besides, we're trying to evaluate the works, not their creators.

This brings us back to that sly trickster Marshall McLuhan and his clever but disastrously misleading maxim, "The medium is the massage." If one is to believe this bit of nonsense, then the meaning of *Yellow Sox 5, Earthworms 3* could easily become *Plaid Sox 6, Surinam Turtles 11* by changing the typeface in which the headline is set. Or *Tofu Burritos 8, Broccoli Stalks 4* by printing with a different color ink. Or *The Gostok Distims the Doshes* by broadcasting the news over cable television.

Balderdash.

Nonsense.

High Olde Academese babble.

Speaking of which, Rabinowitz deserves praise for writing much of her book in fairly plain English. She does have a penchant for words not to be found in the average reader's vocabulary. *Demotic, liminal, copula, periphrases, homology, hermeneutics, homosociality.* In a book written by an academic and meant to be read by academics, such verbiage may be permissible, but Rabinowitz's passionate commitment to "great reading for the millions" would call for a vocabulary accessible to the common man or woman.

And once in a while Professor Rabinowitz does lapse into something that can fairly be described as word-salad. Consider the following:

> "By linking leftist and black authors to Spillane through standardized formats and similar cover art, NAL's works anticipate a new postwar civil rights landscape, in some ways helping make *Brown v. Board of Education of Topeka, Kansas,* the Montgomery Bus Boycott, and their aftermath legible to a largely white working-class readership through detailed chartings of cross-race intimacy."

Indeed. One can well imagine a grease-stained mechanic crawling out from beneath a Mack truck on his lunch break, setting fire to a Lucky Strike gasper, slamming a handy church key through the top of a can of Bud, pulling a copy of *My Gun is Quick* by Mickey Spillane from his pocket and opening it to his dog-eared place, and grunting to himself, "Man, those brave civil rights marchers standing up to Bull Connor are sure a great bunch of Americans!"

Well, there I was, ready to go on record regarding *American Pulp* when I heard of *When Books Went to War,* by Molly Guptill Manning.

Manning's purview is necessarily narrower than Rabinowitz's. Another serious book from a prestigious house, but this time a commercial rather than an academic publisher. The author is an attorney for United States Second District Court of Appeals. She is also an authority on the interface (!) between mystery fiction and the legal world, author of *The Myth of Ephraim Tutt.*

Setting an historical context for her book, Manning describes the frantic pace of mobilization of the US as it became obvious that, like it or not, we were going to have to fight in World War Two. The standing army and navy were tiny, their equipment in short supply and much of it obsolete. There weren't even sufficient facilities to house and feed the vast numbers of newly-fledged servicemen (and women, but the latter were relatively few).

Uncle Sam jerry-built an array of tent cities and acres of wooden barracks. New soldiers and sailors learned the rules of military life, one of which is, *Hurry up and wait!* (Yes, I've been there, done that, and Manning gets it right.) With new recruits often sitting around with time on their hands and nothing to do, there was a desperate demand for books.

Librarians across the country banded together to create the VBCs—Victory Book Campaigns. Civilians were urged to donate books which would be sorted and sent to military bases to provide reading matter for trainees and other service members. Some 10 million books were donated, but while that is indeed an impressive number, there were two major problems with the VBCs:

> Ten million is a lot, but it was nowhere near enough to meet the demand for more and more and more books.

> The books were almost all hardcovers. Military trainees and other servicemen needed smaller, lighter, more flexible books to slide into backpacks or uniform pockets.

The result was the creation of the Council on Books in Wartime. This was an unprecedented cooperative venture by most of the publishers in the nation. With the support and encouragement of the government, the council created a new format for publication. These were paperbacks printed on light stock, set in a horizontal format and bound at the left end. They were printed in large runs and shipped in bundles to military bases and ships throughout the war. Soldiers and sailors were encouraged to read them and swap them. A typical book was usually good for up to six readings before it became unusable.

A set of books were issued each month. The number of titles in a monthly release varied, but generally there were thirty books in a release. Print runs started at 50,000 copies and rose steadily to a high of 155,000 per title in response to ever-increasing demand. Imagine the publication of thirty-odd titles in print runs of 110,000 copies, every month! ASEs were read in foxholes, on board ships, in heavy bombers.

The program was not without controversy. Do-gooders tried to keep "trash" off the lists. Politicians tried to censor the books for political reasons. A provision in the law setting up absentee voting measures for service personal far from home was written to prevent use of the books to influence the Presidential election of 1944.

Still, the books drew remarkable praise from the men they were directed to. There were even special selections designed to appeal to female service personnel.

The program ran from September 1943 to June 1947. Although active hostilities had ceased in August 1945, hundreds of thousands of American troops remained in Europe and Asia—some are still there! In those 46 monthly distributions, a total of 1322 books were issued, including a few titles that were reissued due to great demand.

Molly Guptill Manning is a talented writer with an eye for the dramatic and voice that carries the reader along, seldom if ever lapsing into dry data or clumsy prose. There are a few problems that should probably be attributed to copy-editors or proofreaders rather than the author. For instance in one epigraph the word "solider" appears, that should clearly be "soldier." Elsewhere there's a bizarre bit of pied type: "Servicemen were sexually frustrated, but the idea of providing that catered to such books prurient interests flustered some of the council's staff."

Sure flustered me. (Page 124, you could look it up.) But these flaws are few and minor.

An important executive of the ASE program, one Raymond Trautman, is introduced as a first lieutenant (page 26). By page 28 he is a inexplicably promoted to lieutenant colonel—jumping over captain and major in a single bound—and remains a lieutenant colonel for the rest of the book.

Regarding the choice and effect of the ASEs, Manning addresses the issue far more effectively than Rabinowitz. Rather than push an agenda—remember Rabinowitz's relentless campaign for her own notion of "good" books—Manning provides solid data.

She quotes "One Special Services officer who had worked with combat troops for two years (who) grew so worried about the men he supplied that he wrote the council begging for more books. He insisted there just 'never seemed to be enough,' and that combat troops were 'STARVED' for titles by Thorne Smith, Ernest Hemingway, John Steinbeck, H. Allen Smith, Tiffany Thayer, Sinclair Lewis, and Lloyd Douglas. The men also never stopped asking for *A Tree Grows in Brooklyn, Chicken Every Sunday, Forever Amber,* and *Strange Fruit."*

Gosh, no Henry James, Thomas Hardy, Plato. I'm shocked, shocked!

Month after month the soldiers and sailors gobbled up Westerns by Ernest Haycox, Nelson Nye, Max Brand, Peter Field, Alan LeMay, William Colt MacDonald, and Clarence Mulford; mysteries by Dorothy B. Hughes, Erle Stanley Gardner, Richard and Frances Lockridge, Kelly Roos; jungle adventures by Edgar Rice Burroughs, horror stories by H. P. Lovecraft, even a novelization of *The Adventures of Superman.*

Clearly, the success of the ASEs rested on the pleasure and relief they gave to millions of servicemen and women whose lives were risked—and in far too many cases, lost—defending their nation and its freedoms. Emphatically including the freedom to read uncensored books. Books that they read for entertainment.

Miscellany

BY THE COLUMN INCH

PREP SCHOOL SPORTS. Rings a bell, doesn't it?

When I was a teenager I attended a small boarding school in New Jersey. A number of colleges used to delay the enrollment of incoming freshman athletes, sending them to schools like ours for an extra year of growth and seasoning. A talented kid would use up his high school years, get his diploma, and enroll at a prep school for another year of chemistry or trig, and another season on the gridiron or hardwood before heading off to Ivy League U.

Who paid the tuition fees? Nobody talked about that.

Schools like mine were feeders to colleges in that era—longer ago than you would believe, children—just as the colleges today serve as feeders to the NFL and NBA.

Lots of our students wound up on major college teams, although big Mike Jarmoluk was our only alum to make it in the pros, at least that I know of. In 1946 he was drafted by the Detroit Lions, traded to the Chicago Bears, and played for the Boston Yanks and the New York Bulldogs before finding a home at tackle with the Philadelphia Eagles. They paid him $3,700 a year. In the off-season he worked in a brewery.

Major newspapers and radio stations in New York, Newark, Trenton, and Philadelphia set up networks of stringers at schools throughout the area. At our school a sports-loving teacher named Paul Hartpence—he was also our track and cross-country coach—was the contact point. He recruited a staff of at least slightly literate students to cover games. On a typical autumn Saturday there might be a football game, a soccer match, and a cross-country race to cover. In winter it was basketball, wrestling, riflery. In the spring, baseball, track, tennis.

We learned the jargon of each sport, and were encouraged to use the terminology. Cross-country runners were harriers, wrestlers were grunt-and-groaners, baseball was never played on a field, only on a diamond, and a pitcher wasn't a pitcher, he was a hurler or a fireballer or a wily craftsman.

Mr. Hartpence would assign a writer to each game. I must have been high on the depth chart because I always got the top sport—football, basketball, baseball. I became official scorer for all three. I remember sitting in the "press box"—an elevated section of wooden bleacher—on bitter November afternoons, unable to feel my fingers as I charted the plays, blue for the home team, red for visitors.

We'd trudge back to the press office—occasionally get a lift in Mr. Hartpence's ancient Ford coupe—and have to write multiple versions of the same story, so that each customer got his own text. There were hard deadlines and hard word-counts. "Two hundred words for the *Herald-Tribune* by 5:30 PM." "Two-twenty for the *Inquirer* by 5:45 PM." "One-fifty for the *Times* by 6:00." "Score only for WINS by 6:00 PM, phone this one to the sports desk."

A few customers wanted reports by telephone, but most took them electronically. We had a machine called a Teleprinter, an ancestor of a computer-and-modem. You'd sit in front of it and type in your story and it would print out on telegraph tape in our own office, and do the same in New York or Newark or Philly.

We had an extra day to hand-deliver typewritten copy to the local weekly in our town, and we could stretch out to length. I felt like a big-shot writing for the *Weekly Register*. Even got a by-line there as often as not.

Our customers used to pay by the column-inch. Mr. Hartpence would get a check and cash it and divide the proceeds among his minions. I don't remember how often payday came around, but I used to treasure those payments. Sometimes my share would be fifty cents. Sometimes as much as a dollar or even a dollar and a half.

And our clipping service would send back the proof of our efforts. There I was on the sports pages of the Sunday papers, cheek by jowl with greats like Stanley Woodward and Red Smith. Of course they had big columns with by-lines and photos, and I would have a single anonymous paragraph at the bottom of the page, but still, we were colleagues, weren't we?

I learned a lot from that job. For one thing, it was real work and I received real pay for it. For another, I learned to perform to specs. If the deadline was 6:00 and the customer wanted 185 words, you had your story on the wire on time and it was the prescribed length, not much more and not any less. And there was no not showing up for work because you had a headache or the sniffles, and there was no excuse if the muse wasn't with you that day.

You were a sportswriter. You were a professional, and you did your job.

Those little payments of fifty cents or a dollar were the most precious money I've ever earned, and the pride of performance taught me lessons that I've carried throughout my life as a writer.

NOT EXACTLY A SHOE SALESMAN

FOR A LONG time the only image I'd ever seen of Day Keene was a typical book-jacket photo. There isn't a lot of biographical data available on Keene and I don't know when or where the photo was made, but it has the look of a small-town studio run by a photographer who specialized in documenting weddings and young children for posterity. He might have scored big once every twelve months doing graduation portraits for the local high school's yearbook.

These shots were marked by standard poses and proper lighting. They were technically flawless and utterly unimaginative.

One glance and you'd guess that Keene was a shoe salesman, employed by a shop on the main street of that presumed small town. After twenty years of service—or maybe thirty—Keene would have been promoted to assistant manager, a job which he would hold with pride until reaching retirement age. He was probably a faithful member of Kiwanis, a Mason, and possibly a deacon of the nearby Presbyterian Church.

Bet he drove a six-year-old Plymouth.

Thinking about this some more, he might have been a high school biology teacher rather than a shoe salesman. The kids in his class always giggled a lot when they came to the unit on sexual reproduction. He likely was a scoutmaster as well.

All of this on the basis of one book-jacket portrait.

In it we see a smallish man with thinning, slicked-down hair, a neatly-clipped moustache, and horn-rimmed glasses. He's wearing a white shirt, a really silly polka-dotted bow tie, and a dark jacket. Probably had that photograph taken on his lunch break from the shoe store. Or on Saturday when he didn't have to teach.

In fact, he looked like a cross between H.T. Webster's immortal comic strip character, Caspar Milquetoast, and the brilliant, prissy movie actor, Clifton Webb.

You'd never take him for the prolific author of some of the toughest, nastiest crime fiction of his generation.

And then—*mirabile dictu!*—I came across another photo of Keene. In it he's at least a decade younger than he was in the previous photo. Hair was thicker. Moustache was bushier and less disciplined. No horn-rimmed glasses. And—heaven help us!—no ridiculous bow tie!

Yeah!

That was the Day Keene who wrote *My Flesh is Sweet, The Big Kiss-Off, Bring Him Back Dead, Passage to Samoa, Home is the Sailor,* and dozens of other tough crime novels, most of them flavored with more than a tincture of twisted sexuality.

Yeah! That was Day Keene.

Before going any farther, let's talk about by-lines, especially that peculiar one, Day Keene. It piqued my curiosity when I was a teenager back in Harry Truman's day, and I didn't find out what lay behind it until I got involved in the mystery field myself, not very many years ago.

Biographical data on Day Keene is regrettably sparse. Such fine scholars and critics as Bill Pronzini, Kevin Barton Smith, Al Guthrie, and even the great Bill Crider provide only minimal information. For as prolific and visible an individual as Keene was professionally, he seems to have been remarkably elusive in his personal life.

At least one website asserts that he was born on March 28, 1904, probably in Chicago. His legal name was Gunnar Hjerstedt or maybe Gunard Hjertstedt. He broke into the pulp field with a short story, "Pure and Simple," in *Detective Fiction Weekly* for October 31, 1931. He maintained a steady output of roughly one story a month for five months, all of them published in *DFW*. In Steve Lewis's fine bibliography, there is then a gap until May, 1935, when our boy pops up in *Clues Detective Stories* with "Case of the Bearded Bride."

Then another gap, until he reappeared in *Ace G-Man Stories* for September, 1940 with "It Could Happen Here!" by-lined Day Keene. If you've been following the Keene renaissance you will have seen several stories that he wrote under the name John Corbett between 1942 and 1950. And after that he never stopped running, turning out literally hundreds of criminous yarns for the crime pulps, with an occasional foray into general fiction mags like *Short Stories, Adventure, Argosy,* and slicks or semi-slicks like *Adam, Esquire* and *Man's Magazine.* He even sold stories to *Western Short Stories, Fifteen Western Tales, 10-Story Western,* and *Jungle Tales.*

But what was he doing between May, 1935 and September, 1940? The answer—or at least a partial answer—is provided by golden age radio scholar Victor A. Berch, who discovered that Hjerstedt wrote at least eight dramatic scripts for a radio series called *First Nighter.* He wrote at least one episode for *Behind the*

Camera Lines. He wrote scripts for the *Little Orphan Annie* radio serial, and may have penned as many as several hundred scripts for *Kitty Keene, Incorporated,* a radio series about a female private eye.

The story of how Gunnard Hjertstedt (or however we're spelling it at the moment) was transformed into Day Keene has many variations. Here's the consensus version:

Our boy was visiting the office of one of his pulp publishers, maybe to plead for an advance check. That kind of thing happened all the time. The office was almost certainly that of Popular Publications on 43rd Street in Manhattan. Throughout his career, Popular Pubs was Hjertstedt's favorite outlet. For instance, of the nine stories in the present volume, five were first published in *Detective Tales,* three in *Dime Mystery,* and one in *Popular Detective.* All three magazines were issued by Popular Publications.

That company was headed by Harry Steeger. The top editor was Rogers Terrill, and in all likelihood the person Brother Hjertstedt was there to see was Terrill. I imagine their conversation went something like this:

Terrill: Gunnard, I really like your story "It Could Happen Here!" I'm going to use it in *Ace G-Man Stories* and I want to blurb it on the cover, but your by-line, you know, isn't really very commercial. Half of our customers won't be able to read it and the other half won't be able to pronounce it. Please, buddy, give me a different by-line I can slug on the front of the book.

Hjertstedt: Uh, I dunno, Mr. Terrill, sir. Maybe—uh—do you have any suggestions?

Terrill: How about a family name? What was your mom's maiden name, that's usually a good one.

Hjertstedt: Keeney. Her name is Daisy Keeney.

Terrill: Hmm. Possibilities. Definite possibilities. But it needs work. How about cutting it a little? We certainly don't want a name like Daisy on the cover of *Ace G-Man Stories.*

Hjertstedt: Okay. Let's drop the last syllable of each word. That leaves us with Day Keene. What do you think?"

Terrill: "Okay, I think that's it. Now, how much do you need? How soon can you give me another story? I can't just go writing advance checks to every writer who wanders in here with his hand out!"

And so it was. Or at least, that's how it might have been. Gunnard also wrote as Lewis Dixon, William Richards, and Daniel

White. All pretty generic by-lines. But Day Keene is the one he used for the greatest bulk of his work, and it's the one by which he is remembered.

Unlike many of his pulp-writing colleagues who established popular series characters and returned to them frequently, Keene created few recurring characters. Doc Egg, the Times Square druggist who pops up in several of Keene's New York stories, is an intriguing figure. It's unfortunate that Keene didn't make more use of Doc. And Keene brought back the Chicago private eye firm of McPherson, McCreedy and McCoy more than once, but these characters were never particularly vivid and the stories were carried by their not-especially-startling plots.

By the end of the 1940s the handwriting was on the wall for the pulp magazines, and while many of them survived well into the 1950s—and a few even into the early '60s—most of the better pulpers headed for safe harbor elsewhere. Some, like Howard Browne, wound up in Hollywood writing for the movies or for that new medium called television. Others, including Henry Kuttner, Edmond Hamilton, Alfred Bester and Otto Binder, became comic book scripters either full- or part-time. But the greatest number skedaddled into the book biz, especially the burgeoning paperback field, where Keene eventually wrote something like 50 novels. Exact count is hard to pin down, as publishers came and went pell-mell, sometimes changing titles as they scrambled to survive.

The great majority of Keene's novels were criminous in content, generally set in the more-or-less realistic contemporary world of the 1950s and early '60s. However, he did experiment with other genres.

World Without Women (1960), co-authored with Leonard Pruyn, was Keene's sole foray into science fiction. In this novel, a plague wipes out most of the women in the world and leaves most of the few survivors sterile. Only a few fertile women remain, and hope for the survival of the human species depends on them. The novel focuses on the husband of one of these surviving fertile females. Think half of Philip Wylie's *The Disappearance* (1951) flavored with a tincture of Richard Matheson's *The Shrinking Man* (1956).

Seed of Doubt (1961) is set in a wealthy Florida town. As Keene's plot evolves, a leading male citizen proves to be sterile and his wife conceives through artificial insemination. Why this development should be regarded as a shameful secret and lead to a series of melodramatic and violent acts, is better left unexplored at this late date.

Chautauqua (1961) was co-written with Dwight Babcock, the latter writing as Dwight Vincent. In 1969 this became an Elvis Presley vehicle, and I think I need say no more about it than that.

Guns Along the Brazos (1967), a Western set in northern Mexico and Texas, concerns a onetime rancher and former Confederate army doctor who emigrates to Mexico after the Civil War. Upon returning to Texas to reclaim his ranch he finds that his wife and their ranch foreman have been plotting to betray him.

But let's get back to Day Keene's mainstay, the novel of crime and suspense. Typically, these books are not detective stories or even mysteries as we commonly think of such things. A Keene protagonist is most often a well-intentioned twenty- or thirtyish male who falls under the spell of a sexually dynamic woman of devious motives. Devious to the reader, that is. Keene's hero is so smitten that he follows his new sweetie-pie into trouble that keeps getting deeper and nastier by the page.

A favorite device is to have the mob commit a heinous crime, then frame Keene's protagonist for the dirty deed. Keene's hero tries to determine who really committed the crime and hang the label of guilt upon the real criminal. That's the only way he can clear himself. Of course the mobsters don't want the crime to be solved, and they go after our hero.

At the same time, the cops (variously corrupt, inept, and brutal) are also chasing him. At various times in the book he'll be caught by either the police or the mob and beaten within an inch of his life, only to escape and resume his seemingly hopeless search. All of this action—and tension—is subjected to occasional brief intermissions during which he gets to practice belly-to-belly gymnastics with one or another lubricious young lady.

Keene could occasionally pull a switch on the reader. An example of this was *Who Has Wilma Lathrop?* (1955) a convoluted story of treachery, double-dealing, suspense, and—for once in a Keene opus—some major surprises. It's one of his better efforts.

Trying to pick the best of Keene's many novels is a daunting task, but certainly a leading candidate would be *Death House Doll* (1953). In this book Sergeant Mike Duval, a veteran of both World War Two and Korea, returns to the US on a mission. His brother had been killed in action, and Duval is to visit his deceased sibling's widow. Mike is still in the army, and he has a leave of limited duration.

Problem is, the woman in the case has been convicted of murder and faces electrocution within a matter of days. Duval gets to see her, courtesy of an understanding warden who appreciates Duval's military service. Mike meets the widowed Mona Duval and becomes convinced that she is innocent of the crime for which she is to be executed.

He leaves the prison determined to prove Mona's innocence despite her refusal to cooperate. Before long Mike is being chased by the mob (they want Mona to take the rap), the military police (he's overstayed his leave and is technically AWOL), and the regular cops (okay, so he did beat up a few guys).

The result is a madcap hunt-and-chase novel. Keene somehow manages to keep things under control (sort of) and to tie up a spaghetti-bowl full of loose ends in a mere 140 Ace Double pages. The book is absolutely stunning, unforgettable, Day Keene at his very best.

I should also mention that he created only one continuing character in his novels. This was Johnny Aloha, an LA-based Irish-Hawaiian private eye. Aloha appeared in *Dead in Bed* (1959) and *Payola* (1960). There's a light, tongue-in-cheek feel to these two books. I have a feeling that Keene had encountered the great Richard S. Prather's Shell Scott capers, which were immensely popular at the time. Keene decided to try his hand at something similar. He substituted Aloha's occasional usage of Hawaiian cultural references for Shell Scott's fondness for tropical fish as a character tag or "funny hat." Otherwise, they're just about interchangeable. Big, tough, ex-military, cynical, sexy.

Apparently Keene found the genre uncongenial, as he dropped Aloha after just two books.

Having moved to the Gulf Coast of Florida, where several of his later books are set, Keene joined a congenial group of hardboiled writers who had settled in the Tampa Bay area. To all evidence (of which there is, alas, far too little) he enjoyed the tropical lifestyle and the company of his colleagues. Somewhere along the way he had married and fathered a son. His last new book, *Acapulco G.P.O.*, was published in 1967. He died in Los Angeles on January 9, 1969.

As for the stories in the present collection, I am indebted to our series editor, John Pelan, who tracked down the pulp magazines in which they originally appeared, and assembled them. All else aside, John has made my job incalculably easier by finding the stories in this collection (like many others!). All I've had to do is sit down and enjoy them. And believe me, Day Keene understood the first commandment of the fiction writer: *Give the Readers Something they'll Enjoy!*

The sign over every successful pulp editor's door read, *Fiction is a Medium of Entertainment.* Anything else, if there had to be anything else, was secondary. If you wanted to sell your readers on your philosophy, if you wanted to explain to them your brilliant insight into the human condition, if you wanted them to understand a turning point of history, if you wanted to teach them something about the wonders of chemistry, physics and astronomy . . . all of those goals were okay, provided you showed the customers a good time.

For that matter, if there are any would-be fictioneers in the audience today, I recommend following that same piece of advice.

The stories in the present volume were published over the period a decade, from 1941 to 1951. During this time the pulps had weathered a downturn during the Second World War, due to the rationing of paper supplies. Once the war had ended they came roaring back to life. Despite the outbreak of the Korean War in 1950, they continued to prosper for a while, only to die a lingering death in the 1950s and '60s.

Keene's interests carried his protagonists from Chicago to New York, Florida, and California. The stories are driven, for the most part, by greed. Insurance scams and missing heirs abound. Treacherous, sexually predatory women lurk at every corner. From time to time Keene injects some sly humor, and in at least one instance there's an outrageous lift from a famous Sherlock Holmes story. Or maybe that was homage.

In reading several dozen of Keene's hundreds of stories, I've been deeply impressed by the growth in their quality, from his earliest "Hjertstedt" efforts of the 1930s to the many productions of his mature years. The fact is—and let's be brutally honest about this!—Keene's earliest stories are pretty weak. The ideas are slight and unoriginal, e.g., a dart gun hidden in a camera, a crooked bartender who feeds his customers mickey finns and rolls them for their cash. The characters are very thinly established, e.g., red hair, tall and massive or short, dark, and energetic, given to slang or committed to "proper" English speech. The pacing is jerky and there are technical flaws in the prose that any good high school composition teacher would have red-lined, e.g., changes in narrative viewpoint whenever convenient for the author.

In fact, it's a wonder that Hjertstedt sold those earliest stories at all. I've got a theory which I'll share with you. The pulp magazine field was huge in the 1920s. In the '30s, with the Depression growing ever deeper, there was some shrinkage in the field but the volume of production remained high. Prices, however, dropped. Cover price of many pulps slid from 25¢ down to 20¢, 15¢, 10¢, and in a few cases even to 5¢. Payments to authors dropped from several cents per word to a penny or even a fraction of a cent. Writers' magazines of the era contained letters from pulp authors complaining that publishers were retitling and reissuing their earlier works while making no payments to them at all.

And yet the hungry presses kept churning out a fresh deluge of issues each month. Titles came and went literally by the hundreds. Of all the pulp categories—westerns, science fiction, horror, love stories, sports stories, war stories and so on—mystery and detective magazines were the most popular and consequently the most numerous.

If an average pulp contained ten stories, that meant that the demand for fiction ran to literally thousands of stories per month. In this market, as science fiction writer Robert A. Heinlein theorized a decade later, virtually any story with the faintest glimmer of merit could find a home somewhere, in some periodical, providing only that the author keep it circulating in the face of form rejection slips.

That, at least, is how I believe Gunnard Hjertstedt got his start. Now, more than three quarters of a century later, we can be grateful that he didn't give up. As he learned his craft he learned to create characters with depth and pathos and plots with subtlety and complexity. And he honed his once clunky and graceless prose into a keen-edged instrument to be envied by generations of successors.

It's also my personal belief that Keene's experience writing radio scripts contributed to the development of his talent. Audio drama has the same major ingredients as prose fiction—character, plot, setting—but it also has its own set of requirements. Terseness and clarity are paramount among them. The reader of a novel or a magazine story can linger over a convoluted sentence; the listener cannot. And timing is vital in radio drama. The novelist can go on for another ten pages or another hundred if that will make for a

better book. The radio writer must wrap in time for the proverbial
message from his sponsor.

Above all, Day Keene understood that principle, that principle
that whatever other purposes to which it could be put, fiction always was and still remains a medium of entertainment. For a
demonstration of how well he understood it, simply turn the page
and start reading the stories in this book.

THE MAN IN THE BATHTUB

WHEN PAT AND I moved into our house on Claremont Avenue in Berkeley, California, we soon started meeting our neighbors. In our former hometown, Poughkeepsie, New York, there was very little variety in the neighborhood. It was simple. Everybody worked for the International Business Machines company. Your neighbor was an engineer or a programmer or a manager and the only kind of small talk that occurred at local cocktail parties was shop talk.

On Claremont Avenue, our neighbors to the left were a retired University of California professor and his wife. Professor Stripp was a fascinating man. His father had been a onetime minor league baseball player. He played for Salt Lake City. That meant that young Freddie got to be a batboy, travel with the team, wear a miniature uniform, and fraternize with the players.

A dream job for a ten-year-old.

The Stripps had raised two sons, and I suspect they were suffering with empty nest syndrome. Now Dr. Stripp would join Tommy and me for pitching lessons on many summer afternoons. That was marvelous. He was a lovely old man. His standard greeting any time he passed you in the street was, "Hello, neighbor."

To the right, our neighbors were Don and Alice Schenker, and their striking redheaded daughter. Don and Alice published underground comic books in the 1960s and '70s, including the fabulous *Zap* and many others that are worth a fortune today. Any time I stood in front of my house, struggling with a lawnmower or hedge-clippers, I'd likely see Robert Crumb arriving at or leaving the Schenkers, or S. Clay Wilson, or maybe Moe Moskowitz, proprietor of Moe's Books on Telegraph Avenue.

Our neighbor directly across the street was a colorful Danish immigrant named Birgit Bruno. In her home country, Birgit had loved American jazz and attended shows by touring American jazz orchestras. Years after the fact, once I had become involved with the San Francisco music scene, Birgit told me about her youth in Denmark. She was a band chick—the equivalent of latter-day groupies.

She told me that she had become pregnant after a one-night stand with a member of Count Basie's orchestra. The result was a daughter whom Birgit named Genevieve. Genevieve's father knew nothing about this.

Not very long after Genevieve's birth, Birgit immigrated to the US, bringing her baby with her, and settling in Berkeley.

Eventually she met and married a local resident, a City of Berkeley firefighter and amateur drummer. With her husband Birgit had four more daughters: Sasha, Jeannie, Annie, and Laura. Then Birgit's husband decided that he'd had enough of firefighting. He resigned from the Fire Department, cashed in his retirement fund, gave the money to Birgit for herself and the girls, and moved to New York to pursue his career in music.

Birgit was a remarkably strong, self-reliant person. She had to find a way to support herself and her daughters. Before long she had got a job as a school bus driver. Soon she was able to supplement her salary with some modest fencing and low level dope dealing. At one time I remember Pat getting a beautiful leather coat that had fallen off the back of a truck.

The oldest of Birgit's girls, Genevieve, had developed wanderlust and moved to Alaska. The younger four, grouped closely in age, stayed with their mom and attended a wonderful elementary school just up the street. Pat and I sent our three children to the same school, although at this point only Ken and Kathy were old enough to enroll. Tommy would follow in a few years.

When Kathy discovered that there were four sisters, all of them about her age, attending her school and living across the street from her house, she was delighted. Next thing you knew, the five of them were in and out of each other's houses daily.

Young Tommy, in the meanwhile, had developed a secret language. This is not an uncommon occurrence—science fiction writer David H. Keller wrote one of his best stories about the phenomenon. Tommy would toddle up to Kathy and her closest friend from across the street, Annie, and chatter away to them. Pat and I would be totally mystified by this, but Kathy and Annie understood him perfectly. They would tell us exactly what he had said.

"He's hungry, he wants a cookie, he has to go to the bathroom." Standard toddler stuff, but they could understand him and no one else could.

One day I spent several hours in the yard raking leaves, gathering them up and putting them in garbage pails. At the end of the session I was covered with perspiration and leaf dust. It made a messy coating on my skin. I put away the rake, climbed upstairs, disrobed and lowered myself into a steaming tub.

Ah, bliss.

I started to rub shampoo into my hair.

The door swung open.

What?

I hadn't bothered to lock the bathroom door. I was the only person in the house—I thought. Could this be a daylight home invasion burglary? But school was out for the day, and as I turned toward the door, in marched Kathy.

Followed by Annie.

And Jeannie.

And Laura.

And Sasha.

"Dad," Kathy said, "these are my friends." And she proceeded to introduce them to me.

Annie. Jeannie. Laura. Sasha.

I kept my cool as best I could. The Bruno girls weren't really very interested in me. Very soon they trooped out. I climbed out of the tub, dried myself off, and dressed.

Nobody said much about the incident for a couple of days. I told Pat about it and we shared a good laugh.

Then, a couple of afternoons later, the doorbell rang. I think I'd been auditioning the latest shipment of LP's to arrive. I was working as a pop media journalist and sometime music critic in those days, and it was a very pleasant way to earn a few dollars. All too few, alas, but that's another matter.

Birgit was a heavy-boned, broad-shouldered woman. She filled the doorway. I invited her into the living room and turned the music down. "I want to talk to you," Birgit said.

I thought, "Uh-oh. Here it comes!"

Something about my being a dirty old man and how dare I expose myself to a room full of innocent little girls and . . . jeez, what next? This woman was nearly as tall as I was, and must have outweighed my by close to forty pounds. One hard punch and . . .

But that wasn't what I got. What I got was, "The girls told me about visiting you in the bathtub and it was so kind of you to let them. You know, how are they going to learn how men are made if they never get to see one?"

One weekend not long after this, I noticed that the Count Basie Orchestra was scheduled to perform in Berkeley. Birgit told me that she planned to attend. The show took place on a Saturday night.

The next day, I saw Birgit. "How was the Basie show?"

She told me that it was wonderful.

"Did you see your old friend from Denmark?"

"He's still in the band. You know, I couldn't pick him out by his face, but I recognized him by his trombone."

UNCLE EDDIE

FOR STARTERS, HE wasn't really my uncle. My mother, Sylvia, had died when I was six years old. My father, Sol, waited a few years, then remarried. He was a successful business executive and his second wife was his longtime secretary's younger sister. Eddie was her younger brother, which made him, I suppose, my "uncle in-law." If there is such a thing. To me, he was just Uncle Eddie.

Eddie had been a machinist working at the IBM manufacturing facility in Poughkeepsie, New York, before the Second World War. When the US got into the war and Eddie wound up in uniform, the personnel officers took one look at Eddie's skills and decided to make him an aircraft mechanic. He wound up spending the war in England, servicing B-17's.

If you've ever seen one of those wartime movies claiming to portray the suffering and heroism of bomber crews—*Twelve O'Clock High* or *Memphis Belle*—you surely saw the greasemonkeys who kept the engines running and patched up the bullet-holes and sent the aircrews off to destroy Hitler's tank factories and welcomed them home when they staggered back over the English Channel and pancaked on their landing fields while the crash wagons raced to pull wounded crewmen out of the planes.

In 1945 the war ended and Uncle Eddie came to see me. I was ten years old. Eddie was still wearing his uniform, his sergeant's chevron's proudly displayed on his sleeves, the olive green shirt and trousers spotless, creases pressed to knife-blade sharpness. He showed me how they made their beds for inspection in the army. I was certain that he'd won the war singlehanded. I'm still halfway convinced of that.

Somehow Eddie and his sister, my father's second wife, didn't get along very well. It took me several decades to learn the reason. My father's second wife was the youngest of four girls born to her parents. The three older girls were fairly close in age. There was a gap of several years, then the fourth girl arrived. For several years, as she told me long afterwards, she was treated as the Little Princess of her family.

Then arrived the bonus baby: Eddie. After all those years and all those girls, here was the gift of heaven: a boy! Eddie, of course, became instantly the Little Prince, and the youngest girl became just another girl.

She decided to do something about this. She decided to kill her baby brother. Details were never revealed to me, and now I'm sure I'll never learn them. But the attempt must have been pretty severe. Three quarters of a century later, when my Eddie's sister died and I telephoned to ask him to the funeral he said, "That's too bad but I'm too busy," and hung up.

But back to England and the days of those bomber raids on wartime Germany.

In 1994 I was researching a novel that would eventually become part of my Lindsey-and-Plum series under the title *The Bessie Blue Killer.* It involved the air war of half a century earlier, and I spent a good deal of time at the Oakland International Airport. There were several fly-ins of historic aircraft and the men who had flown them in the 1940s.

I got to meet several of the famous Tuskegee Airmen and to crawl around lovingly restored bombers including a B-17 Flying Fortress and a B-29 Superfortress. I encountered a onetime bombardier whom I'll call Luther Simpson (not his real name), an energetic bantam of an old-timer who proved to be a born raconteur.

I asked if by any chance he'd ever encountered my Uncle Eddie—stranger things have happened—but he had not. However, Luther realized that he had a willing audience and he proceeded to tell his stories.

One involved a staff sergeant who'd run the squadron office. He was a nasty martinet if ever there was one. He was a stickler when it came to army paperwork, leave requests, and promotions. He was in charge of the squadron mail clerk, and insisted that the clerk follow every army regulation to the last microscopic footnote.

Sergeant Young was his name. He was a middle-aged army lifer. His favorite stunt came if an airman stopped at the company office before boarding a plane for a bombing mission. The airman asked if the day's mail from home had arrived and Sergeant Young—he was a staff sergeant, three chevrons and two rockers, bucking for master sergeant—shook his head.

"You know better than that, Private, mail call isn't till 0900 and it's only 0630."

"I know that, Sarge. But we're going up at 0700. By 0900 we'll be over Nice headed for Hamburg."

"Not my fault, sonny. You can get your letters when you get back from Germany."

Funny thing was, Luther Simpson told me, Sergeant Young was jealous of the flyers who risked their lives day after day. He was always trying to hitch a ride on a B-17 or a B-24 Liberator. The 17s carried a crew of nine, Luther said. Pilot, co-pilot, navigator, flight engineer, bombardier, two side gunners, tail gunner, belly gunner.

The pilot was always an officer, generally a colonel, designated as aircraft commander. He'd have to approve carrying a passenger, and he always turned down Sergeant Young's pleas. And Sergeant Young kept being a complete s.o.b. Everybody knew Sergeant Young, by reputation if not by personal experience.

But one day the guys in a particular crew decided they'd had enough of Sergeant Young's nastiness. Luther Simpson seemed a little reluctant to tell me the details, but there seemed to be something to do with rejecting the paperwork on some poor gunner who really needed the few extra bucks that an added stripe on his sleeve would bring him every month. It sounded like a bit of petty meanness to me, but as Luther Simpson told the story this airman really needed the extra money and Sergeant Young took particular glee in screwing up the guy's promotion.

All the guys in the crew with Young's victim got together. All the enlisted men in the crew, that is. The officers didn't know anything about this, or at least they weren't supposed to. The gunners and the navigator and the bombardier and the flight engineer got together and invited Sergeant Young along on their next mission. Young was delighted. I guess he wanted to go home after the war and parade around like a hero.

The next morning, just as the sun was rising over the rolling hills behind the airfield, ten men instead of nine climbed aboard one of the 17s. They flew in formation with hundreds of other American bombers. They were escorted by P-51 Mustangs that fought off German fighters as best they could, supplemented by the machine ginners in the bombers. They dropped their bombs and circled around for the return flight to England.

Sergeant Young couldn't have been happier, until he found himself gripped by both elbows. The bomb bay doors were still open. The two airmen who had Young by the arms lifted him, threw him forward, and down through the open bomb bay he went, screaming all the way.

Luther swore the story was true. As for me, I wouldn't know. Most of the people I dealt with when I was in the army were pretty good people, but there were a few rotten eggs, one captain named—oh, never mind. This is Luther Simpson's turn in the spotlight, not mine.

The B-17s were called Flying Fortresses, and when I was a kid and the war was going on, several thousand miles from my school in New Jersey, we were encouraged to think of them as mighty aerial dreadnaughts. The first time I saw one on the ground in Oakland, and got to climb into it as make my way around, I was startled by how small it was.

I stood in the middle of the fuselage and stood with my fingertips outstretched like that fellow in the da Vinci drawing, and I could touch the inside skin of the airplane with both hands. And the skin wasn't impervious armor, it was thin metal, aluminum I think, and I could have poked a dimple in it if I'd tried.

The B-29s were pressurized and heated, which did a lot for the crew who flew them. But the 17 was an older model. Flyers had to wear oxygen masks and electrically heated flying suits. Those suits had actually been invented during the First World War; they were designed to keep the flyers from freezing at altitudes of 20,000 feet or even higher.

They were modular. The boots zipped onto the pants, which zipped onto the torso, as did the sleeves.

Luther told me that he'd been on a bombing raid on Berlin, and as the squadron turned back to return to base he discovered that one of his legs was getting very cold. He checked his suit and discovered that there was a short circuit and his lower leg wasn't getting any heat.

He must have said something panicky into the plane's intercom, because the flight engineer—a pal of his—made his way into the nose of the plane, where Luther's flight station kept him, and made some gestures to Luther.

The engineer unzipped one of his own boots and pointed to Luther's. It didn't take long for Luther to get the message. He unzipped his faulty boot and swapped with his pal. Within minutes he could feel the warmth and life coming back into his foot.

Twenty minutes later the engineer was back and they swapped boots again. And so on, until they were safely on the ground once again.

"Saved my leg," Luther told me. "I would have lost it to frostbite if my friend hadn't swapped boots with me."

I hope my Uncle Eddie was at the Enlisted Men's Club that night, and shared a drink with those airmen.

CLUB FIGHTER

BY 1953 I WAS a college student, struggling to rehabilitate myself from a horrendous school experience of the previous years. My mother was deceased, my father had remarried and I didn't get along with his second wife, and our household seemed to operate in a state of quiet tension and suppressed hostility. This was not good.

Then my father did something surprising. He invited me to attend the local boxing matches with him. We were living in South Florida. I was attending the University of Miami. And there was a weekly boxing card at the Miami Beach Auditorium, a modern, comfortable venue that was used for everything from symphony concerts to basketball games.

The bouts at the auditorium featured a variety of club fighters, and in case you're unfamiliar with the concept, let me put it this way. A club fighter is the boxing equivalent of a career minor league baseball player. Club fighters perform frequently, they make a fair living, and sometimes they even develop a loyal fan base.

But they seldom rise above this level, and the lucky ones retire to a second career with their brains unscrambled and their intellects intact. They're the guys who fill the records of champions who compile long strings of victories as they rise to the top of their profession.

In fact I'd had a very brief and utterly undistinguished fling as a boxer in my teens. One of the best decisions I've made in my life was, not to pursue that career.

The most popular regular on boxing cards at the Miami Beach Auditorium was a middleweight billed as Yama Bahama. His real name was William Horatio Butler, Jr. Born on the island of Bimini on February 16, 1933, he engaged in a local sport called "battle royals." In a battle royal six boys, typically twelve years old, would fight at one time, bare knuckled and blindfolded. Last boy standing was declared the winner. And this was all for fun.

Young William had two older brothers who were skilled amateur boxers. He followed them to the gym, started training, and developed his talent.

His first professional bout took place at the Miami Beach Auditorium in November, 1953. He won on a first round technical knockout.

He was a hard worker, sometimes fighting as often as three times in a month. His first eight bouts were all at the Miami Beach Auditorium, and he won them all. He quickly became a crowd favorite.

In the meanwhile, my father and I were getting back together emotionally. I started to realize that he was not the unfeeling tyrant I'd thought him to be. He discovered that I wasn't the rebellious sluggard he'd thought.

And Yama Bahama's career was taking off. He fought in Detroit, Chicago, Honolulu, and Madison Square Garden. He even had bouts at one of boxing's holiest shrines, the St. Nicholas Arena in New York. He traveled to Europe and fought in Rome, and returned to his home in the Bahamas for bouts in Nassau and Bimini.

In the meanwhile, my father and I were getting along better. Boxing matches at the Miami Beach Auditorium became a father-and-son ritual. My brother, Jerry, was serving in the United States Navy and my father's second wife had no desire to attend these pugilistic events. But Dad and I would keep score of each bout and compare notes with each other and with the official judges.

I suppose I identified with Yama. Seeing him box week after week, I studied his style. He was a skillful boxer, not overwhelmingly powerful, but he had quick hands and was capable of delivering a combination of lefts and rights in what seemed like split seconds. His footwork was excellent—that had been my greatest weakness in the ring. This morning—literally!—I came across a video of one of his bouts on YouTube. For a few moments I was back in the Miami Beach Auditorium and it was the 1950s again.

Unfortunately my father's health was increasingly fragile in those years. At the same time I was completing my undergraduate efforts at college while earning a small income working at a local movie theater. In January, 1956, I received my degree; by April of that year I was in the United States Army.

Not long after that, my father passed away. I'd been back on leave several times, and we had good conversations, even talking about plans to start a family business once both Jerry and I were home and out of uniform. That was never to be. Still, these were important occasions. The last time I saw my father alive, he talked about his first wife, my mother. She had been a taboo topic in the sixteen years since her death. In all those years I'd never heard him speak of her. On this day he said wistfully, "She was the sweetest person I ever knew."

Yama Bahama must have had the greatest night of his career on June 18, 1958. He fought the great Kid Gavilan at the Miami Beach Auditorium and won a unanimous decision. I would have loved to be there with my Dad, but he was no longer living and I was many miles from home defending my country from Nikita Khrushchev and his evil minions. But reading about that match in the next day's paper, I almost felt as if we'd been there, keeping score for ourselves, just to keep the judges honest.

As for history's judgment of Yama Bahama—he was more than a typical club fighter. Over a professional career that lasted for a decade he compiled a record of 77 wins, 14 losses, and three draws. In those 94 bouts he had scored 26 knockouts and been kayoed only twice, one of them a TKO when he bled from a cut over one eye. I suspect that was the result of a head-butt, but after all these years there's no point in making an issue of the foul. Yama's last bout was fought in Bimini in March of 1963. He won it by a TKO—as he had won his first bout, in Miami Beach, in 1953. He died in June, 2009, at the age of 76.

I will confess that I've forgotten the names of Yama's opponents—with the exception of Kid Gavilan, of course. They were typically club fighters, not nearly as good as Yama Bahama. But as a modest bow to these fallen heroes, I will list the opponents whom Yama defeated in that first rush of matches in Miami Beach, between November 17, 1953 and March 2, 1954: Henry Lee Irwin (points), Eddie Armstrong (points), Humphrey Humphries (points), Phil Brick (knockout), Baldwin Deveaux (points), Baldwin Deveaux again (points), Johnny Williams (knockout), and Jimmy Wilson (knockout)—all within the space of three and half months.

In the boxing record books Yama Bahama was an above-average club fighter, but in my memory and in my heart, he was a champion.

Think Pieces

Ethan Lupoff reading his grandfather's writing

LEARNING TO READ

I'VE WRITTEN ELSEWHERE about the experience of learning to read. In case you haven't read the story, here it is in a nutshell: One of my earliest recollections is of lying on the living room rug on a Sunday morning next to my brother. The newspaper comic section was spread in front of us. No less a personage than Fiorello LaGuardia, the Mayor of the City of New York, was reading the comics over the radio.

The mayor was reading Flash Gordon. Jerry and I were focused on the story. I can still hear the mayor's odd, funny voice after all these years. I can still see those wonderful Alex Raymond drawings: handsome Flash, lovely Dale, bearded Doctor Zarkov, saturnine Emperor Ming. I can see the soaring architecture and the Art Deco spaceships (even though, at that age, I'd never heard of Art Deco).

But there was something missing. There were all those little squiggles, hooks and curves and lines and dots, that I knew were words. The mayor, miles away in his radio studio, could read them. My brother, lying next to me, could read them. But I couldn't read them.

I very nearly went mad with jealousy. I demanded that someone, anyone, teach me the great secret of turning those hooks and curves and lines and dots into words. I was told that I would learn to read when I started school, just as Jerry had learned to read when he started school. But Jerry was three years older than I, and to a small child three years is an inconceivable stretch of time.

The result was a stalemate, and there was no peace in our house until my grandmother, the softest-hearted member of the family, gave in. We sat down together after lunch one day, and she showed me the letters, and told me their sounds, and how they went together to make words. By dinner time I knew how to read.

Some thoroughly educated friends of mine have heard this story and told me that it's untrue. I've created a false memory, they tell me. Learning to read in a single afternoon is quite impossible. But other friends have told me that it is indeed possible. They've done it themselves.

I've seen my children and my grandchildren learning to read, and although they've done so over a period of many years and a distance of many miles, they've all followed the same process.

277

First you learn the letters and their sounds.
This is the letter "a" and it sounds like this:____
This is the letter "b" and it sounds like this:____
. . . and so on.

Once you've learned the letters and their sounds, you learn to put them together to make words:
The letters "c" and "a" and "t" go together and they spell "cat."

But now, thinking about it, I find myself wondering, How does a child who is deaf from birth learn to read? She could see the letters, see the word "cat" and see a picture of a cat (or a real cat, if one were available). I suppose the process would be similar to the "flash card" method that was foisted on the public some years ago, and seems, happily, to have gone to the trash-bin of pedagogical history along with the New Math and other cock-eyed nostrums.

Maybe this process is more like the method used to teach children to read Chinese or other character-based or pictographic languages, rather than phoneme-based languages like English. In a way this would be a more difficult method, as each new word would have to be learned as a separate unit. A hearing child, having learned the letters and their sounds, could "sound out" c-a-t-t-a-i-l and get "cat-tail," but a "whole-word" oriented child, even if she knew "cat," would be baffled by "tail."

On the other hand, I think that people who have learned reading by the sound-it-out method are inevitably and permanently slowed down by the mental process, even if it is subconscious, of working through the sound-it-out process whenever they read. But a deaf person, never having been exposed to that process, would read far faster than a hearing person. She would go directly from the three black squiggles that spell "cat" to the concept of "cat" without all of that mental processing of letters-into-words-into-mental-images.

As a consequence, I am inclined to think that deaf persons are intrinsically smarter—or at least, faster—than hearing persons.

I don't know if this is true. I don't know if it's been researched. Maybe there's a good topic there for a graduate student's thesis. If you figure this out, please let me know.

TRIANGLE ON THE SIDEWALK

PAT AND I have lived in our present home for a long time—since 1970. I don't know how many times I've walked from our house to the corner of the nearest cross-street. In forty-four years, averaging at a guess four times a day, that would be . . . hmm, something like 58,240 times.

And that's not even allowing for leap years.

Just a few steps from my driveway there's a triangle very neatly impressed in the cement. In simple, sans serif capital letters, it says

THE OAKLAND
PAVING
CO.

Directly above the triangle in a neat rectangular box is recorded the year the sidewalk was laid down and the triangle placed there by conscientious workers. 1912.

For most of the years I've lived here I never noticed the triangle, its legend and the date, but lately every time I've walked over it I read the message and the date.

1912.

Assuming that even the youngest of the workers—probably all of them work*men*, I doubt that women had broken through the cement ceiling by 1912—were about twenty years old in that halcyon year, they would be 122 years old in this year, 2014. Very, very unlikely that any of them survive.

That sidewalk must have felt the tread of millions of shoes in the past 102 year. Certainly children's shoes as they made their way to the elementary school a few blocks up Claremont Avenue from here. I don't think that John Muir School is a century old—not yet—but it's been there for a long time. It was already a neighborhood institution when our children attended John Muir in the early 1970s.

Plenty of University of California students, and the leather bluchers and high-heel pumps of alumni returning every other year to attend the Big Game between Cal and rival Stanford.

Soldiers' boots during two World Wars, and the Korean War, and the Vietnam War, and the first Gulf War and the second Gulf War. My own boots for several years during the Cold War, but I was lucky—neither clever nor virtuous—enough to get into uniform and back out again between wars.

Hippies' sandals and techies' sneakers.

And what have I left out?

The lives that have passed in front of my house. The generations of adolescents and adults, young couples starting out on the exciting adventure of shared lives, becoming parents and grandparents in turn, and then giving way to newer generations.

Claremont Avenue is a broad thoroughfare. The late novelist and poet Stanton A. Coblentz told me that his mother sent him across San Francisco Bay to find safety with relatives in Oakland after that April day when the earth shook and the sky burned and San Francisco lay in ruins. He lived in Oakland for some years, commuting to classes at the new University of California campus in Berkeley.

A horse car line ran up the middle of Claremont Avenue in those days. That's why the street is wide.

Radio was a novel toy when the sidewalk was laid down in front of my house, although even the house wasn't yet here. It was built in 1925. There were a fair number of telephones; surely I need not say that they were all landlines. There were motion pictures—silent—and automobiles but still more horses than autos.

Television was a wild dream and if you'd asked a resident in that era what he thought about computers he would have thought you were talking about the young ladies who worked for the United States government compiling columns and columns of figures.

The airplane had been invented, but it was still a flimsy thing of struts and fabric, not yet introduced to aerial combat, as it would be in Europe a few years later.

And—astronauts on the moon and satellites in orbit?

What do you think the Kaiser and his cousin the Tsar would have thought of that?

My doorbell rang this afternoon and there stood an earnest young man—well, young compared to me, anyway!—accompanied by his even younger-looking female campaign manager, soliciting my vote in the coming City Council election. How many elections have come and gone while people walked on that triangle in front of my house? How many Presidents have sworn the oath of office?

Wilson, Harding, Coolidge, Hoover, Roosevelt, Truman, Eisenhower, Kennedy, Johnson, Nixon, Ford, Carter, Reagan, Bush, Clinton, another Bush, Obama.

And the triangle endures there. I walk over it every day. I haven't counted the number of people who walk over it every day. Surely hundreds if not thousands.

Living and growing and aging and dying, and the triangle is still there.

THE OAKLAND
PAVING
CO.

And above the triangle, in a small rectangular box, the year it was laid down. 1912.

Dick & Pat Lupoff

SOURCES OF CONTENTS OF

WRITER: Volume 3

\-

'The Two-Timers: Ray Cummings & Malcolm Jameson' - First published in the book of the same name (Surinam Turtle Press, 2014).

'Editing a Titan' - First published in *Paperback Parade,* edited by Gary Lovisi, 2014.

'The Key to Lafferty' - Introduction to *The Man with the Speckled Eyes: The Collected Short Fiction, Volume Four* (Centipede Press, 2017).

'Frank M. Robinson (1926-2014)' - Original to *Writer: Volume 3*

'We Didn't Know' - Original to *Writer: Volume 3.*

'An ERB Addict Gets His Fix' - First published in *Locus* magazine, 2015.

'The Iceman Cometh' - Introduction to *The Crackpot and other twisted tales of greedy fans and collectors*, by John E. Stockman (Surinam Turtle Press, 2015).

'Howard Browne, Paul Pine and the Halo Novels' - Introduction to *Howard Browne: the Collected Paul Pin Novels,* edited by Stephen Haffner, forthcoming.

'Life on a Buck-Slip' - Introduction to *Win, Place and Die* by Milton K. Ozaki (Surinam Turtle Press, 2013).

'In Another World . . .' - *Christopher Weills' Sports Weekly,* 2014.

'The A's Bionic Pitcher' - *The Ultimate Sports Guide,* edited by Christopher Weills, 2014.

'In a Zone' - *Christopher Weills' Sports Weekly,* 2015.

'That Kid in the Outfield' - *Christopher Weills' Sports Weekly.* 2014.

'Gonna Rattle Them Bones' - *Christopher Weills' Sports Weekly*, 2014.

'Kendell and Magga and Milo and Me' - Original to *Writer: Volume 3.*

'My Favorite Captain Marvel Story' - Original to *Writer: Volume 3.*

'When is a Pulp not a Pulp?' - *Pulp Adventures* Number 17, 2015, edited by Audrey Parente.

'The AICFAD Style Sheet' - First published in *Flier* (fanzine) in 1961.

'Crashing Comets, Blasting Rockets, Blazing Ray Guns, Hideous Monsters and Gorgeous, Gorgeous, Gorgeous Women' - First published in *Roy Thomas Presents Planet Comics, Volume 8,* 2015.

'The Propwash Patrol' - First published in *The Comic-Book Book,* edited by Don Thompson & Richard A. Lupoff (1973)

'The Propwash Patrol Flies Again' - First published in *The Comic-Book Book,* edited by Don Thompson & Richard A. Lupoff (1973)

'It's Magic' - First published in *The Comic-Book Book,* edited by Don Thompson & Richard A. Lupoff (1973)

'The Big Red Cheese' - First published in *Xero* (fanzine) Number 1, 1960.

'Frozen Fingers' - *The Ultimate Sports Guide* edited by Christopher Weills (forthcoming)

'I Coulda Had a Three-Pointer' - First published in *Christopher Weills' Sports Weekly,* 2015.

'The Black Hood' - First published in *Locus* magazine, 2014.

'Captain Future, Vol.3' - Original to *Writer: Volume 3.*

'Captain Future's Back' - First published in *TOR.com* (forthcoming)

'Two to Keep' - First published in *Paperback Parade,* edited by Gary Lovisi, 2015.

'By the Column Inch' - Original to *Writer: Volume 3.*

'Not Exactly a Shoe Salesman' - Introduction to *Homicide House: Day Keene in the Detective Pulps, Vol.6* (Ramble House, 2015)

'The Man in the Bathtub' - Original to *Writer: Volume 3.*

'Uncle Eddie' - Original to *Writer: Volume 3.*

'Club Fighter' - First published in *Christopher Weills' Sports Weekly.*

'Learning to Read' - Original to *Writer: Volume 3.*

'Triangle on the Sidewalk' - Original to *Writer: Volume 3.*

RAMBLE HOUSE's

HARRY STEPHEN KEELER WEBWORK MYSTERIES

(RH) indicates the title is available ONLY in the RAMBLE HOUSE edition

Keeler Related Works

A To Izzard: A Harry Stephen Keeler Companion by Fender Tucker — Articles and stories about Harry, by Harry, and in his style. Included is a compleat bibliography.

Wild About Harry: Reviews of Keeler Novels — Edited by Richard Polt & Fender Tucker — 22 reviews of works by Harry Stephen Keeler from *Keeler News*. A perfect introduction to the author.

The Keeler Keyhole Collection: Annotated newsletter rants from Harry Stephen Keeler, edited by Francis M. Nevins. Over 400 pages of incredibly personal Keeleriana.

Fakealoo — Pastiches of the style of Harry Stephen Keeler by selected demented members of the HSK Society. Updated every year with the new winner.

Strands of the Web: Short Stories of Harry Stephen Keeler — 29 stories, just about all that Keeler wrote, are edited and introduced by Fred Cleaver.

RAMBLE HOUSE's LOON SANCTUARY

A Clear Path to Cross—Sharon Knowles short mystery stories by Ed Lynskey.

A Corpse Walks in Brooklyn and Other Stories—Volume 5 in the Day Keene in the Detective Pulps series.

A Fair Californian—Novel by Olive Harper about a young woman's quest for gold — a quest that turns into something completely unexpected.

A Jimmy Starr Omnibus—Three 40s novels by Jimmy Starr.

A Niche in Time and Other Stories—Classic SF by William F. Temple.

A Shot Rang Out—Three decades of reviews and articles by today's Anthony Boucher, Jon Breen. An essential book for any mystery lover's library.

A Smell of Smoke—A 1951 English countryside thriller by Miles Burton.

A Snark Selection—Lewis Carroll's *The Hunting of the Snark* with two Snarkian chapters by Harry Stephen Keeler—Illustrated by Gavin L. O'Keefe.

A Young Man's Heart—A forgotten early classic by Cornell Woolrich.

Alexander Laing Novels—*The Motives of Nicholas Holtz* and *Dr. Scarlett*, stories of medical mayhem and intrigue from the 30s.

An Angel in the Street—Modern hardboiled noir by Peter Genovese.

Automaton—Brilliant treatise on robotics: 1928-style! By H. Stafford Hatfield.

Away From the Here and Now—Clare Winger Harris stories, collected by Richard A. Lupoff

Beast or Man?—A 1930 novel of racism and horror by Sean M'Guire. Introduced by John Pelan.

Black Hogan Strikes Again—Australia's Peter Renwick pens a tale of the 30s outback.

Black River Falls—Suspense from the master, Ed Gorman.

Blondy's Boy Friend—A snappy 1930 story by Philip Wylie, writing as Leatrice Homesley.

Blood in a Snap—The *Finnegan's Wake* of the 21st century, by Jim Weiler.

Blood Moon—The first of the Robert Payne series by Ed Gorman.

Bogart '48—Hollywood action with Bogie by John Stanley and Kenn Davis

Butterfly Man—1930s novel by Lew Levenson about a dancer who must come to terms with his homosexuality.

Calling Lou Largo!—Two Lou Largo novels by William Ard.

Cathedral of Horror—First volume of collected stories by weird fiction writer Arthur J. Burks.

Chalk Face—Curious supernatural murder thriller by Waldo Frank.

Cornucopia of Crime—Francis M. Nevins assembled this huge collection of his writings about crime literature and the people who write it. Essential for any serious mystery library.

Corpse Without Flesh—Strange novel of forensics by George Bruce

Crimson Clown Novels—By Johnston McCulley, author of the Zorro novels, *The Crimson Clown* and *The Crimson Clown Again.*

Dago Red—22 tales of dark suspense by Bill Pronzini.

Dark Sanctuary—Weird Menace story by H. B. Gregory.

David Hume Novels—*Corpses Never Argue, Cemetery First Stop, Make Way for the Mourners, Eternity Here I Come.* 1930s British hardboiled fiction with an attitude.

David&Son: Peregrine Parentus and other tales—Collection of tales and memoirs by Avram Davidson and Ethan Davidson, some published for the first time. Introduced by Grania Davidson Davis.

Dead Man Talks Too Much—Hollywood boozer by Weed Dickenson.

Death in a Bowl—1930's murder mystery by Raoul Whitfield.

Death Leaves No Card—One of the most unusual murdered-in-the-tub mysteries you'll ever read. By Miles Burton.

Death March of the Dancing Dolls and Other Stories—Volume Three in the Day Keene in the Detective Pulps series. Introduced by Bill Crider.

Deep Space and other Stories—A collection of SF gems by Richard A. Lupoff.

Detective Duff Unravels It—Episodic mysteries by Harvey O'Higgins.

Devil's Planet—Locked room mystery set on the planet Mars, by Manly Wade Wellman.

Dime Novels: Ramble House's 10-Cent Books—*Knife in the Dark* by Robert Leslie Bellem, *Hot Lead* and *Song of Death* by Ed Earl Repp, *A Hashish House in New York* by H.H. Kane, and five more.

Doctor Arnoldi—Tiffany Thayer's story of the death of death.

Don Diablo: Book of a Lost Film—Two-volume treatment of a western by Paul Landres, with diagrams. Intro by Francis M. Nevins.

Dope and Swastikas—Two strange novels from 1922 by Edmund Snell

Dope Tales #1—Two dope-riddled classics; *Dope Runners* by Gerald Grantham and *Death Takes the Joystick* by Phillip Condé.

Dope Tales #2—Two more narco-classics; *The Invisible Hand* by Rex Dark and *The Smokers of Hashish* by Norman Berrow.

Dope Tales #3—Two enchanting novels of opium by the master, Sax Rohmer. *Dope* and *The Yellow Claw*.

Double Hot & Double Sex—Two combos of '60s softcore sex novels by Morris Hershman.

Dr. Odin—Douglas Newton's 1933 racial potboiler comes back to life.

E. C. R. Lorac — *Black Beadle*, *The Case in the Clinic*, *Slippery Staircase* and *The Devil and the C.I.D.*

E. R. Punshon novels—*Information Received*, *Crossword Mystery*, *Dictator's Way*, *Diabolic Candelabra*, *Music Tells All*, *Helen Passes By*, *The House of Godwinsson*, *The Golden Dagger*, *The Attending Truth*, *Strange Ending*, *Brought to Light*, *Dark is the Clue*, *Triple Quest*, and *Six Were Present*: featuring Bobby Owen.

Ed "Strangler" Lewis: Facts within a Myth—Authoritative illustrated biography of the famous American wrestler Ed Lewis, by noted historian Steve Yohe.

Evangelical Cockroach—Jack Woodford writes about writing.

Evidence in Blue—1938 mystery by E. Charles Vivian.

Fatal Accident—Murder by automobile, a 1936 mystery by Cecil M. Wills.

Fighting Mad—Todd Robbins' 1922 novel about boxing and life

Five Million in Cash—Gangster thriller by Tiffany Thayer writing as O. B. King.

Food for the Fungus Lady—Collection of weird stories by Ralston Shields, edited and introduced by John Pelan.

Francis M. Nevins—Two omnibus volumes of novels featuring his legal sleuth Loren Mensing: *Publish and Perish / Corrupt and Ensnare* and *Into the Same River Twice / Beneficiaries' Requiem*.

Freaks and Fantasies—Eerie tales by Tod Robbins, collaborator of Tod Browning on the film FREAKS.

Gadsby—A lipogram (a novel without the letter E). Ernest Vincent Wright's last work, published in 1939 right before his death.

Gelett Burgess Novels—*The Master of Mysteries, The White Cat, Two O'Clock Courage, Ladies in Boxes, Find the Woman, The Heart Line, The Picaroons* and *Lady Mechante*. Recently added is A Gelett Burgess Sampler, edited by Alfred Jan. All are introduced by Richard A. Lupoff.

Geronimo—S. M. Barrett's 1905 autobiography of a noble American.

Gordon Eklund—*Second Creation, Retro Man* and *Stalking the Sun*: three volumes of the author's best short stories.

Go Forth and Multiply—Anthology of science fiction tales of repopulation, edited by Gordon Van Gelder.

Hake Talbot Novels—*Rim of the Pit, The Hangman's Handyman.* Classic locked room mysteries, with mapback covers by Gavin O'Keefe.

Hands Out of Hell and Other Stories—John H. Knox's eerie hallucinations

Hell is a City—William Ard's masterpiece.

Hollywood Dreams—A novel of Tinsel Town and the Depression by Richard O'Brien.

Homicide House—#6 in the Day Keene in the Detective Pulps series.

Hostesses in Hell and Other Stories—Russell Gray's most graphic stories

House of the Restless Dead—Strange and ominous tales by Hugh B. Cave

Inclination to Murder—1966 thriller by New Zealand's Harriet Hunter.

Invaders from the Dark—Classic werewolf tale from Greye La Spina.

J. Poindexter, Colored—Classic satirical black novel by Irvin S. Cobb.

Jack Mann Novels—Strange murder in the English countryside. *Gees' First Case, Nightmare Farm, Grey Shapes, The Ninth Life, The Glass Too Many, Her Ways Are Death, The Kleinert Case* and *Maker of Shadows.*

Jake Hardy—A lusty western tale from Wesley Tallant.

James Corbett—*Vampire of the Skies, The Ghost Plane, Murder Begets Murder* and *The Air Killer* – strange thriller novels from this singular British author.

Jim Harmon Double Novels—*Vixen Hollow/Celluloid Scandal, The Man Who Made Maniacs/Silent Siren, Ape Rape/Wanton Witch, Sex Burns Like Fire/Twist Session, Sudden Lust/Passion Strip, Sin Unlimited/Harlot Master, Twilight Girls/Sex Institution.* Written in the early 60s and never reprinted until now.

Joel Townsley Rogers Novels and Short Stories—By the author of *The Red Right Hand: Once In a Red Moon, Lady With the Dice, The Stopped Clock, Never Leave My Bed.* Also two short story collections: *Night of Horror* and *Killing Time.*

John Carstairs, Space Detective—Arboreal Sci-fi by Frank Belknap Long

John G. Brandon—*The Case of the Withered Hand, Finger-Prints Never Lie*, and *Death on Delivery*: crime thrillers by Australian author John G. Brandon.

John S. Glasby—Two collections of Glasby's Lovecraftian stories: *The Brooding City* and *Beyond the Rim.* Introduced by John Pelan.

Joseph Shallit Novels—*The Case of the Billion Dollar Body, Lady Don't Die on My Doorstep, Kiss the Killer, Yell Bloody Murder, Take Your Last Look.* One of America's best 50's authors and a favorite of author Bill Pronzini.

Keller Memento—45 short stories of the amazing and weird by Dr. David Keller.

Killer's Caress—Cary Moran's 1936 hardboiled thriller.

Knight Asrael and Other Stories—Collection of fourteen fantasy tales by Una Ashworth Taylor

Knowing the Unknowable: Putting Psi to Work—Damien Broderick, PhD puts forward the valid case for evidence of Psi.

Lady of the Yellow Death and Other Stories—More stories by Wyatt Blassingame.

Laughing Death—1932 Yellow Peril thriller by Walter C. Brown.

League of the Grateful Dead and Other Stories—Volume One in the Day Keene in the Detective Pulps series.

Library of Death—Ghastly tale by Ronald S. L. Harding, introduced by John Pelan

Lords of the Earth—A novel of meddling dabblers in the occult invoking the ancient powers of Atlantis. J.M.A. Mills' sequel to *The Tomb of the Dark Ones*.

Mad-Doctor Merciful—Collin Brooks' unsettling novel of medical experimentation with supernatural forces.

Malcolm Jameson Novels and Short Stories—*Astonishing! Astounding!, Tarnished Bomb, The Alien Envoy and Other Stories* and *The Chariots of San Fernando and Other Stories.* All introduced and edited by John Pelan or Richard A. Lupoff.

Man Out of Hell and Other Stories—Volume II of the John H. Knox weird pulps collection.

Marblehead: A Novel of H.P. Lovecraft—A long-lost masterpiece from Richard A. Lupoff. This is the "director's cut", the long version that has never been published before.

Mark of the Laughing Death and Other Stories—Shockers from the pulps by Francis James, introduced by John Pelan.

Mark Hansom Novels—*Master of Souls, The Ghost of Gaston Revere, The Madman, The Shadow on the House, Sorcerer's Chessmen & The Wizard of Berner's Abbey.*

Max Afford Novels—*Owl of Darkness, Death's Mannikins, Blood on His Hands, The Dead Are Blind, The Sheep and the Wolves, Sinners in Paradise* and *Two Locked Room Mysteries and a Ripping Yarn* by one of Australia's finest mystery novelists.

Mistress of Terror—Fourth volume of the collected weird tales of Wyatt Blassingame.

Molly and her Man of War— Romantic novel with a difference, by Arabella Kenealy.

Money Brawl—Two books about the writing business by Jack Woodford and H. Bedford-Jones. Introduced by Richard A. Lupoff.

More Secret Adventures of Sherlock Holmes—Gary Lovisi's second collection of tales about the unknown sides of the great detective.

Muddled Mind: Complete Works of Ed Wood, Jr.—David Hayes and Hayden Davis deconstruct the life and works of the mad, but canny, genius.

Murder among the Nudists—1934 mystery by Peter Hunt, featuring a naked Detective-Inspector going undercover in a nudist colony.

Murder in Black and White—1931 classic tennis whodunit by Evelyn Elder.

Murder in Shawnee—Two novels of the Alleghenies by John Douglas: *Shawnee Alley Fire* and *Haunts.*

Murder in Silk—A 1937 Yellow Peril novel of the silk trade by Ralph Trevor.

Murder in Suffolk—A 1938 murder mystery novel by the mysterious 'A. Fielding.'

My Deadly Angel—1955 Cold War drama by John Chelton.

My First Time: The One Experience You Never Forget—Michael Birchwood—64 true first-person narratives of how they lost it.

My Touch Brings Death—Second volume of collected stories by Russell Gray.

Mysterious Martin, the Master of Murder—Two versions of a strange 1912 novel by Tod Robbins about a man who writes books that can kill.

Norman Berrow Novels—*The Bishop's Sword, Ghost House, Don't Go Out After Dark, Claws of the Cougar, The Smokers of Hashish, The Secret Dancer, Don't Jump Mr. Boland!, The Footprints of Satan, Fingers for Ransom, The Three Tiers of*

Fantasy, The Spaniard's Thumb, The Eleventh Plague, Words Have Wings, One Thrilling Night, The Lady's in Danger, It Howls at Night, The Terror in the Fog, Oil Under the Window, Murder in the Melody, The Singing Room. This is the complete Norman Berrow library of locked-room mysteries, several of which are masterpieces.

Old Faithful and Other Stories—SF classic tales by Raymond Z. Gallun

Old Times' Sake—Short stories by James Reasoner from Mike Shayne Magazine.

One Dreadful Night—A classic mystery by Ronald S. L. Harding

Pair O' Jacks—A mystery novel and a diatribe about publishing by Jack Woodford

Pawns of Destiny—Psychological drama by Kay Seaton.

Perfect .38—Two early Timothy Dane novels by William Ard. More to come.

Prince Pax—Devilish intrigue by George Sylvester Viereck and Philip Eldridge

Prose Bowl—Futuristic satire of a world where hack writing has replaced football as our national obsession, by Bill Pronzini and Barry N. Malzberg.

Red Light—The history of legal prostitution in Shreveport Louisiana by Eric Brock. Includes wonderful photos of the houses and the ladies.

Researching American-Made Toy Soldiers—A 276-page collection of a lifetime of articles by toy soldier expert Richard O'Brien.

Reunion in Hell—Volume One of the John H. Knox series of weird stories from the pulps. Introduced by horror expert John Pelan.

Ripped from the Headlines!—The Jack the Ripper story as told in the newspaper articles in the *New York* and *London Times*.

Rough Cut & New, Improved Murder—Ed Gorman's first two novels.

R. R. Ryan Novels — *Freak Museum, The Subjugated Beast, Death of a Sadist, Echo of a Curse, Devil's Shelter* and *No Escape*. Introduced by John Pelan.

Roland Daniel Novels — *Ruby of a Thousand Dreams, The Girl in the Dark*, and *A Roland Daniel Double: The Signal and The Return of Wu Fang*.

Ruled By Radio — 1925 futuristic novel by Robert L. Hadfield & Frank E. Farncombe.

Rupert Penny Novels — *Policeman's Holiday, Policeman's Evidence, Lucky Policeman, Policeman in Armour, Sealed Room Murder, Sweet Poison, The Talkative Policeman, She had to Have Gas* and *Cut and Run* (by Martin Tanner.) Rupert Penny is the pseudonym of Australian Charles Thornett, a master of the locked room, impossible crime plot.

Sacred Locomotive Flies — Richard A. Lupoff's psychedelic SF story.

Sam — Early gay novel by Lonnie Coleman.

Sand's Game — Spectacular hardboiled noir from Ennis Willie, edited by Lynn Myers and Stephen Mertz, with contributions from Max Allan Collins, Bill Crider, Wayne Dundee, Bill Pronzini, Gary Lovisi and James Reasoner.

Sand's War — More violent fiction from the typewriter of Ennis Willie

Satan's Den Exposed — True crime in Truth or Consequences New Mexico — Award-winning journalism by the *Desert Journal*.

Satan's Secret and Selected Stories — Barnard Stacey's only novel with a selection of his best short stories.

Satans of Saturn — Novellas from the pulps by Otis Adelbert Kline and E. H. Price

Satan's Sin House and Other Stories — Horrific gore by Wayne Rogers

Second Creation — The first volume of selected short stories by Gordon Eklund.

Secrets of a Teenage Superhero — Graphic lit by Jonathan Sweet

Sex Slave — Potboiler of lust in the days of Cleopatra by Dion Leclerq, 1966.

Sideslip — 1968 SF masterpiece by Ted White and Dave Van Arnam.

Slammer Days — Two full-length prison memoirs: *Men into Beasts* (1952) by George Sylvester Viereck and *Home Away From Home* (1962) by Jack Woodford.

Star Griffin — Michael Kurland's 1987 masterpiece of SF drollery is back.

Stakeout on Millennium Drive — Award-winning Indianapolis Noir by Ian Woollen.

Strands of the Web: Short Stories of Harry Stephen Keeler — Edited and Introduced by Fred Cleaver.

Summer Camp for Corpses and Other Stories — Weird Menace tales from Arthur Leo Zagat; introduced by John Pelan.

Suzy — A collection of comic strips by Richard O'Brien and Bob Vojtko from 1970.

Tail of the Lizard King / Kaliwood — Two novellas by Adam Mudman Bezecny paying homage to the sleaze genre.

Tales of the Macabre and Ordinary — Modern twisted horror by Chris Mikul, author of the *Bizarrism* series.

Tales of Terror and Torment Vols. #1 & #2 — John Pelan selects and introduces these samplers of weird menace tales from the pulps.

Tenebrae — Ernest G. Henham's 1898 horror tale brought back.

The Alice Books — Lewis Carroll's classics *Alice's Adventures in Wonderland* and *Through the Looking-Glass* together in one volume, with new illustrations by O'Keefe.

The Amorous Intrigues & Adventures of Aaron Burr — by Anonymous. Hot historical action about the man who almost became Emperor of Mexico.

The Anthony Boucher Chronicles — edited by Francis M. Nevins. Book reviews by Anthony Boucher written for the *San Francisco Chronicle,* 1942 – 1947. Essential and fascinating reading by the best book reviewer there ever was.

The Barclay Catalogs — Two essential books about toy soldier collecting by Richard O'Brien

The Basil Wells Omnibus — A collection of Wells' stories by Richard A. Lupoff

The Beautiful Dead and Other Stories — Dreadful tales from Donald Dale

The Best of 10-Story Book — edited by Chris Mikul, over 35 stories from the literary magazine Harry Stephen Keeler edited.

The Bitch Wall — Novel about American soldiers in the Vietnam War, based on Dennis Lane's experiences.

The Black Dark Murders — Vintage 50s college murder yarn by Milt Ozaki, writing as Robert O. Saber.

The Book of Time — The classic novel by H.G. Wells is joined by sequels by Wells himself and three stories by Richard A. Lupoff. Illustrated by Gavin L. O'Keefe.

The Broken Fang and Other Experiences of a Specialist in Spooks — Eerie mystery tales by Uel Key.

The Strange Case of the Antlered Man — A mystery of superstition by Edwy Searles Brooks.

The Case of the Bearded Bride — #4 in the Day Keene in the Detective Pulps series.

The Case of the Little Green Men — Mack Reynolds wrote this love song to sci-fi fans back in 1951 and it's now back in print.

The Charlie Chaplin Murder Mystery — A 2004 tribute by noted film scholar, Wes D. Gehring.

The Cloudbuilders and Other Stories — SF tales from Colin Kapp.

The Collected Writings — Collection of science fiction stories, memoirs and poetry by Carol Carr. Introduction by Karen Haber.

The Compleat Calhoon — All of Fender Tucker's works: Includes *Totah Six-Pack, Weed, Women and Song* and *Tales from the Tower,* plus a CD of all of his songs.

The Compleat Ova Hamlet — Parodies of SF authors by Richard A. Lupoff. This is a brand new edition with more stories and more illustrations by Trina Robbins.

The Contested Earth and Other SF Stories — A never-before published space opera and seven short stories by Jim Harmon.

The Corpse Factory — More horror stories by Arthur Leo Zagat.

The Crackpot and Other Twisted Tales of Greedy Fans and Collectors — The first retrospective collection of the whacky stories of John E. Stockman. Edited by Dwight R. Decker.

The Crimson Butterfly — Early novel by Edmund Snell involving superstition and aberrant Lepidoptera in Borneo.

The Crimson Query — A 1929 thriller from Arlton Eadie. A perfect way to get introduced.

The Daymakers, City of the Tiger & Perchance to Wake — Three volumes of stories taken from the influential British science fiction magazine *Science Fantasy*. Compiled by John Boston & Damien Broderick.

The Devil Drives — An odd prison and lost treasure novel from 1932 by Virgil Markham.

The Devil of Pei-Ling — Herbert Asbury's 1929 tale of the occult.

The Devil's Mistress — A 1915 Scottish gothic tale by J. W. Brodie-Innes, a member of Aleister Crowley's Golden Dawn.

The Devil's Nightclub and Other Stories — John Pelan introduces some gruesome tales by Nat Schachner.

The Disentanglers — Episodic intrigue at the turn of last century by Andrew Lang

The Dog Poker Code — A spoof of *The Da Vinci Code* by D. B. Smithee.

The Dumpling — Political murder from 1907 by Coulson Kernahan.

The End of It All and Other Stories — Ed Gorman selected his favorite short stories for this huge collection.

The Evil of Li-Sin — A Gerald Verner double, combining *The Menace of Li-Sin* and *The Vengeance of Li-Sin*, together with an introduction by John Pelan and an afterword and bibliography by Chris Verner.

The Fangs of Suet Pudding — A 1944 novel of the German invasion by Adams Farr

The Finger of Destiny and Other Stories — Edmund Snell's superb collection of weird stories of Borneo.

The Gold Star Line — Seaboard adventure from L.T. Reade and Robert Eustace.

The Great Orme Terror — Horror novel by Garnett Radcliffe.

The Hairbreadth Escapes of Major Mendax — Francis Blake Crofton's 1889 boys' book.

The House That Time Forgot and Other Stories — Insane pulpitude by Robert F. Young

The House of the Vampire — 1907 poetic thriller by George S. Viereck.

The Illustrious Corpse — Murder hijinx from Tiffany Thayer

The Incredible Adventures of Rowland Hern — Intriguing 1928 impossible crimes by Nicholas Olde.

The John Dickson Carr Companion — Comprehensive reference work compiled by James E. Keirans. Indispensable resource for the Carr *aficionado*.

The Julius Caesar Murder Case — A 1935 retelling of the assassination by Wallace Irwin that's more fun than Shakespeare's version.

The Kid Was a Killer — Caryl Chessman's only novel, based on his own experiences.

The Koky Comics — A collection of all of the 1978-1981 Sunday and daily comic strips by Richard O'Brien and Mort Gerberg, in two volumes.

The Lady of the Fjords — Barnard Balogh's novel of Norse gods and heroes, reincarnation, and a love affair transcending mortality.

The Lady of the Terraces — 1925 missing race adventure by E. Charles Vivian.

The Lord of Terror — 1925 mystery with master-criminal, Fantômas.

The Man who was Murdered Twice — Intriguing murder mystery by Robert H. Leitfred.

The Melamare Mystery — A classic 1929 Arsene Lupin mystery by Maurice Leblanc

The Man Who Was Secrett — Epic SF stories from John Brunner

The Man Without a Planet — Science fiction tales by Richard Wilson

The N. R. De Mexico Novels — Robert Bragg, the real N.R. de Mexico, presents *Marijuana Girl, Madman on a Drum, Private Chauffeur* in one volume.

The Night Remembers — A 1991 Jack Walsh mystery from Ed Gorman.

The One After Snelling — Kickass modern noir from Richard O'Brien.

The Organ Reader — A huge compilation of just about everything published in the 1971-1972 radical bay-area newspaper, *THE ORGAN*. A coffee table book that points out the shallowness of the coffee table mindset.

The Place of Hairy Death — Collected weird horror tales by Anthony M. Rud.

The Poker Club — Three in one! Ed Gorman's ground-breaking novel, the short story it was based upon, and the screenplay of the film made from it.

The Private Journal & Diary of John H. Surratt — The memoirs of the man who conspired to assassinate President Lincoln.

The Ramble House Coloring Book — Twenty illustrations to color in, each adapted from one of Gavin L. O'Keefe's RH cover designs.

The Ramble House Mapbacks — Recently revised book by Gavin L. O'Keefe with color pictures of all the Ramble House books with mapbacks.

The Secret Adventures of Sherlock Holmes — Three Sherlockian pastiches by the Brooklyn author/publisher, Gary Lovisi.

The Secret of the Morgue — Frederick G. Eberhard's 1932 mystery involving murder and forensic science with an undercurrent of the malaise that's driven by Prohibition.

The Sign of the Scorpion — A 1935 Edmund Snell tale of oriental evil.

The Silent Terror of Chu-Sheng — Yellow Peril suspense novel by Eugene Thomas.

The Singular Problem of the Stygian House-Boat — Two classic tales by John Kendrick Bangs about the denizens of Hades.

The Smiling Corpse — Philip Wylie and Bernard Bergman's odd 1935 novel.

The Sorcery Club — Classic supernatural novel by Elliott O'Donnell.

The Spider: Satan's Murder Machines — A thesis about Iron Man.

The Stench of Death: An Odoriferous Omnibus by Jack Moskovitz — Two complete novels and two novellas from 60's sleaze author, Jack Moskovitz.

The Story Writer and Other Stories — Classic SF from Richard Wilson

The Strange Thirteen — Richard B. Gamon's odd stories about Raj India.

The Technique of the Mystery Story — Carolyn Wells' tips about writing.

The Tell-Tale Soul — Two novellas by Bram Stoker Award-winning author Christopher Conlon. Introduction by John Pelan.

The Threat of Nostalgia — A collection of his most obscure stories by Jon Breen

The Time Armada — Fox B. Holden's 1953 SF gem.

The Tomb of the Dark Ones — Adventure in Egypt where ancient forces are roused from æons of slumber. A J. M. A. Mills novel from 1937.

The Tongueless Horror and Other Stories — Volume One of the series of short stories from the weird pulps by Wyatt Blassingame.

The Town from Planet Five — From Richard Wilson, two SF classics, *And Then the Town Took Off* and *The Girls from Planet 5*

The Tracer of Lost Persons — From 1906, an episodic novel that became a hit radio series in the 30s. Introduced by Richard A. Lupoff.

The Trail of the Cloven Hoof — Diabolical horror from 1935 by Arlton Eadie. Introduced by John Pelan.

The Triune Man — Mindscrambling science fiction from Richard A. Lupoff.

The Unholy Goddess and Other Stories — Wyatt Blassingame's first DTP compilation

The Universal Holmes — Richard A. Lupoff's 2007 collection of five Holmesian pastiches and a recipe for giant rat stew.

The Werewolf vs the Vampire Woman — Hard to believe ultraviolence by either Arthur M. Scarm or Arthur M. Scram.

The Whistling Ancestors — A 1936 classic of weirdness by Richard E. Goddard and introduced by John Pelan.

The White Owl — A vintage thriller from Edmund Snell

The White Peril in the Far East — Sidney Lewis Gulick's 1905 indictment of the West and assurance that Japan would never attack the U.S.

The Wonderful Wizard of Oz — by L. Frank Baum and illustrated by Gavin L. O'Keefe.

The Yu-Chi Stone — Novel of intrigue and superstition set in Borneo, by Edmund Snell.

They Called the Shots — Collection of authoritative articles by Francis M. Nevins exploring the action movie directors of the late silents through to the late 1960s.

Time Line — Ramble House artist Gavin O'Keefe selects his most evocative art inspired by the twisted literature he reads and designs.

Tiresias — Psychotic modern horror novel by Jonathan M. Sweet.

Tortures and Towers — Two novellas of terror by Dexter Dayle.

Totah Six-Pack — Fender Tucker's six tales about Farmington in one sleek volume.

Tree of Life, Book of Death — Grania Davis' book of her life.

Trail of the Spirit Warrior — Roger Haley's saga of life in the Indian Territories.

Twelve Who Were Damned — Collection of weird menace tales by Paul Ernst.

Two Kinds of Bad — Two 50s novels by William Ard about Danny Fontaine

Two Suns of Morcali and Other Stories — Evelyn E. Smith's SF tour-de-force

Two-Timers — Time travel double: *The Man Who Mastered Time* by Ray Cummings and *Time Column* and *Taa the Terrible* by Malcolm Jameson. Introduced by Richard A. Lupoff.

Ultra-Boiled — 23 gut-wrenching tales by our Man in Brooklyn, Gary Lovisi.

Up Front From Behind — A 2011 satire of Wall Street by James B. Kobak.

Victims & Villains — Intriguing Sherlockiana from Derham Groves.

Wade Wright Novels — *Echo of Fear, Death At Nostalgia Street, It Leads to Murder* and *Shadows' Edge*, a double book featuring *Shadows Don't Bleed* and *The Sharp Edge*.

Walter S. Masterman Novels — *The Green Toad, The Flying Beast, The Yellow Mistletoe, The Wrong Verdict, The Perjured Alibi, The Border Line, The Bloodhounds Bay, The Curse of Cantire, The Baddington Horror* and *Death Turns Traitor.* Masterman wrote horror and mystery, some introduced by John Pelan.

We Are the Dead and Other Stories — Volume Two in the Day Keene in the Detective Pulps series, introduced by Ed Gorman. When done, there may be 11 in the series.

Welsh Rarebit Tales — Charming stories from 1902 by Harle Oren Cummins

West Texas War and Other Western Stories — Western hijinks by Gary Lovisi.

What Was That?—Ghostly murder mystery from 1920 by Katharine Haviland Taylor.

What If? Volume 1, 2 and 3 — Richard A. Lupoff introduces three decades worth of SF short stories that should have won a Hugo, but didn't.

When the Bat Man Thirsts and Other Stories — Weird tales from Frederick C. Davis.

When the Dead Walk — Gary Lovisi takes us into the zombie-infested South.

Whip Dodge: Man Hunter — Wesley Tallant's saga of a bounty hunter of the old West.

Win, Place and Die! — The first new mystery by Milt Ozaki in decades. The ultimate novel of 70s Reno.

Writer, Volumes 1, 2 & 3 — A *magnus opus* from Richard A. Lupoff summing up his life as writer.

You'll Die Laughing — Bruce Elliott's 1945 novel of murder at a practical joker's English countryside manor.

You're Not Alone: 30 Science Fiction Stories from *Cosmos Magazine*, edited by Damien Broderick.

RAMBLE HOUSE

www.ramblehouse.com   fender@ramblehouse.com

10329 Sheephead Drive, Vancleave MS 39565

Made in the USA
Las Vegas, NV
23 July 2021